BRICHAH

Or

בריחה

(Hebrew for Escape or Flight)

By William Leibner

Edited by Phyllis Oster

Published by JewishGen

**An Affiliate of the Museum of Jewish Heritage - A Living Memorial to the Holocaust
New York**

Brichah - Hebrew for Escape or Flight

Brichah (Hebrew for Escape or Flight

Written by: William Leibner (Jerusalem, Israel)
Edited by Phyllis Oster
Layout: Joel Alpert
Cover Design: Jan R. Fine
Indexing: Sue Cohen

Published by JewishGen, Inc.
An Affiliate of the Museum of Jewish Heritage
A Living Memorial to the Holocaust
36 Battery Place, New York, NY 10280

"JewishGen, Inc. is not responsible for inaccuracies or omissions in the original work and makes no representations regarding the accuracy of this translation. Digital images of the original book's contents can be seen online at the New York Public Library Web site."

The mission of the JewishGen organization is to produce a translation of the original work and we cannot verify the accuracy of statements or alter facts cited.

Printed in the United States of America by Lightning Source, Inc.

Library of Congress Control Number (LCCN): 2017947391
ISBN: 978-1-939561-57-2 (hard cover: 296 pages, alk. paper)

Cover photograph: Front and back Courtesy of Yad Vashem

JewishGen and the Yizkor-Books-in-Print Project

This book has been published by the **Yizkor-Books-in-Print Project,** as part of the **Yizkor Book Project** of **JewishGen, Inc**.

JewishGen, Inc. is a non-profit organization founded in 1987 as a resource for Jewish genealogy. Its website [www.jewishgen.org] serves as an international clearinghouse and resource center to assist individuals who are researching the history of their Jewish families and the places where they lived. JewishGen provides databases, facilitates discussion groups, and coordinates projects relating to Jewish genealogy and the history of the Jewish people. In 2003, JewishGen became an affiliate of the **Museum of Jewish Heritage - A Living Memorial to the Holocaust** in New York.

The **JewishGen Yizkor Book Project** was organized to make more widely known the existence of Yizkor (Memorial) Books written by survivors and former residents of various Jewish communities throughout the world. Later, volunteers connected to the different destroyed communities began cooperating to have these books translated from the original language—usually Hebrew or Yiddish—into English, thus enabling a wider audience to have access to the valuable information contained within them. As each chapter of these books was translated, it was posted on the JewishGen website and made available to the general public.

The **Yizkor-Books-in-Print Project** began in 2011 as an initiative to print and publish Yizkor Books that had been fully translated, so that hard copies would be available for purchase by the descendants of these communities and also by scholars, universities, synagogues, libraries, and museums.

These Yizkor books have been produced almost entirely through the volunteer effort of researchers from around the world, assisted by donations from private individuals. The books are printed and sold at near cost, so as to make them as affordable as possible. Our goal is to make this important genre of Jewish literature and history available in English in book form, so that people can have the personal histories of their ancestral towns on their bookshelves for themselves and for their children and grandchildren.

A list of all published translated Yizkor Books in the project with prices and ordering information can be found at:

http://www.jewishgen.org/Yizkor/ybip.html

Lance Ackerfeld, Yizkor Book Project Manager

Joel Alpert, Yizkor-Book-in-Print Project Coordinator

JewishGen
Yizkor Book Project

This book is presented by the
Yizkor Books in Print Project
Project Coordinator: Joel Alpert

Part of the
Yizkor Books Project of JewishGen, Inc.
Project Manager: Lance Ackerfeld

These books have been produced solely through volunteer effort
of individuals from around the world. The books are printed and
sold at near cost, so as to make them as affordable as possible.

Our goal is to make this history and important genre of Jewish
literature available in English in book form so that people can have
the near-personal histories of their ancestral towns on their bookshelves for themselves and for their children and grandchildren.

Any donations to the Yizkor Books Project are appreciated.

Please send donations to:
Yizkor Book Project
JewishGen
36 Battery Place
New York, NY 10280

JewishGen, Inc. is an affiliate of the
Museum of Jewish Heritage
A Living Memorial to the Holocaust

Acknowledgements

The staff at Yad Vashem was most helpful in the research necessary for this book, including Avner Shalev, chairman of the Yad Vashem Directorate, Dr. Robert Rozette, Director of the Yad Vashem library, Rachel Cohen secretary of the library, Mimi Ash at the Yad Vashem center in Jerusalem, Dr. Daniel Uziel head of the archive division at Yad Vashem and the entire staff at the library of Yad Vashem.

Special thanks to Dr. Zvi Fine who provided excellent background information on the activities of the Joint Distribution Committee operations in Europe.

Zvi Oren director of the Museum at the Kibbutz Lochamei Hagetaot.

Special thanks to Mrs. Claudette Leibner for her patience in listening to the material.

Thanks to Emil Leibner who constantly provided technical assistance and helped to see the project completed.

Special thanks are in order for Phyllis Oster who edited the text.

We would also like to thank all the interviewed people and those who helped with our work.

William Leibner

William Leibner wrote the following books:
> The Nowy Zmigrod Yizkor Book
> Krosno by the Wislok River, a Yizkor Book
> The Zabrze-Hindenburg Yizkor Book
> The Unlikely Hero of Sobrance, Slovakia with Larry Price

William Leibner translated the following books:
> The Korczyna Yizkor Book from Yiddish to English
> The Yizkor Book of Jaslo from Hebrew to English
> Blood Stained Feathers from Hebrew to English

Brichah - Hebrew for Escape or Flight

Notes to the Reader:

A list of this book and all books available in the Yizkor-Book-In-Print Project along with prices is available at:

http://www.jewishgen.org/Yizkor/ybip.html

Brichah - Hebrew for Escape or Flight

Brichah - Hebrew for Escape or Flight

BRICHAH

Or

בריחה

Hebrew for Escape or Flight

By

WILLIAM LEIBNER

Edited by

Phyllis Oster

TABLE OF CONTENTS

*Mass movement of Jews across Polish-Czech
border under the leadership of the Brichah*

The situation of the Jewish survivors following World War II was very traumatic especially in Eastern Europe. Most felt guilty about having survived when their families perished. The common question was why did I survive, why do I deserve to live. Of course there was no answer. The survivors returned to find their homes occupied by strangers. They were often received coldly and many times were threatened and told not to return. On occasion surviving Shoah Jews were physically chased out of the hamlets and occasionally killed. Survivors had no choice but to move to bigger cities where there were more Jews. Small communities of survivors began to form in cities like Lemberg, Rowno and Kowno. The Russian secret police kept a close watch on these communities and had spies who reported on the activities of the survivors. Some of the Shoah survivors were former Zionists who still had dreams of going to Palestine. It was obvious from their treatment in the camps that no one cared about the Jews. Many became convinced that salvation lay in Palestine helping to build a Jewish state. This idea arose in several places especially the former Polish areas that were now part of the Soviet Union.

The Soviet life style did not permit Zionist or Jewish activities except those approved by the Communist party. All freedom of expression was suppressed except for Communist Party doctrine. Jewish religious life was strictly controlled as were all non-party activities. The Shoah survivors felt lonely and desperate without any links to the outside Jewish world. They began to look for ways to establish contact with other Jewish communities in the region but most important, they sought contact with Jewish communities outside the Soviet Union.

The efforts were successful and contacts were established with an office of the Jewish Agency of Palestine in Bucharest, Romania, just emerged from underground to encourage Jews to move to Palestine. The American Joint Distribution Committee (JDC) also had opened offices to help needy Jews. Ties were strengthened over time and a new organization named *"The Brichah"* or escape emerged, dedicated to helping Jews leave the Soviet controlled areas in Eastern Europe. The heroic organization functioned along spartan military lines: no formal organization or offices, no official records, and no reports. But the organization achieved results, in spite of the enormous logistical, political and administrative obstacles. At first dozens of Jews left their homes, then hundreds and eventually thousands.

Brichah entered the lexicon of the Jewish World. Its motto was "Between Mountains and Borders, in starless nights, we will lead Jewish convoys". Most of the members of the organization were former partisans, discharged soldiers from the Polish, Russian and Allied armies Jewish Brigades. The secret organization led about 300,000 Jews from Eastern Europe to Central Europe mainly Germany and Austria. Most of the survivors lived in Displaced Person (DP) camps hoping to reach Palestine. Many Jewish refugees found new homes in the United States, Canada, South America, England and Australia but most of the Jewish survivors did reach Palestine, legally or illegally. Some Brichah members were caught and paid a heavy price for their activities but this did not deter others from taking their place.

This book describes the activities of the Brichah organization from 1945-1948. With the establishment of the State of Israel, the Brichah was dissolved, the members returned home to resume their normal life. The organization existed a short time but achieved heroic results. It led the Jewish masses from the DP camps to defeat the British naval blockade of the Palestinian borders.

The organization and its members inscribed a golden page in Jewish history and in the pages of the History of Israel.

Chapter I
The Origins Of The Brichah

The Brichah movement first arose in places like Baranowice, Rowno, and Wilno, formerly Poland, and Czernowitz, Romania, in the aftermath of the Shoah. As a result of rampant anti-Semitism and Russian repression, desperate and isolated Jewish survivors banded together to form a heroic movement that quickly transitioned into a major enterprise that would help thousands of Jews reach Palestine and other safe havens.

Baranowice began in 1871 as a railroad station on the Smolensk-Brest route. On August 1, 1919, Baranowice received city rights and became a poviat (county) center in Nowogródek Voivodship. Control of Baranowice changed multiple times. In 1919 it was in Polish hands, then Soviet troops retook the city in July of 1920, only to have the Poles retake it in September.

In 1921 Baranowice had over 11,000 inhabitants (67% Jews, with the rest being mostly Belarusians, Poles and Russians). Soon the city started to grow and became an important center of trade and commerce for the area. The city's Orthodox cathedral was built in the neoclassical style in 1924-1931; it was decorated with mosaics that had survived the demolition of the Alexander Nevsky Cathedral in Warsaw. The city was also an important military garrison. Because of the fast growth of local industry, in 1938 a local branch of Polish Radio was opened. In September 1939, Soviet forces occupied the city and immediately introduced Communist order. All Jewish clubs and activities were closed. All Zionist activities were forbidden. The Jewish press was censored or closed. All Jewish political organizations like the "Bund" (Jewish socialist movement) were closed.

Eliezer Lidkowsky refused to abide by the new rules. Lidkowsky was born in 1908 in the small hamlet of Jeslo in present day Belarus and later moved to Baranowice. He was an active leader of the "Dror" or "Freiheit" Zionist youth movement that called for young Jews to go to Palestine and build the land along Socialist lines.[1] Lidkowsky was soon arrested by the Soviet secret police for conducting Zionist activities and was sentenced to 18 months in prison. He served his term and was released, joining his wife and children.

---

[1] Bauer, Yehuda. Flight and Rescue: Brichah. New York: Random House, 1970, pp 3-5.

Eliezer Lidkowsky

The City of Baranowice prior to World War II

Five days after the Germans invaded the Soviet Union, they entered the city of Baranowice. At the start of the city's occupation by the Germans there were some 12,000 Jews living there, of whom about three thousand were refugees from Western Poland. The German soldiers – together with local Poles and Byelorussians – began breaking into Jews' homes, intent on robbery, looting, and abusing their occupants. Anti-Jewish regulations were promulgated daily including curfews and arm bands.

In September 1941 a Judenrat or council of Jewish elders was established that carried out Nazi orders regarding Jewish citizens. Soon after, a ghetto was created. The Judenrat and the ghetto police had their headquarters at the main gate, across the street from the Gestapo building. The ghetto was terribly overcrowded, but actions and selections began to drastically reduce the Jewish population.

Many Jews actually worked for the German army, among them Eliezer Lidkowsky. Eliezer and his brother Abraham saw the helplessness of the Jewish situation and began to organize a group of Jews to defend themselves. The brothers eventually left the ghetto to join the partisans in the forest, but were not welcomed by the non-Jewish partisans. Other Jewish groups organized and headed to the forests. Slowly the Jewish partisans increased in number and formed their own unit. They fought in spite of the daily difficulties and blatant anti-Semitism among the non-Jewish partisans.

In July 1942, the Jewish ghetto population was sent somewhat further, 70 km (43 miles) north to Kostopil where they were all killed. Mrs. Lidkowsky had refused to join her husband in the forest and decided to remain in Baranowice where she was murdered with her children. The ghetto was subsequently liquidated.

The city of Baranowice was liberated by the Red Army on July 6, 1944. A significant part of the Polish population of the city had been expelled by Soviet authorities to Siberia and Kazakhstan between 1939 and 1941. The remaining Polish population was being squeezed out of the city and forced to move to Poland proper. About 250 Jews survived the Shoah and soon also left for Poland. The area became Soviet territory according to the Potsdam Agreement. Later on, a memorial complex of 20 thousand square meters was established, commemorating the killing of 17,500 Jews during the Holocaust.

Eliezer Lidkowsky and his brother Abraham survived the war with the partisans and helped liberate the city of Rowno, near Lwow. Rowno had been captured by the Nazis in June of 1941. Anti-Jewish policies immediately affected the Jews. Mass selections and killings took place. At the time, roughly half of Rowno's inhabitants were Jewish; of these, about 23,000 were taken to a pine grove in Sosenki and killed between November 6th and 8th.

Liquidation of the ghetto of Rowno on July 13, 1943. Notice the
carts lined to haul the few possessions and the people carrying bags.

Rowno is first mentioned in 1283 as one of the inhabited places of Halych-Volhynia. From the second half of the 14th century it was under the Great Duchy of Lithuania and from 1569 it was in the Polish-Lithuanian Commonwealth. Following the partition of Poland in 1793, Rowno became part of the Russian Empire. In April-May 1919 Rowno served as the temporary capital of the Ukrainian People's Republic. With the Riga Peace Treaty of 1921 it became a part of Poland. In September 1939, the city of Rowno was occupied by the Soviet Army.

On February 2, 1944, the Red Army entered the city of Rowno. Only 30 or 40 Jews from Rowno had survived the Shoah and they warmly greeted the Jewish partisans who arrived with the Russians. About 250 Jewish partisans including the Lidkowsky brothers remained in the desolate city. With the help of another partisan, Itzhak Reichman, the brothers began to organize a Jewish community. Meetings were held and the group soon had 12 members. They received permission to open an artisan cooperative where Jewish survivors worked for a living. The workshop became the Jewish refugee center where survivors flocked to get information or help. The Jewish population grew and soon located a rabbi who took over the local synagogue and began to organize Jewish religious life.

Eliezer needed money to expand the services of the Jewish community in Rowno, so he went to Moscow seeking funds. He met the famous Yiddish actor Salomon Mikhoels and the Yiddish writer Itsik Fefer, both members of the Anti Fascist Committee set up by Stalin to gain Western support and sympathy for the Soviet Union during the war. However, he returned to Rowno empty handed. Meanwhile Jews continued to arrive in Rowno seeking help.

Lidkowsky and the other Jews in the community felt isolated and this feeling increased daily. The surrounding areas had been cleansed of Jews. Survivors would arrive in the Rowno area, see the desolation, and quickly leave for cities with a larger Jewish population. The Soviet Administration did not provide help to restore the communities, especially Jewish communities. So it was left up to Jewish individuals who were closely watched by the secret police. Zionist activities were totally forbidden.

Lidkowsky and some of the partisans did not want to remain in Rowno. They saw the Poles leaving for Poland and they too wanted to leave, but to Palestine, not an easy thing to accomplish since the war still raged in Europe. Suddenly a window opened. The Soviet Army liberated the city of Czernowitz on March 28, 1944. Czernowitz was close to the Romanian border where the Port of Constantsa or Cernauti was located on the Black Sea. Lidkowsky remembered the period when ships used to leave the Romanian port with Jews heading for Palestine. The idea was discussed among the partisans. They agreed to send a group under the leadership of Abraham Lidkowsky to the city of Czernowitz and if feasible further on to Romania. The young partisans were determined to head to Palestine and live in a Jewish environment despite the tremendous obstacles and dangers along the way. And their efforts would help create a safe route for groups of Jewish Shoah survivors to follow.

The group set out along a southern route in the direction of the Romanian border. The train tracks were dislocated and bands of Bandera supporters, extreme Nationalist Ukrainians bitterly opposed to the Soviet regime, spread terror throughout the countryside. Stalin was vehemently opposed to a separate Ukrainian state. Slowly the Jewish group made headway, often stopping in places where there were once large Jewish communities, now desolate. A few survivors were seen here and there. Finally the group reached Czernowitz.

Prior to the war Czernowitz had been a major Jewish center. A 1930 census indicated that 42,592 Jews resided in the city (representing 37% of the total population). After being designated the capital of the new Habsburg crown province of Bucovina in 1849, Czernowitz enjoyed several decades of development, a process stimulated by the economic and political emancipation of Jews, which was completed after 1867. The Jewish population increased significantly from 4,678 (out of a total 20,467) in 1850 to 14,440 (out of 45,600) in 1880 and 28,610 (out of 87,235) in 1910. The proportion of entrepreneurs who were Jewish reached approximately 90 percent after 1900. It was therefore not by chance that parliamentary representatives of the Chamber of Industry and Commerce, founded in 1850, were mainly Jews.

In 1930, the majority of the Jewish population of Czernowitz declared Yiddish as their mother tongue. There were disputes between the Yiddishists and Hebraists, as well as among Zionists, social democrats and supporters of the Union of Romanian Jews. The squabbles weakened the ability of the community to react to increasingly virulent anti-Semitic manifestations, events that occasionally had the passive or even active support of the authorities. The Jewish population consisted of Orthodox Jews, Hasidim, Zionists, (ranging from Revisionists on the right, to Shomer Hatzair, Bundists and assimilated Jews on the left).

In June 1940 Czernowitz was occupied by the Soviet Union. As in other cities Soviet authorities immediately implemented a Communist order, resulting in the deportation of about 3,000 wealthy Jews to Siberia. Romanian and German forces reoccupied the city on July 5, 1941, with precise orders from the pro-Nazi Romanian government of Ion Antonescu to punish Jews for their apparent attachment to the Soviet Union. Following a wave of assassinations, culminating in the murder of Chief Rabbi Abraham Mark and the torching of the temple, a series of repressive measures was instituted, depriving Jews of civil and economic rights. On October 11, 1941, a ghetto was established that concentrated approximately 5,000 people in the former Jewish district of the city, serving as a transit point before their deportation across the Dniester River. From October 1941 to May–June 1942, more than 32,000 people were deported to various camps and ghettos in Transnistria.

To prevent a complete paralysis of local affairs, several Romanian notables, led by Mayor Traian Popovici, managed to obtain approval for 17,000 Jews to remain in Czernowitz, where they were to perform compulsory labor. It is estimated that after the city was reoccupied by the Soviet Army in 1944, approximately 30 percent of the Jewish population had survived.

A group of Jewish writers with the Yiddish newspaper
Tshernovitser bleter *(Czernowitz Pages), Czernowitz, 1930s.*
(Left to right): Itsik Manger, Josef Lerner, S. A. Sofer, Naftali Herz Kon.
(The Ghetto Fighters' Museum/Israel)

With the liberation of Czernowitz, the surviving Jews began to breath. The Jewish community started to organize and some synagogues began to function. Zionist clubs were still forbidden and all Jewish activities were controlled by the Soviet government. Czernowitz Jews who had been sent to Siberia and Kazakhstan began to return home. Abraham Lidkowsky and his team began to look for jobs since they had to support themselves, and everyone had to work in the Soviet Union in order not to attract attention from the authorities. Abraham sent one team member back to Rowno to report to Eliezer that he could begin to send small groups of partisans to Czernowitz. Meanwhile Abraham connected with local Jews in Czernowitz and was soon introduced to Rabbi Meir Kahan, with whom he shared their plans. Rabbi Kahan was a Zionist sympathizer who introduced Abraham to other local Zionists. They began to organize places for the incoming groups of Rowno partisans. Arrangements were also made with border smugglers to help cross the Soviet-Romanian border. All these activities had to be done in total secrecy, for the Soviet secret police were everywhere. Unexpectedly, a group of partisans headed by Ruzhka Korczak and Dr. Samuel Amarant arrived from Vilnius (Wilno). They were a part of the Abba Kovner group of partisans in Wilno who were looking for a way to reach Romania and the port of embarkation for Palestine.

There were disagreements in the Vilnius group over the direction they should take. Most of the partisans saw no hope for a Jewish life in post-war Lithuania, but some wanted to continue to fight Germany and others wanted to avenge Jewish deaths. Finally they reached a decision to head to Palestine. This decision was supported by Abba Kovner, Vitka Kempner and Ruzhka Korczak and most of the members of the Vilnius Jewish partisan group.[2]

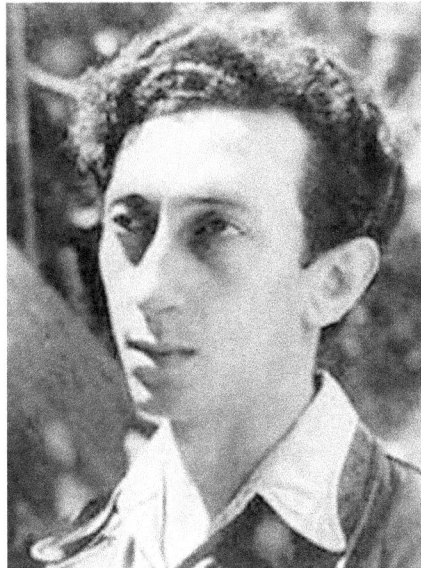

Abba Kovner

Abba Kovner was born in 1918 in Sebastopol, Crimea, on the shores of the Black Sea. His early life was the typical model of Jewish youth of the time. He was raised in Vilnius, which had been the preeminent center of Jewish learning since the seventeenth century. While there he was exposed to every variety of Jewish thought and the teachings of traditional and modern persuasions, from orthodoxy to socialism. Kovner attended the University of Vilnius as an art student, learning to sculpt, and later developed a passion for poetry. Like many other boys his age Kovner became interested in the Zionist movement and joined a local youth group of the "Ha-Shomer ha-Tzairr." or the Young Guard.

---

[2] Bauer, Flight, p.16

On June 24, 1941, the Germans occupied Vilnius. Several thousand Jews fled eastward with the Soviet Army, but the rapid German advance trapped the majority of the Jews in Vilnius and almost 60,000 Jews remained in the city at the time of the German occupation. Less than a month after the Germans occupied the city, they conducted their first Aktion. Einsatzkommando 9 rounding up 5,000 Jewish men and sent them to Ponary, an abandoned Soviet oil storage facility with large pits designed to house fuel.

On August 31, 1941, led by SS officer Einsatzkommando 9 Oberscharführer Horst Schweinberger, the SS established two ghettos in Wilno, referred to as Ghetto No. 1 and Ghetto No. 2. The following day they swept through the city and forced the remaining Jews into the newly created ghettos. About 30,000 Jews were forced into Ghetto No. 1 and between 9,000 and 11,000 Jews into Ghetto No. 2. Kovner and 16 other members of the Ha-Shomer Ha-Tzairr fled the city. Hiding out in a convent of Dominican nuns a few miles outside of Wilno from where they watched as the Nazis conducted a series of actions, against the Jewish community. Jews were then dragged to the Ponary site and murdered.

Abba Kovner had no illusions about the German intentions for the Jews of Wilno. He saw the German behavior against the Jews and was convinced that they intended to kill all Jews. Kovner urged the remaining Jews to organize and resist. A secret meeting was held on December 31, 1941, where many of the youth groups and activists advocating resistance came together to discuss defensive efforts. Although not all in attendance agreed to stay and fight, Abba Kovner took it upon himself to urge what remained of the Ghetto inhabitants to rise up and fight from within the ghetto itself. In an impassioned speech delivered at one of the ghetto soup kitchens, he shouted to those around him:

"Jewish youth! Do not trust those who are trying to deceive you. Out of the eighty thousand Jews in the 'Jerusalem of Lithuania' only twenty thousand are left... Ponary is not a concentration camp. They have all been shot there. Hitler plans to destroy all the Jews of Europe, and the Jews of Lithuania have been chosen to be the first in line. We will not be led like sheep to the slaughter! True, we are weak and defenseless, but the only reply to the murderer is revolt! Brothers! Better to fall as free fighters than to live by the mercy of the murderers. Arise! Arise with your last breath!"

Shortly thereafter the United Partisan Organization or Fareinikte Partisaner Organizatzie (FPO) was formed on January 21, 1942, in the

Wilno Ghetto. "We will not go like sheep to the slaughter" was its motto. It was decided that the FPO would be led by a "staff command" made up of Kovner, Josef Glazman and Yitzhak Wittenberg, with the "chief commander" being Wittenberg. Later, two more members were added to staff commandnamely Abraham Chwojnik of the Bund and Nissan Reznik of the HaNoar Ha-Tzioni or Zionist Youth – expanding the leadership to five. The goals of the FPO were to establish a means for the self defense of the ghetto population, to sabotage German industrial and military activities and to join the partisan fight against the Germans.

Itzhak Wittenberg, Head of Jewish military resistance in the Wilno ghetto

The Wilno Judenrat was totally opposed to the military partisan activities. The head of the Judenrat, Yaacov Gens, waged a bitter campaign against armed resistance. The Germans cooperated with him and Wittenberg was sacrificed to the Gestapo, who killed him. One of Wittenberg's last moves was to appoint Abba Kovner as head of the Wilno ghetto partisans.

During the summer and fall of 1943, Kovner and his resistance fighters carried out acts of sabotage against German military trains and equipment transports, and even set up an illegal printing press outside of the ghetto. One of their key goals was to establish ties to the partisan forces in the forests that were supported by Russia. Kovner also sent emissaries to the Warsaw and Bialystok ghettos to warn the Jewish inhabitants about the mass killings of Jews by Germans in Russia and urged active military resistance. On September 1, 1943, German forces began the final destruction of the Wilno ghetto. Kovner and the FPO made a concerted effort to try and persuade the ghetto residents not to gather for the deportation because they were in actuality being sent to their deaths. The majority of the Jewish ghetto inhabitants refused to believe Kovner, who ordered his forces to attack the Germans. The Wehrmacht brought in light artillery and explosives to flush out the ghetto fighters. But as soon as it grew dark, the Germans pulled out of the ghetto and left it to the Jewish Police.

Abba Kovner, FPO leader

After the initial skirmish with the Germans, Gens, the head of the Judenrat, tried to prevent further destruction by offering to provide additional Jews for forced labor in Estonia, if only the Germans would leave the ghetto. The Germans agreed and Yaacov Gens was given a quota of Jews to be deported. But the Germans ended up seizing every Jew in Wilno to meet their quota. Only 12,000 Jews remained in the city. Yaacov Gens was killed and the ghetto was liquidated a few days later.

Kovner and hundreds of the ghetto fighters escaped through the city's sewers and other outlets to the Rudniki forests where they joined Soviet partisans on many combat missions. There Kovner and his followers operated a partisan division comprised solely of Jews and performed many heroic acts of sabotage. The division played a key role in destroying power installations, water infrastructures and supply depots. They blew up German transport trains and even rescued groups of prisoners from the Kalais labor camp.

Map of the route that Jewish partisans from Vilnius, Baranowice and Rowno used to reach Czernowitz or Cernauti and then Bucharest, Romania.

With the liberation of Wilno, Kovner, Ruzhka Korczak and Vitka Kempner, began to activate what remained of the decimated Jewish community. The young partisans began to ponder their future. Did they want to fight the German army and exact revenge or try to escape the madness? Some of the partisans argued that they wanted to head to Palestine to fulfill their ideal of building a Jewish nation. The promise of a true homeland won out and Kovner sent Korczak and Dr. Amarant to Czernowitz to explore the possibility of crossing the Soviet-Romanian border. Two Jewish partisan leaders had the same object yet were hundreds of kilometers from each other. Both delegations met in

Czernowitz. They worked together to create an organization that would absorb transports of illegal Jews in the city and send them onward to Romania. Many local Zionists in Czernowitz assisted the newcomers, facilitated by Rabbi Kahan. Both Abraham Lidkowsky and Korczak dispatched messages to start sending groups of Jews. Meanwhile, Abraham Lidkowsky, Korczak and some Zionist youths managed with the help of smugglers to cross the border to Romania where they took a train to Bucharest. The road was now clear to Palestine. At last there was an opening of hope for those Jewish Shoah survivors who wanted to go to Palestine and fulfill their dreams.

List of Brichah agents in the Soviet Union

Last Name	First Name	G		Area of Operation
ABRAHAM	Hersh	M		Romania
AST	Awrham	M		Sov .Union
ECKSTEIN	Haya	F		Sov Union
EHERENPREISS	Joseph	M		Sov Union
EHRENHAFT	Sarah	F		Sov Union
FARBER	Fishel	M		Sov .Union
FELDMAN	Raphael	M		Sov .Union
FRANKFURTER	Yehoshua	M	Rabbi	Sov .Union
KAHAN	Meier	M	Rabbi	Sov Union
KARMIL	Moshe	M		Sov Union
KARMIL	Akiva	M		Sov Union
KLESS	Shlomomo	M		Sov .Union
KLESS-VULKAN	Genia	F		Sov .Union
LEONEK		F		Sov Union
LEV	Fima	M		Sov Union
MELLER	Yossef	M		Sov .Union
RITTER	Zeev	M		Sov Union
ROZMAN	Mordechai	M		Sov .Union
SCOTT	Kopel	M		Sov Union
SHEVAH	Ze'ev	M		Sov .Union
SHIMONOW	S	M		Sov Union
SHREIBER	Itzhak	M		Sov .Union
SURKISS	Mordecha	M		Sov .Union

Chapter II
Bucharest, Romania

Abraham Lidkowsky and Ruzhka Korczak arrived in Bucharest and located the Palestine office headed by the legendary **Moshe Auerbach** (later changed to Agami). Auerbach was born in Latvia and came to Palestine in 1926 and settled in "kfar" or village Giladi along the Syrian border near the old settlement of Tel Chai. Yosef Trumpeldor had fallen in Battle defending the settlement. The area was constantly exposed to marauding bands of Bedouins and the Kibbutz was forced to devote a great deal of energy to defense. Agami joined the local Haganah branch and quickly rose through the ranks. He showed exceptional leadership qualities and in 1936 he was chosen by the Jewish Agency of Palestine to head the Vienna office, where his main job was to help Austrian Jews leave for Palestine, legally or illegally. He actually met on several occasions with Nazi leader and future Shoah executor Adolf Eichmann in Vienna and walked away alive.

אגמי משה

Moshe Auerbach, later Moshe Agami

His activities increased greatly when the Jewish Agency of Palestine under the leadership of David Ben Gurion decided to abandon the policy of co-operation with Britain, following various measures Britain adopted aimed at Jews, including the drastic reduction of entrance certificates to Jews wanting to go to Palestine, even though the number of Jews trying to leave Europe grew daily. The British were determined to stop all Jewish immigration to Palestine and adopted pro-Arab policies hoping to gain the favor of the Arab world.

Shaul Avigur, head of the "Mossad"
which organized the smuggling of Jews into Palestine

The Jewish Agency decided to attack British policies in Palestine. A special office named the "Mossad" was created and empowered to use all means possible to bring Jews to Palestine. The Mossad organization was headed by **Shaul Avigur,** who organized a network of offices throughout Europe for this effort. The Mossad began to buy ships and load them with Jews headed to Palestine. At first, there was some success but soon Britain ordered its Mediterranean fleet to patrol the approaches to Palestine. Still, boats with illegal immigrants kept arriving. British ambassadors intervened everywhere diplomatically to stop the departure of ships but Jews kept coming to Romania where they hoped to board ships for Palestine. Agami was very busy expediting Jewish transports from Austria to Romania until he was finally kicked out of Austria as a foreign Jew. He moved his office to Greece, then to Yugoslavia, Bulgaria and Turkey. Everywhere he tried to buy ships and load them with Jews. The task was very difficult. British agents followed him and managed to destroy many deals by the mere threat that the ship would be confiscated on arrival in Palestine. The British agents also publicized when ships with Jews were expected to leave the European shores. No European country wanted problems with England. Meanwhile, Germany expanded control over Europe. Mossad offices kept closing one after the other as the Germans advanced. Agami and other Mossad agents arrived in Turkey where they tried to continue their activities, now limited to countries bordering the Black Sea: Bulgaria, Romania and Turkey.

Brichah - Hebrew for Escape or Flight

The Bulgarian Jews had been Zionist sympathizers since the days of the Hovevei Zion, forerunners of the political Zionism created by Theodor Herzl. They supported the Zionist movements and participated in Zionist activities. They also helped the Mossad acquire ships and increase the illegal shipping activities as the German threat spread throughout Europe. The first ship to leave Bulgaria was the *Velos* in 1934. The following ships left Bulgaria with Jews aboard heading for Palestine. Despite all the obstacles, quite a number of ships left for Palestine, mostly financed by the Jewish Agency and the JDC.

June 1938	*Karlica Maria*
June 1939	*Aghios Nicolaos*
July 1939	*Colorado*
August 1939	*Rudnitchar*
August 1939	*Krotova*
November 1939	*Rudnitchar*
December 1939	*Rudnitchar*
January 1940	*Rudnitchar*
May 1940	*Libertad*
December 1940	*Salvador*

The *Salvador* was the last ship to leave the Bulgarian port of Varna. In December 1940, with 352 refugees bound for Palestine, the boat ran aground 100 meters off the coast of Silivri, west of Istanbul, and sank. Two hundred twenty-three passengers drowned or died of exposure in the frigid waters. Half the survivors were sent back to Bulgaria while the remainder were allowed to board the Darien II, and landed in Palestine but were imprisoned at Atlit detention camp as illegal refugees. Eventually they would be released from the camp against certificates of entrance that the British mandate issued each month. Following the departure of the ship, the climate in Bulgaria began to change rapidly. Germany pressured Bulgaria to join the Axis countries, dangling territorial concessions and influencing public opinion through propaganda. Bulgaria officially joined the Tripartite Agreement on March 1, 1941.

<>

The illegal ship Salvador that left Bulgaria with Jewish refugees
for Palestine in December 1940 (Yad Vashem Archives)

In 1941, the Bulgarian parliament and Tsar Boris III began to enact anti-Jewish laws. Jews were prohibited from voting, running for office, working in government positions, serving in the army, marrying or cohabitating with ethnic Bulgarians, using Bulgarian names or owning rural land. Authorities began confiscating all radios and telephones owned by Jews. All Jewish organizations were disbanded. All Zionist offices were ordered closed. All non-Bulgarian Zionist officials had to leave the country and Mossad activities came to an end. Most young Jews were drafted into labor battalions and forced to work on big projects. The Germans began to demand that Bulgaria send their Jews to Poland and other areas of the Reich. Serious discussions continued on the subject between the governments. The Germans meanwhile detained all the Jews in the areas that they had given to Bulgaria like parts of Macedonia and deported them to Poland where they all perished.

Brichah - Hebrew for Escape or Flight

German pressure continued but the Bulgarian government was divided on the issue and the Bulgarian Church was totally opposed to the deportation of Bulgarian Jews. Meanwhile Germany suffered some military setbacks and victory became uncertain. The Bulgarians procrastinated and finally decided not to deport its Jews. Bulgaria's 48,000 Jews were saved from deportation to Nazi concentration camps with the help of Dimitar Peshev, an influential political figure in Bulgarian politics, leaders of the Bulgarian Church, led by Metropolitan Stefan of Sofia, Tsar Boris, and ordinary citizens. Most of the Jews would leave Bulgaria for Israel following the establishment of the Jewish State.

Romania was also an important port of embarkation for Jews to Palestine. The Palestine office was very active in Bucharest and helped many ships leave Romania via the port of Constanta. Below is a list of the ships that left Romania for Palestine.

November 1938	*Draga B*and the *Delpha*
December 1938	*Chepo*
January 1939	*Katina*
February 1939	*Chepo*
March 1939	*Astir*, the *Sandu*, the *Agios Nicolaos* and the *Asimi*
May 1939	*Liesel* and the *Frosula*
June 1939	*Las Perlas* and the *Rim*
July 1939	*Parita*
August 1939	*Tiger Hill*, the *Aghios Nicolaos* and the *Noe Mijulia*
January 1940	*Hilda*
February 1940	*Saraya* and the *Pentcho*
October 1940	*Pacific*
November, 1940	*Atlantic* and the *Milos Nou*
March 1941	*Darien* and *Mihai*
April 1941	*Mirceal*
May 1941	*Dor de Val*
December 1941	*Struma*
August 1942	*Dora*
September 1942	*Vitrol* and the *Europa*

Most of these ships reached the Palestinian coast where the Mandate authorities detained the passengers and placed them in detention facilities but at least they were saved. The extent of illegal shipping was carried out against huge obstacles by a vast operation involving many groups and individuals to find the ships and bring the refugees aboard the vessels. Even the war that started in September 1939 did not stop the movement of ships and the rescue operations. On the contrary, the war increased the activities. The Palestinian Office was flooded with applicants but the lack of ships limited the number of sailings.

The Jewish situation in Romania went from bad to worse. Anti-Jewish legislation started as early as 1937 with the exclusion of Jews from professional associations. On September 14, 1940, General, later Marshal, Ion Antonescu seized power in Romania. He forced King Carol to abdicate in favor of his 18 year-old son Michael. Romania then adopted the Romanian version of the Nuremberg laws in Germany. The "Iron Guard" or extreme nationalist and anti-Semitic members of the government pressed for more anti-Jewish laws that were constantly issued by the government. These acts made life very difficult for the Jews in the old provinces of Romania. Most of the Jewish organizations, including Zionist groups, were dissolved. In the new areas that Romania acquired – Bukovina, Bessarabia and Transnistria – the Jews were decimated by the Romanian and German armies. A zone was created between the Bug and Dniester Rivers where all Jews of the new areas were sent and eventually perished. But the regime actually encouraged all Jewish emigration or aliyah activities. The anti-Jewish campaign intensified with Romania's participation in the attack against Russia. Romania committed large forces and supplies to the attack. The Romanian economy could barely keep pace with the expenses of the war. Marshal Antonescu was determined to stay with Germany and kept a close eye on the young Romanian King.

Some Jewish organizations in Romania refused to close down and went underground, like the Council of Jewish Communities that was able to maintain contact with the JDC. The Palestine office headed by Leo Eisnercontinued to function and successfully organized many ships to get Jews out of Romania. The Revisionist Zionist organization in Romania headed by Samuel Klamart also continued to function underground. Illegal ships continued to leave Romania until the *Struma* was torpedoed.

Brichah - Hebrew for Escape or Flight

The Struma

The *Struma* was an old vessel built in 1867. The Mossad had to use what was available and the *Struma* with a crew was ready. Apart from the crew and 60 Betar youth (members of the Revisionist Zionist youth movement), there were over 700 passengers who had paid large fees to board the ship. Antonescu's Romanian government approved the voyage. The diesel engine of the *Struma* failed several times between her departure from Constanta on the Black Sea on December 12, 1941, and its arrival in Istanbul on December 15, 1941. The ship had to be towed by a tug both to leave Constanta and to enter Istanbul. On February 23, 1942, with its engine still inoperable and its refugee passengers aboard, Turkish authorities towed the Struma from Istanbul through the Bosporus to the Black Sea. Within hours, in the morning of February 24, a Soviet submarine torpedoed the ship, killing passengers and crew, making it the Black Sea's largest exclusively civilian naval disaster of World War II. David Stoliar, age 19, was the only survivor.

It was obvious that the *Struma* had needed major repairs to continue the journey. The passengers had been stripped of all their possessions by Romanian customs officials, so the ship had no money to undertake repairs. The Turks wanted the ship to continue its voyage unless the passengers had certificates for Palestine. Britain refused to issue certificates although it had plenty in reserve. A small number of passengers had Palestinian visas so survived along with Stoliar. Turkey and Britain tried to hide the disaster. Stoliar was kept in a Turkish prison for some time until Britain issued him a certificate to enter Palestine. The Jews in Palestine were furious and expressed it through posters plastered on the walls of buildings across Palestine.

MURDER!

SIR HAROLD MAC MICHAEL

Known as High Commissioner for Palestine

WANTED for MURDER

OF 800 REFUGEES DROWNED IN THE
BLACK SEA ON THE BOAT .STRUMA

Poster that appeared after the sinking of the Struma.
Mac Michael was the head of the Palestinian Mandate Authority.

The terrible sea disaster forced the Mossad and the Revisionists to stop sending illegal ships since the risks were too high. Illegal shipping to Palestine came to a total standstill except for some small private boats. The Mossad resumed sending ships from Romania to Palestine in March 1944. Most of the transports actually left Turkey although the paperwork and preparations were made in Romania. With the military defeats suffered by the Axis forces, the winds of war shifted and so did the policy of Turkey regarding Jews heading to Palestine. Turkey consented to be a transit country and the Mossad took full advantage of the situation with eleven ships leaving that year.

March 1944	*Milka* A
April 1944	*Meritza A*, the *Bilasitza*, the *Milka B* and the *Meritza B*
April 1944	*Bilasitza*
May 1944	*Meritza B*
July 1944	*Kazbek*
August 1944	*Moriana*, the *Bulbul*, the *Mefakure* and the *Salah El Din*
December 1944	*Taurus*

The Soviet armies were driving toward the Romanian borders, the Allies were bombing the industrial sites in Romania, particularly the Pelosi oil fields. The Antonescu regime in Romania was weakening by the day. On August 23, 1944, the young King Michael assumed power, joined the allies and dismissed Marshal Antonescu from office. The JDC, the American Jewish Congress (AJC), the Palestine Office, Zionist organizations and the Hechalutz all reopened their offices and functioned in the open again.

The various Romanian Jewish organizations, including the Union of Jews in Romania under the leadership of **Wilhelm Filderman**, also started to work once again. Filderman, a well-known and respected community leader since 1919, had protected and fought for the rights of Jews in Romania. He was a lawyer by profession and was well connected with leading Romanian personalities. He retired to France where he continued to live until April 8, 1963.

Wilhelm Filderman

Moshe Auerbach was assigned to head the Palestine Office and he galvanized the bureau into activity. All Zionist groups that dealt with aliyah formed a common front. The aim was to expedite as many Jews as possible to Palestine. Bucharest had thousands of illegal Jews; some had escaped from Transnistria camps, others from Romanian labor battalions, still others from Poland. All these people wanted desperately to leave Romania since they were surviving on false papers. The demand for seats aboard the illegal ships far exceeded the available space.

Then Lidkowsky and Korczak showed up in Auerbach's office. This was the first contact between a Palestinian Jewish official and Jewish partisan survivor in Eastern Europe. They talked for hours and explained the present chaotic situation in the area. Auerbach decided to send both representatives aboard the Taurus to Palestine where they would be able to explain what had happened in Eastern Europe. Most of Palestine and the Jewish world knew very little if anything of what had happened to the Jews. Auerbach knew it was vital that eye witnesses share their stories. Both men arrived December 12, 1944 in Haifa, Palestine.[3] Lidkowsky and Korczak quickly met with important Jewish leaders and shared their knowledge of the dire situation of post-war Jewish Europe.

Auerbach enlarged the Palestinian Office in Bucharest and created a Brichah office whose task was to bring Jews out of the Transnistria area camps to Bucharest where they could be helped and shipped onwards to Palestine. Auerbach, Kovner and Lidkowsky all worked together with the JDC providing assistance to Shoah survivors. The Council of Jewish Communities under the leadership of Wilhelm Filderman pushed the government to help return the surviving Romanian Jews from the death camps of Transnistria.[4] Small groups of Jews also began to arrive from Rowno and Vilnius through the route established by Lidkowsky and Korczak. Jews in other cities such as Lwow heard of the possibility of going to Palestine and decided to join the exodus.

Remnants of the pre-war Zionist movements began to move to Bucharest via Czernowitz, part of the Soviet Union. The city became an important Brichah center from where Jews would be smuggled into Romania. It is estimated that by April 1945 there were 2,000 to 3,000 new Jewish arrivals in Bucharest.[5] The Soviet secret police began to take an active interest in the aliyah movement and managed to plant an agent within the Brichah organization in Czernowitz. He was a local Jewish doctor who professed to be a Zionist sympathizer and actually helped the smuggling operations. When Dr. Amarant, a close associate of Kovner, arrived with a sizable group of Jewish partisans from Wilno, they were surrounded by Soviet secret police who knew where to look. There was a great deal of confusion and some of the new arrivals managed to disappear but 11 people were arrested, including Dr. Amarant, and Rabbi Kahan. While on their way to prison Dr. Amarant managed to send a cable to the community in Lwow that they had been arrested.[6] Word soon spread to all Brichah units: Stop sending Jews to Czernowitz. The

---

[3] Bauer, Flight, p. 17.

[4] Israel Defense Ministry. The Brichah Movement from Europe to Israel 1945-1948. 1998, p. 59.

[5] Bauer, Flight. p. 31.

[6] Bauer, Flight, p. 17.

Jews who arrived in Czernowitz and were not arrested by the police were eventually smuggled to Romania. But the Czernowitz Brichah operation center was destroyed. On May 11, 1945, proceedings started against the arrested Brichah leaders in Czernowitz, most of whom faced serious charges of counterrevolutionary activities, and some received up to two years in jail. The Soviet police interrogations revealed the activities of Lidkowsky in Rowno and Kovner in Wilno. They and some of their associates became wanted men and left for Poland.

The Czernowitz Brichah center was shut dealing a serious blow to the entire Brichah movement, for the route of hope for many Jews in Eastern Europe was now closed. The Brichah organization in Romania continued to expand and create more illegal routes leading to Hungary and Yugoslavia. The port of Constanta in Romania that once handled ships leaving for Palestine was now almost entirely closed to civilian shipping; the Soviet navy kept expanding its presence in the port and the government slowly closed private shipping companies.

Incomplete list of Brichah agents who operated in Romania

Some of the names have been altered or changed or are intentionally incorrect for safety reasons.

Last Name	First Name	Code name	G	Area of Operation
ABRAHAM	Hersh		M	Romania
ARTZI-HERTZIG	Itzhak		M	Romania
ASHMAN	Frida		F	Romania
ASHMAN	Chaim		M	Romania
AUERBACH	Moshe	Agami	M	Romania
BEN EPHRAIM	Itzhak	Meno	M	Romania
BIELSKI		Hatzair	M	Romania
BITESH				Romania
BREITNER	Shimon		M	Romania
BURSHTEIN	Mordechai		M	Romania
CHERMATZ	Julek		M	Romania
COMIN	Baruch		M	Romania
COMIN	Ariela		F	Romania
DAVID	Dov		M	Romania
ELDAR	Arieh		M	Romania
FARKASH	Laci		M	Romania
FELDMAN	Raphael		M	Romania
FELLER	Neta		F	Romania
FERBER	Fishel		M	Romania
GARFUNKEL	Sulka		F	Romania

GELBER-YACOBI	Bruria		F	Romania
GENOSSAR	Menashe		M	Romania
GOLDSTEIN	Baruch		M	Romania
GOLDSTEIN	Reisel		F	Romania
HALPERIN	Rachel		F	Romania
HAMEL	Itzhak		M	Romania
HELLER	Bumek		M	Romania
HENDLER	Oskar		M	Romania
HERTZIG	Shimon		M	Romania
KLARMAN	Yossef		M	Romania
KLEIDMAN	Lionka		M	Romania
KLESS	Shlomo		M	Romania
KEMPNER KOCHBA	Eliezer		M	Romania
KOVNER	Abba		M	Lithuania
KRAUSS	Erica		F	Romania
KUPPERSTEIN	Meir		M	Romania
LAHAV	Tzivia - Bri		F	Romania
LAZAR	Chaim		M	Romania
LEVI	Yehuda	Pitzi	M	Romania
LEVIPENSE	Moshe		M	Romania
LITVAK	Itzhak		M	Romania
LUPOVIC	Chico		M	Romania
MUNKATCH	Mordechai		M	Romania
PELED	Chaim		M	Romania
RABINOWICZ	Shimon	hanita	M	Romania
RABINOWICZ	Zeev		M	Romania
REICH	Herman-Gav		M	Romania
REZNIK	Nissan		M	Romania
ROSENBERG	Raphael	ReJo	M	Romania
ROSENBERG	Yaakov		M	Romania
ROTEM	Kazik		M	Romania
ROZMAN	Mordechai		M	Romania
RUCHMAN	Pasha		M	Romania
SHAPIRO	Cila		F	Romania
SHIBA	Hanah		F	Romania
SHNIRSKA	Mira		F	Romania
STEINMAN	Baruch		M	Romania
TCHITINSKY	Klaman	Katzetnik	M	Romania
TREIMAN	Fink		M	Romania
TRICHTER	Poldi		M	Romania
TZIMAND	David		M	Romania
WINKLER-YATIR	Yael		F	Romania
WITZMAN	Zelig		M	Romania
WURTZEL	Chaim		M	Romania

Brichah - Hebrew for Escape or Flight

הלפרין רחל

דב דוד

גלברג-יעקבי ברוריה

ברייטנר שמעון

טריימן פינק

וורצל חיים

וינקלר-יתיר יעל

הרציג שמעון

לוי יהודה (פיצי)

להב צביה ברינה

כוכבא אליעזר

טריכטר פולדי

Some pictures of Brichah agents in Romania.

Top row, left to right:
Rachel Halpern, Dov David, Bruria Gelber-Jacobi and Shimon Breitner.

Second row, left to right:
Treiman Fink, Chaim Wurtzel, Yael Winkler-Yatir, Shimon Hertzig

Last row, left to right:
Yehuda Levi (Pitzi). Tzivia Lahav-Brina, Eliezer Kochba, Poldi Trichter.

Brichah - Hebrew for Escape or Flight

Chapter III
The Brichah In Poland

Map labels: Szczecin, Gdańsk, Wilno, Baranowicze, Białystok, Poznań, Brześć, WARSZAWA, 1947 border, Łódź, Wrocław, Lublin, Curzon line "B", Kraków, Lwów, Stanisławów

annexed by Poland in 1945

annexed by Soviet Union in 1945

THE CURZON LINE

Poland's old and new borders, 1945

The territorial changes of Poland immediately after World War II were very extensive. In 1945, after the defeat of Nazi Germany, Polish borders were redrawn in accordance with the decisions made by the Allies at the Potsdam Conference at the insistence of the Soviet Union. The prewar eastern Polish territories of Kresy, which the Red Army had invaded in 1939, were permanently annexed by the USSR, and most of their Polish inhabitants expelled. Today, these territories are part of sovereign Belarus, Ukraine and Lithuania.

The Government of the Republic of Poland in Exile, also known as the Polish government-in-exile, headquartered in London, refused to recognize the new Polish borders and began a steady opposition campaign within Poland to the changes. Joseph Stalin was determined to change the borders and since Soviet troops controlled the areas, the changes were immediately implemented. Stalin obtained full agreement from the provisional government of Poland, and with his approval, Wanda Wasilewska, a native of Krakow, became the head of the newly formed Związek Patriotów Polskich ("Society of Polish Patriots"), a Soviet-created provisional government that was to control Poland. In 1944, she also became the Deputy Chief of the Polish Committee of National Liberation (PKWN), another Soviet sponsored provisional government that opposed the Polish government-in-exile headed by Stanislaw Mikolajczyk. These entities fought each other for international recognition as the legal government of Poland. The London exile government had the support of the Western powers and the Polish population at large while Wasilewska had the support of the Soviet Union and the Polish Communist Party. The latter decided to bring into the Polish government known non-communist ministers to boost its international standing, notably Emil Sommerstein.

Wanda Wasilewska

Dr. Emil Sommerstein, a minister in the temporary Polish government and the Chairman of the Central Committee of Jews in Poland

Dr. Emil Sommerstein, born in the village of Chleszczewa near Lwow, was an attorney but devoted himself to Zionism and politics. Sommerstein was elected to the Polish Senate, serving as a deputy from 1922 to 1927 and again from 1929 to 1934. He was also a member of several important parliamentary commissions. In 1939 Sommerstein was arrested by the Soviet authorities, underwent severe interrogations and was sent from gulag to gulag. Suddenly, he was released from prison, flown to Moscow, shaved, showered, dressed and appointed as a member of the provisional Polish cabinet, the first Polish Jew to hold such office in Poland. Stalin was determined to control Poland since he needed a bridge between the Soviet Union and East Germany where his army was stationed. He decided to rehabilitate well-known Polish political figures[7].There were a few other Polish non-communists in the cabinet, but the majority were Communist Party members or communist sympathizers answerable to Moscow.

Sommerstein was familiar with Soviet political tactics and knew full well that he was being used for propaganda purposes. He decided to play along and try to obtain as many benefits as possible for Jewish Shoah survivors. He was instrumental in the creation of the Provisional Central Committee of Polish Jews in October 1944 under the umbrella of the PKWN. The name of the Jewish organization was soon altered to the Central Committee of Polish Jews, also referred to as the Central Committee of Jews in Poland and abbreviated CKŻP (Polish: Centralny Komitet Żydów w Polsce, Yiddish: צענטראל קאמיטעט פון די יידן אין פוילן Centraler

---

[7] Bauer, Flight, p24

Komitet fun di Jidn in Pojln). A state-sponsored political representation of Jews in Poland, it was established on November 12, 1944. The Central Committee established Jewish community centers throughout liberated Poland and assisted Jewish Shoah survivors in resuming their lives in Poland. It legally represented all CKŻP-registered Polish Jews in their dealings with the new government and its agencies. Initially, a Provisional Committee of Polish Jews (Tymczasowy Komitet Żydów Polskich) was convened in Lublin, chaired by Emil Sommerstein, with Michał Shuldenfrei as Vice Chairman. Shuldenfrei, a Polish lawyer, was an active Bund leader and a member of the Polish Parliament after the war.

In February 1945, the Committee was reorganized in Warsaw as the Central Committee of Jews in Poland. Its presidium included an uneasy coalition of Jewish representatives who defined themselves as Communist, Bundist, Left and Right Poalei Tzion, Iḥud, He-Ḥaluts, Ha-Shomer ha-Tzair, the Union of Jewish Partisans, and the Jewish Fighting Organization. Sommerstein remained the chairman, with Marek Bitter, Adolf Berman (President 1946–1949) and Szlomo Herszenhorn his deputies, and Paweł Zelicki as Secretary General. The CKŻP integrated local Jewish committees into a new multilevel hierarchy consisting of local, district, provincial and central echelons. It also appointed supervisors for local Jewish committees. The Committee created an Education Department headed by Szlomo Herszenhorn, an active Bundist educator who established the first Jewish orphanage in liberated Poland.

The Jewish Shoah survivors were shadows of themselves.[8] They were afraid of everything. Their families murdered, their homes gone, they faced the hostile street alone. Sommerstein felt that the Jews needed a spiritual or religious uplift to get back on their feet. He insisted that the Polish government appoint a Chief Chaplain of the Polish Army to meet the spiritual needs of the Jewish soldier.[9] There were about 13,000 registered Jewish soldiers in the Polish Army while some Jewish soldiers passed themselves off as Poles.[10] The Chaplain would become the spiritual head of the Jewish community in Poland. Sommerstein contacted Dr. Rabbi David Kahane in Lwow and asked him to come to Lublin where the Soviet backed Polish government was headquartered.

---

[8] Anna Cichopek-Gajraj. Beyond Violence. Cambridge University Press, 2014. p.35
[9] David Kahane, Rabbi. After the Deluge, Jerusalem, 1981. pp, 10-14. Hebrew
3 Cichopek-Gajraj. Violence. p. 44

Rabbi Dr. Major David Kahane in his military uniform (with his family)

Dr. Rabbi David Kahane was at the time one of the few rabbis in Poland to have survived while hiding during the Shoah.[11] Rabbi Kahane later became Chief Rabbi of the Israeli Air Force and then Chief Rabbi of Buenos Aires, Argentina. He was born March 15, 1902 in the village of Grzymalow in the Tarnopol region of Eastern Galicia.[12] He was ordained as a rabbi in 1929 in Vienna where he also received his Ph.D. After his studies, Kahane settled in Lwow (Lemberg), Poland, and became the rabbi of the Sistoska synagogue.[13] He held that position until the Nazi invasion of Poland in September 1939.

In his memoir "Lwow Ghetto Diary," Rabbi Kahane describes how he survived the war by playing cat and mouse with the Nazi troops searching the city for Jews.[14] At one point, Kahane describes how he scurried out from behind a place he was hiding and ran while Nazi soldiers shot at him. But Kahane was soon captured, and moved with the other Jews of Lwow to the ghetto built by the Nazis. Eventually he was deported from the ghetto and wound up in the Janowska labor camp outside the city of Lwow.[15] Janowska was also a transit camp. From there Jews unfit to work were sent to the death camp of Belzec. According to Rabbi Kahane, conditions in the camp were so horrible they defied description. Kahane escaped the Janowska camp and pleaded for refuge in the palace of Lwow's Ukrainian Metropolitan Archbishop

---

[11] William , Leibner, Mass Exit Transport of Jewish Children from Poland, Jerusalem: Yad Vashem, 2010.

12 David Kahane, Rabbi. After the Deluge, Jerusalem, Israel 1981 pp, 12-14.

13 Ibid, pp .12-14.

14 David Kahane, Rabbi. Lwow Ghetto Diary. Jerusalem, 1978, p.87

15 Ibid, p.125

Andreas Sheptytsky. During the war Sheptytsky harbored hundreds of Jews in his residence and in Greek Catholic monasteries. He also issued the now famous pastoral letter, "Thou Shalt Not Kill" to protest Nazi atrocities.

By the end of World War II, over one and a half million innocent Jewish children had been slaughtered by the Nazis. But some Jewish children survived because parents rushed to neighbors and friends, even to the local priests, monasteries and convents, begging shelter for the children. If possible, parents trekked to peasant farmers they knew in the Polish countryside and paid to have the children hidden. Reportedly, some parents tossed their children over walls the Nazis had built around Jewish ghettos in hopes the children would be picked up by a passing tender-hearted Pole.

According to later testimony by Rabbi Kahane, the Jewish religious establishment of the city debated whether it was permissible to hide Jewish children in Christian institutions. Kahane said most of the rabbis were in favor of the move, "believing that, if the children survived, someone would remove them from the convents and return them to the fold." Several rabbis, however, believed it preferable for the children to die with the rest of their families and their people rather than be placed in a convent. Rabbi Kahane disagreed, believing the highest duty of a Jew was to save the children's lives. He arranged with the Archbishop to place his own daughter in a convent. She survived the Shoah, as did Kahane's wife, who was admitted to a Uniate institution under orders of Archbishop Sheptytsky. The Archbishop also issued orders to the Uniate convents of the Studite order in Eastern Galicia to accept Jewish children and hide them. Mother General Josefa-Helena Witer, head of the Convents of the Uniate Studite Order in Eastern Galicia, personally greeted Jewish children and distributed them among her institutions, ensuring their safety. Archbishop Sheptytsky died in 1944 and is buried in St. George's Cathedral in Lwow.

Kahane's experience led him to a deep understanding of the complexities the Jewish community faced following the war. Having survived with his family due to the good offices of the Christian community, he respected any Christian family or institution that harbored Jews during the Nazi terrorist rule. With the liberation, Lwow became Soviet territory and Rabbi Kahane began the uphill battle of reviving the decimated Jewish community.

One day Kahane was surprised to receive an invitation to come to Lublin to meet Emil Sommerstein, head of the temporary Central Organization of Polish Jews in liberated Poland, and a member of the Soviet-sponsored Polish government.[16] Sommerstein had convinced the government of the need to establish a Jewish chaplaincy in the Polish Army. When Kahane arrived, Sommerstein took him to meet the Polish Minister of Defense, General Rola-Zymierski, who offered Kahane the job of Chief Military Chaplain of the Polish Army, with the rank of Major (later promoted to Colonel). The Rabbi thanked the Polish Minister but insisted that he be given permission to revitalize the destroyed Jewish religious communities in liberated Poland. His request was granted and he appointed Chaplain Aaron Becker to organize the Association of Jewish Religious Community Centers (AJRCC).

The CKŻP received money allocations from the Polish government to be distributed to the Jewish survivors in Poland to get them started. The CKŻP also began to publish a Yiddish newspaper entitled "Dos Naye Leben" or the New Life. The number of Jewish survivors in Poland increased by the day. Of the over three million Jews who were living in Poland when the Nazis invaded on September 1, 1939, only 10,000 Jews remained in liberated Poland in January 1945, according to Anna Cichopek-Gajraj in "Beyond Violence."[17] By June 1945 that number had jumped to 68,500. The increase was due to surviving Jews who had returned to Poland from the camps and the forests, and demobilized Polish Jewish soldiers. By the end of 1945, the number of Jews in Poland would reach 81,593.[18]

The Polish Jewish population would also increase with the expulsion of Polish citizens from the areas that the Soviet Union annexed. The Soviet authorities forced many Poles and Polish institutions to move to Poland. Many Polish Jews, including Eliezer Lidkowsky and Abba Kovner, left the Soviet Union and arrived in Poland. By January 1946 the number of Jews in Poland increased to 106,492 with the discharge of Jewish soldiers from the Polish and Soviet armies. By June 1946, the number of Jews in post-war Poland peaked at 240, 489.[19] By 1948 the Polish repatriation commission had repatriated 175,000 Jews who had spent the war years in the Soviet Union. The majority of these repatriated

16 Kahane, Deluge, pp12-14.
17 Cichopek-Gajraj, Violence, p.44
18 Ibid., Violence, p.44
19 Ibid., Violence, p.44

Jews were sent to the new areas that Poland received in the post-war settlement. Non-Jewish Poles were also sent to the new areas. The Polish government insisted on settling Poles in the new areas to take the place of the Germans who were expelled from these areas.

The members of the Central Committee were mostly unknown to the Jewish survivors of Poland with some exceptions, such as Sommerstein and Shuldenfrei. Sommerstein decided to popularize the Committee and added two famous members who would later become a family, Antek or Itzhak Zuckerman and Zivia Lubetkin. Both were young leaders who had fought the Germans and were well known names among the Jews.

Yitzhak Zuckerman, Polish hero also known as
Yitzhak Cukierman and Antek Zuckerman

Yitzhak Zuckerman was born in 1915 in Warsaw, Poland. He was a hero of Jewish resistance to the Nazis in World War II and one of the few survivors of the Warsaw Ghetto Uprising. Zuckerman was active in a federation of young Zionist organizations, Hehalutz, and was an early advocate of armed resistance to Nazi depredations against the Jews. He was quick to interpret the first mass executions of Jews as the beginning of a systematic program of annihilation. Perceiving the full scope of Nazi plans and realizing that the Jews had nothing left to lose, in March 1942 Zuckerman represented Hehalutz at a meeting of Zionist groups and urged the creation and arming of a defense organization. Others feared that resistance would provoke the Nazis to greater violence. But on July 28, soon after the first trainload of 5,000 Jews had left the Warsaw ghetto to be gassed at the death camp of Treblinka, Jewish leaders accepted his view and created the Jewish Fighting Organization (Żydowska Organizacja Bojowa or ŻOB) under the leadership of

Mordechai Anielewicz. Zuckerman became one of his three co-commanders and also helped lead a political affiliate founded at the same time, the Jewish National Committee (Żydowski Komitet Narodowy). Zuckerman fought in the Polish uprising of 1944 in Warsaw and survived the war.

Zivia Lubetkin was also invited to join the Central Committee. She was born in Byeten near Slonim on November 9, 1914.

Zivia Lubetkin

She joined the Labor Zionist Movement at an early age. In her late teens she joined the Zionist youth movement, Dror, and in 1938 became a member of its Executive Council. After Nazi Germany and later the Soviet Union invaded Poland in September 1939 she made a perilous journey from the Soviet occupied part of the country to Warsaw to join the underground (ŻOB). She fought in the Polish uprising in Warsaw in 1944 and survived the war.

The CKŻP tried to cope with the needs of the Jewish Shoah survivors as well as with the Jews who were repatriated from the Soviet Union but the funds available from the Polish government were limited. **David Guzik**, a prewar official of the American Jewish Joint Distribution Committee (JDC) in Poland emerged from hiding and took matters into his own hands.[20] Throughout the war he had been active raising money for the Jewish ghetto of Warsaw and later for the Jewish revolt in Warsaw. Following the war, he assumed the post of Director of JDC in Poland. Guzik was well connected and keenly aware of the problems that Jews faced in liberated Poland. He organized an extensive system of

---

[20] William. Leibner, Zabrze-Hindenburg-Zabrze Yizkor Book. Jerusalem: Yad Vashem, pp.50-54

welfare assistance to the surviving Jewish communities in Poland. He gave aid to Jewish old age homes and orphanages and organized an extensive operation to bring food, medicines and money that was so desperately needed by Polish Jews. He died tragically in a plane accident on March 5, 1946 in Prague.

David Guzik

The Jewish pre-war organizations began to reappear in cities that had Jewish populations, particularly Zionist youth organizations such as Hashomer HaHatzair, Hehalutz, Betar and Bnei Akiva. A big debate began among Polish Zionists about their future: Should they stay in Poland or go to Palestine? Lidkowsky and Kovner participated in the debates and urged all Zionists to make aliyah, that is, emigrate to Palestine. They even met with Sommerstein and urged him to support their cause.[21] The meeting did not produce positive results since Sommerstein was a general Zionist who preferred that Zionists decide for themselves what to do. He himself saw the possibility of a revitalized Jewish community in Poland that would continue to live and forge ahead despite the Shoah. He was a Zionist but could stay in Poland just like a French Zionist could stay in France. Sommerstein had to be cautious because he did not want to antagonize the Polish government who supported his activities and the organizations that dealt with helping

---

[21] Bauer, Flight, p.19

Jewish Shoah survivors. He also had to be diplomatic around members of the Central Committee who were mostly communists and Bundist and vehemently opposed to Zionism.

Sommerstein did not commit himself to Lidkowsky and Kovner's ideas. The Brichah activists had not come to Poland to settle down but wanted action. They decided to leave Lublin, then the center of Polish government activities, and move to the quiet provincial city of Krakow where there was less police supervision. Kovner was well respected by the Brichah membership but wanted the younger members to assume leadership.

Mordechai Rosman

Kovner recommended that **Mordechai Rosman** assume the running of the Brichah in Poland. Rosman was a partisan who had fought in the war with Kovner.

Meanwhile, the road to Bucharest remained closed and a new route had to be found for the refugees. Kovner sent a team headed by Ze'ev Rabinowitz, better known as "Velvele," to explore the possibility of a new route to Romania. The team left Lublin and headed to Krosno, or Sanok, Poland, where they crossed the Carpathian Mountains to reach Humenne, Czechoslovakia and then on to Chust in Ukraine, and then to Baia Mare and Bucharest in Romania. The team reached Moshe Auerbach in Bucharest and a new path was created for Jews wanting to go to Palestine.

Map of the new route to Bucharest

Ze'ev Rabinowitz returned to Krakow and reported to Mordechai Rosman and Abba Kovner, who at this point was head of the Brichah organization in Europe. Preparations were immediately made to establish safe places stacked with food and clothing along the road, to sustain the refugees during their climb over the Carpathian Mountains. A Brichah team was sent to the city of Krosno to organize the necessary preparations. Groups of Polish Jewish refugees soon started to arrive in Krosno where they were briefed about the trip and provided with food bought on the black market. The refugees were also provided with the necessary forged papers that were printed in Krakow.

Groups of Jews began to arrive in Bucharest but there was no exit from Romania. The port of Constanta was closed to private shipping since the Soviet and Romanian military fleets were in control. Besides, it was almost impossible to rent or buy boats since British agents were everywhere and used their influence to torpedo shipping deals. Meanwhile, more Polish Jews arrived in Bucharest and were joined by the Shoah survivors from the Transnistria camps. The Jewish Agency and the Romanian office of the JDC worked hard to support them. But the situation in Romania was getting out of hand. The reception centers were overflowing and there was no solution in sight.

The Krakow Brichah office produced a multitude of official stamps and documents that were used by the Brichah transports to ship Jews from place to place.

Members of the executive office of the Brichah in Poland.

Seated from left to right: Tuvia Hacohen, Yochanan Cohen, Isser Ben-Zvi, and Netzer Alexander.
Second row standing from left to right: Gershon Lev, David Weinshelbaum, Israel Hershkowitz, David Meller.
Third row standing left to right: Shlomo Brandt, Nachum Blumenkrantz and Misha Krawtchik.

Kovner arrived in Romania to assess the situation. There was no possibility that the port of Constanta would be viable. He saw two possible routes, through Yugoslavia and Hungary. He sent one of his lieutenants, Mula Ben Haim, with some men to Belgrade. They reached the city and made inquiries regarding transportation to Palestine. Ben Haim then sent Pinhas Zeitag, known as "Pinieh the Yellow," to the city of Split, Yugoslavia (present day Croatia) near the Italian border. He reached the city on May 13, 1945, five days after the end of the war[22]. The Jewish Brigade had a big base at Treviso not far from Split. The Brigade was a Jewish fighting force, mainly from Palestine, formed in 1944 under the auspices of the British Army. With the war over, the soldiers were free to take day trips into the area and met Zeitag on one of the outings. They were eager to help the effort. The Brigade became the key link that would open the route from Romania to Italy and establish contact between the East European Brichah and Palestinian Jewry. The route was difficult but effective, starting in Arad-Timisoara, Romania, then to Belgrade and Zagreb, Yugoslavia and then to Trieste, Italy.

Rosman was ordered to leave Poland and move to Budapest where he would try to open another route to Italy from Romania. Budapest had a well-organized Zionist community with active Zionist youth groups who helped the many Jewish refugees in the city. Joel Palgi, a Palestinian Jewish parachutist helped organize the Jewish community and especially the Zionist movements. Rosman began to contact people and offices to get the necessary papers to create a new refugee route. He established a route that began in Romania and headed to Budapest, Hungary, then to Graz, Austria, and to Italy. The Jewish transports rolled across Europe to Italy where they hoped to sail to Palestine. The numbers were still small but the Brichah managed to establish an effective organization that would soon play a very important role in Jewish history.

Events in Poland soon overtook all plans and decisions, namely the Kielce pogrom. Under the pretext that a Christian child was kidnapped by Jews for ritual purposes, the Poles attacked the surviving Jews of Kielce. The fact that Polish security and police forces joined the mob sent alarm warnings to all Jews of Poland. Fear gripped the surviving Polish Jews that were mostly sitting on their suitcases not sure whether to stay in Poland or go west. The pogrom of July 4, 1946 settled the issue. Polish Jews headed for the Czech-Polish and Polish-German borders en masse.

---

[22] Bauer, Flight, p.41

Brichah - Hebrew for Escape or Flight

The Brichah established two routes out of Romania. One started in Romania headed to Belgrade, Serbia then Zagreb, Croatia, then Italy. The second route also started in Romania and headed to Budapest, Hungary, then to Graz, Austria and finally to Italy. Both routes were long and difficult but gave the Brichah a way to transport many Jews out of Romania.

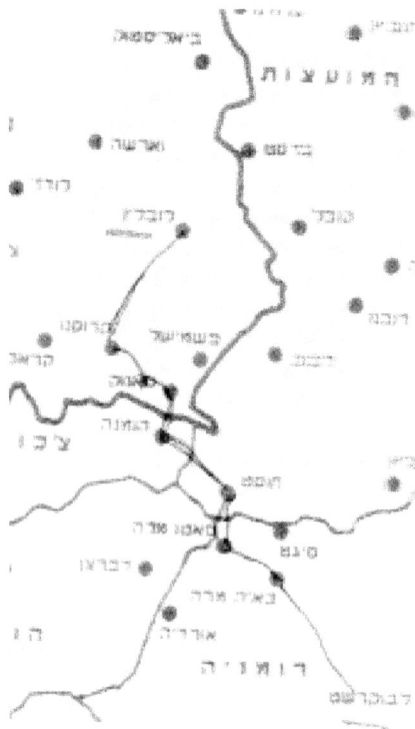

*Crossing points of the Brichah at Krosno and Sanok, Poland
to Slovakia, Subcarpathia and Romania.*

Starting July 1945, about 4,600 Jews left Poland and crossed illegally to Czechoslovakia, in August, 9,875 left, September, 6,745 left, October, 9,760, November 5,200 and in December, 2050 Jews left. The stream became stronger and in May of 1946, 3,052 Polish Jews entered Czechoslovakia. By June the number had jumped to 8,000. After the pogrom in Kielce, the tide turned to a tsunami. Nineteen thousand Jews left Poland in July; 35,346 in August; and 12,379 in September of 1946. During 5 months, 77,700 Polish Jews crossed the border at Nachod in Czechoslovakia, one of several major crossing points that included Kladzko, Walbrzych, Wroclaw, Krosno and Sanok. According to American Joint records, it is estimated that 90,000 Jews left Poland in 1946[23].

As mentioned before, the old Brichah road via Czernowitz was closed with the arrest of the Brichah leaders (Ref: Bauer, Flight p. 28) A new route had to be established to Romania(Ref: Bauer, Flight p. 28)-29). The Brichah leader, Abba Kovner, ordered 3 of his assistants to explore a new route that led to Romania. He selected Velvele Rabinowitz from Wilno as head of the group and sent them to Krosno, across the Carpathian Mountains to Humenne,

---

23 Bauer, Flight, p. 119

48

Slovakia, Chust in Subcarpathia and Sato Mare in Romania. The group reached Bucharest and met Moshe Auerbach, Romanian Brichah Chief. Rabinowitz returned to Krakow, Poland and reported to the Brichah that the route was now open for Polish Jews to head to Romania and eventually to Palestine. Mordechai Rosman head of the Polish Brichah decided to open permanent bases for Jews, crossing the border at Rzeszow and at Tarnow in Galicia.

A group of Polish Brichah agents, including Moshe Meiri,
known as Ben (right bottom row), head of Krosno Brichah station.

From there small groups would proceed to Krosno or Sanok where they would rest and then proceed cross the border to Slovakia where the Slovakian Brichah would take over. Ben proceeded to Krosno and organized a base where the Brichah brought small groups of Jews that were about to cross the Carpathian Mountains. They had to rest, stock up on food and prepare for as long trip over the mountains. The Krosno station grew in importance as the number of Jewish refugees increased, but became less important as the crossing points shifted west due to the Constanta port facilities being closed to the Brichah. Instead of Romania, the refugees were now sent to Czechoslovakia, then Germany and Austria where they entered DP camps mainly in the American zones. Jews continued to live in the big cities like Krakow, Warsaw, Lodz, and Wroclaw. But the Polish countryside slowly became clear of Jews.

Brichah - Hebrew for Escape or Flight

Brichah agents in Krosno; from right to left; Sarah Pressman, Lena Hemel, Stefan Grajek, Vi Feishter and a police official. The city of Krosno was located near the Polish-Czechoslovakian (presently Slovakian) border. The Brichah would bring groups of Jews that wanted to go to Palestine. In Krosno they received their final directions and instructions.

With the liberation of the city of Krosno, some Jewish survivors began to appear, amongst them **Salek Berger**, a native of Krosno, who survived the war in Eastern Ukraine and with the liberation of the area was drafted into the Polish Army. He fought the Germans and was discharged at the end of the war. He returned to Krosno but decided not to stay in the city. Berger joined the local "Brichah" and led transports of Jews across the Polish–Czech border in the area of Krosno where he knew the paths. The work was difficult, dangerous and illegal.

The members of the organization were ex–partisans, camp survivors, discharged soldiers from the Jewish brigade and discharged soldiers from the Polish and Russian armies like Berger himself. He remained with the organization for some time and then was replaced by another volunteer. Berger was sent to one of the DP camps in Italy where he remained for several years. He eventually reached the US.

The Brichah was very active escorting thousands of Jews across the Czech-Polish borders. Entire Polish regions became devoid of Jews. The repatriation of Polish citizens from the Soviet Union slowed to a trickle.

The number of Jews crossing the borders decreased steadily as the number of Jews declined drastically in Poland. With the end of the Spychalski-Zuckerman agreement, the Polish government closed all borders but continued to grant exit visas to Jews wanting to leave the country. The Polish Brichah organization slowly dismantled their operations and closed the Krosno office. The Brichah left Poland and shifted all its energies to Austria, Germany and Italy.

Brichah - Hebrew for Escape or Flight

Incomplete list of Brichah agents in Poland. The large number of people indicates the extensive operations of the Brichah in Poland.

Last Name	First Name	Code name	G	Area of Operation
APPFEL	Zacharia		M	Poland
APPFELHOLTZ	Chaim		M	Poland
AWIROW	Itzhak	Pasha	M	Poland
BAUER	Arieh		M	Poland
BEN-ZVI	Iaaer	Shimon	M	Poland
BIATOS	Feliks		M	Poland
BLUMENKRANTZ	Nahum		M	Poland
BOXER	Zvi		M	Poland
BRANDT	Shlomo	Jozek	M	Poland
BRAT	Hanke		F	Poland
BRAT	Zvi		M	Poland
BRONEK		Stettin		Poland
CARMI	Itzhak		M	Poland
CHMIELNIK	Chaim		M	Poland
COHEN	Yochanan	Gideon		Poland
DAVID		Stettin		Poland
DIAMANT	Sarah		F	Poland
DOLEK		Stettin		Poland
DOLEK			M	Poland
DORA		Stettin		Poland
DOVELAH		Kattowice		Poland
DWORKIN	Yerachmiel		M	Poland
EINHORN-STRASBERG	Rina		F	Poland
ENGLANDER		Jozek	M	Poland
ERNA	Yaacov		M	Poland
FEISHTER	W		M	Poland
FLINKER-KLEINBERG	Regina		F	Poland
FREILICHMAN	Yossef		M	Poland
GEITER	Menashe		M	Poland
GELIBTER	Bronek		M	Poland
GELLER	Martin		M	Poland
GELLER	Liuba		F	Poland
GITTELMAN	Shimshon		M	Poland
GLIGSBERG	Sarah		F	Poland
GOLDSTEIN	Shlomo		M	Poland
GOREN-GRINSHPAN	Ron		M	Poland
GRAYEK	Stephan		M	Poland
GRAYEK	Shulem	Stefan	M	Poland
GRINBERG-BAR-GRA	Kanda		M	Poland
GRINGROSS	Shenia		M	Poland
GRISHA		Stettin	M	Poland

GROSS	Nechemia		M	Poland
GROSSMAN	Shoshana		F	Poland
HACOHEN	Rachel		F	Poland
HACOHEN	Tuvia		M	Poland
HALB		Walbrzych		Poland
HALPERIN	Yossef		M	Poland
HALPERT	Eliezer		M	
HELLER	Awraham		M	Poland
HEMEL	Lena		F	Poland
HERSHKOWITZ	Israel		M	Poland
ISRAEL		Stettin		Poland
JAFFA		Krakow		Poland
JEDINOWITZ	Ephraim		M	Poland
JOHANES	Dov		M	Poland
JOSEPH		Klatzko		Poland
KALMAN		Stettin		Poland
KAMINSKY	Dov		M	Poland
KASPI	Avraham		M	Poland
KIHEN	Shlomo		M	Poland
KLEIMAN	Julek		M	Poland
KOPLOWITZ	Yehuda		M	Poland
KRAWTCHIK	Misha		M	Poland
KREIZER	Itzhak		M	Poland
KRIKON	Zv		M	Poland
KROCHMAL	Maks		M	Poland
KROLITZKI	Shoshana		M	Poland
KROLITZKI	Chaim		M	Poland
KROLOWSKI	Israel		M	Poland
LASKER	Peretz		M	Poland
LAZAR	Chaim		M	Poland
LEV	Fima		M	Poland
LEV	Gershon		M	Poland
LITVAK		Katowice		Poland
LUST	Ephraim		M	Poland
MAIMON	Yehusa	Poldi	M	Poland
MANKOTA	Yehusa		M	Poland
MANN	Shlomo		M	Poland
MEIRFELD	Chaim		M	Poland
MEIRI	Moshe	Ben	M	Poland
MELETZ	Mitek		M	Poland
MELLER	Yossef		M	Poland
MELLER	David		M	Poland
MENDEL		Krosno		M	Poland
MITTELMAN	Max	Mietek	M	Poland
MOSHE		Klacko		Poland
MOSHE		Stettin		M	Poland
NAHUM		Krakow		Poland
NATHAN		Zbonshin		Poland

NEIMAN	Mordechai		M	Poland
NETZER	Zvi	Alexander	M	Poland
NISSAN	Mordechai		M	Poland
NISSENBLAT	Hanah		M	Poland
OICHENWALD	Janek		M	Poland
OLIWITZKI	Zvi	Heniek	M	Poland
ORLINSKI	Riszek		M	Poland
OZICHOWSKI	Nahum		M	Poland
PERLMUTTER	Yehoshua		M	Poland
PHIL	Jozek		M	Poland
PIPI		Stettin		Poland
PODHORTZER	Shlomo		M	Poland
PRESSMAN	Sarah		F	Poland
RABINOWITZ	Reuven		M	Poland
RAKOWER	Shalom		M	Poland
RAPAPPORT	Monia		M	Poland
REITZES	Buria		M	Poland
REZNIK	Nissan		M	Poland
RIM	Poldek		M	Poland
ROSA		Stettin		Poland
ROZA			M	Poland
ROZMAN	Mordechai		M	Poland
RUBINSTEIN	Eliezer		M	Poland
RUCHMAN	Pasha		M	Rumania
RUDELNIK	Israel		M	Poland
SADEH	Avraham		M	Poland
SARA		Stettin		Poland
SCHECHTER	Bracha		F	Poland
SCHECHTER	Yossef		M	Poland
SCHIFF	David	Dudek	M	Poland
SCHOCHET	Nach	Jingi	M	Poland
SCHOCHET	Zalman		M	Poland
SCHWARTZ	Yaacov		M	Poland
SEGAL	Pessah		M	Poland
SHALOM		Stettin		Poland
SHARON		Vienna		Austria
SHARON	Menachem		M	Poland
SHAUL		Krakow		Poalnd
SHELET	Mark		M	Poland
SHENKMAN	Kuba		M	Poland
SHENOON	Avinoam		M	Poland
SHIMONOW		Krakow		Poland
SHTILER	Arieh		M	Poland
SONIA		Rzeszow		Poland
STASHEK	Stief		M	Poland
TCHATCHKES	Fishel		M	Poland
TEITELBAUM	David		M	Poland
VERED-WERTZEISER	Awraham		M	Poland

WALDMAN	A		M	Poland
WARSZAWCIK	Hasia		F	Poland
WEINSHELBAUM	David		M	Poland
WEISSMAN	Nachman		M	Poland
WEIZER	David		M	Poland
WERMAN	Munia		M	Poland
WINTZELBERG	Karol		M	Poland
WOLBERSTEIN	Moshe		M	Poland
YAFAH		Krakow		Poland
YEHOSHUA			M	Poland
ZAGMIROWSKI	Tanchum		M	Poland
ZEIDEL	Hillel		M	Poland
ZILBERSTEIN	Mark		M	Poland
ZIMAN	Rosa		F	
ZISKIND	IRA		M	Poland
ZOHAR-ZLOTO	Zvi		M	Poland
ZUCKERMAN	Antek		M	Poland
ZVI		Krakow		Poland

Brichah - Hebrew for Escape or Flight

Chapter V
Transit Station; Czechoslovakia

Following the Kielce pogrom thousands of Polish Jews headed to the Polish –Czech and Polish-German borders.

Brichah roads leading Polish Jewish survivors out of Poland.
In the North, the roads from both Szczecin or Stettin, and
Glogow, led to the Soviet zone of Germany. Roads from
Wroclaw or Breslau, Katowice and Krakow led to Czechoslovakia.

In March 1939 Germany occupied the remaining parts of the Czech provinces of Bohemia and Moravia, and a puppet Slovak state was established in Slovakia. As already mentioned, some Jewish survivors who returned from the camps to their homes in Poland, Slovakia, Lithuania and Latvia (and elsewhere) decided to leave these new homes and return to the labor or concentration camps (converted into refugee centers) in Austria and Germany. Most of the returnees were escorted by the Polish Brichah to the Polish-Czech borders where the Czech Brichah headed by **Moshe Govsman** awaited them. Govsman was a Palestinian farmer familiar with military operations and he ran the Brichah like a military unit. Some of the Jewish returnees went to Romania as mentioned earlier while others proceeded to Czechoslovakia under

Brichah guidance. There were also private groups that organized border crossings. In 1945, about 5,000 Polish Jews left Poland, crossed illegally into Czechoslovakia and then continued to Germany and Austria. Baltic, Ukrainian, Slovak, Hungarian and Romanian Jews joined this ever-growing trickle of illegal Jewish Shoah survivors who entered Czechoslovakia.[24] Most of them reached the small Czechoslovak town of Nachod where the Czech Repatriation Office and the American Jewish Joint Distribution Committee (JDC) had established a small reception camp for refugees.[25] The hamlet had 20 Jewish inhabitants who had survived the war out of a pre-war community of 300 Jews. These Jews helped the refugees on their way. The camp consisted of two barracks but would expand with time. The exit of Jews from Poland would continue until 1972 although through regular channels between Israel and Poland starting in 1949. About 243,511 Jews would leave Poland (see chart below[26]). Most of them emigrated to Israel while others went to the United States, South America and Europe.

Moshe Govsman, head of the Czechoslovakia Brichah organization

---

[24] Cohen, Yochanan. Chart of Jews Leaving Poland p.108 in the text
[25] Szulc, The Secret Alliance, p.137
[26] Cohen, Yochanan. Brichah Gdola Mepolin, Jerusalem: Attachment number 13, p.471

סה״כ	בדרכים אחרות²	ע״י "הבריחה"¹	התקופה
5.000‑3.500	1.000‑500	כ‑2.500	משלהי 1944 עד מאי 1945 מאי ויוני
10.500‑9.000	4.000‑2.500	כ‑6.500	1945 יולי‑סוף
38.775‑37.775	5.500‑4.500	33.275	1945
88.717‑86.717	6.000‑4.000	82.717	1946
2.730	————	2.730	ינואר‑פברואר 1947
144.222‑139.222	16.500‑11.500	127.722	
	⁵39.000		1952‑1949
	⁴42.289		1959‑1956
	⁵4.000		1967‑1960
	⁶14.000		1972‑1967
99.289	99.289		
243.511‑238.511	115.789‑110.788	127.722	סה״כ

Details of Jews that left Poland after WWII

- *Column on the right represents period from 1944-May 1945.*
- *Next colum represent Brichah transports.*
- *Next colum represent independent smuggling operations.*
- *Last colum represent total number of Jews that left Poland.*

- *From 1944-May 1945, 5000 Jews left Poland.*
- *From May-June 1945, 10,500 Jews left Poland*
- *From July- December 1945, 38,775 Jews left Poland*
- *During 1946, 88,716 Jews left Poland.*
- *From January-February 1947, 2,730 Jews left Poland.*

Between 1945 and 1947, 127,722 Jews were safely taken out of Poland by the Brichah. This was quite an achievement for a relatively small organization that worked in secret with the financial help of the Jewish Agency in Palestine and the JDC in Poland. Many of the Brichah members volunteered and barely covered their minimal expenses. In places where JDC had offices, Brichah members would be on their payrolls. The Brichah volunteers faced serious dangers as they illegally crossed the various borders. For example, on May 2, 1946, a transport of Gordonia Zionist youth members was ambushed near Nowy Targ, Poland, and murdered along with their Brichah guides. Still, the Brichah continued with its task of leading Jews out of Eastern Europe to Central Europe.

Joseph Schwartz, Director of JDC European Joint Operations became alarmed at the large numbers of Jews leaving Poland. Schwartz was a brilliant and exceptional man. Known as "Packy" to those close to him, he was born in Ukraine and moved to Baltimore at an early age. A distinguished educator and scholar and an authority on Semitics and Semitic Literature, Schwartz received his doctorate from Yale following his graduation from the Rabbi Isaac Elchanan Seminary of Yeshiva University. Schwartz taught at the American University in Cairo and at Long Island University and then served as Director of the Federation of Jewish Charities in Brooklyn. He served the JDC from 1939-1950 and then went on to become the Executive Vice Chairman of the United Jewish Appeal and later the Vice President of Israel Bonds. Schwartz died in 1975.

Joseph Schwartz, Director of European Joint Operations
(dressed in a military uniform).

Schwartz saw the growth of the illegal border crossings and decided to call on Gaynor Israel Jacobson who was in the USA recuperating from a serious disease he contracted in Greece. Jacobson had proved himself capable of handling very difficult situations. Schwartz saw that he needed an exceptional man to head the office in Prague as the number of Jewish refuges kept growing in Czechoslovakia.

Brichah - Hebrew for Escape or Flight

In March 1939 Germany occupied the remaining parts of the Czech provinces of Bohemia and Moravia. According to the official records there were 118,310 Jews in these provinces according to the Nuremberg laws[27]. Only 3010 Czech Jews survived the Shoa most of them were married to non-Jews[28]. As already mentioned, some Jewish survivors who returned from the camps to their homes in Poland, Chechia ,Slovakia, Lithuania and Latvia and Ukraine decided to leave these new homes and return to the labor or concentration camps (converted into refugee centers) in Austria and Germany. Most of the returnees were escorted by the Polish Brichah to the Polish-Czech borders where the Czech Brichah headed by **Moshe Govsman** awaited them. Govsman was a Palestinian farmer familiar with military operations and he ran the Brichah like a military unit. Some of the Jewish returnees went to Romania as mentioned earlier while others proceeded to Czechoslovakia under Brichah guidance. There were also private groups that organized border crossings. In 1945, about 5,000 Polish Jews left Poland, crossed illegally into Czechoslovakia and then continued to Germany and Austria. Baltic, Ukrainian, Slovak, Hungarian and Romanian Jews joined this ever-growing trickle of illegal Jewish Shoah survivors who entered Czechoslovakia.[29] Most of them reached the small Czechoslovak town of Nachod where the Czech Repatriation Office and the American Jewish Joint Distribution Committee (JDC) had established a small reception camp for refugees.[30] The hamlet had 20 Jewish inhabitants who had survived the war out of a pre-war community of 300 Jews. These Jews helped the refugees on their way. The camp consisted of two barracks but would expand with time. The exit of Jews from Poland would continue until 1972 although through regular channels between Israel and Poland starting in 1949. About 243,511 Jews would leave Poland (see chart above). Most of them emigrated to Israel while others went to the United States, South America and Europe.

Between 1945 and 1947, 127,722 Jews were safely taken out of Poland by the Brichah. This was quite an achievement for a relatively small organization that worked in secret with the financial help of the Jewish Agency in Palestine and the JDC in Poland. Many of the Brichah members volunteered and barely covered their minimal expenses. In places where JDC had offices, Brichah members would be on their payrolls. The

27 Bondi, Ruth, Uprooted Roots, Jewish chapters in the History of Czechoslovakia, Jerusalem, p.205
28 Ibid., p.210
29 Cohen, Yochanan. Chart of Jews Leaving Poland p.108 in the text
30 Szulc, The Secret Alliance, p.137

Brichah volunteers faced serious dangers as they illegally crossed the various borders. For example, on May 2, 1946, a transport of Gordonia Zionist youth members was ambushed near Nowy Targ, Poland, and murdered along with their Brichah guides. Still, the Brichah continued with its task of leading Jews out of Eastern Europe to Central Europe.

Schwartz saw the growth of the illegal border crossings and decided to call on Gaynor Israel Jacobson who was in the USA recuperating from a serious disease he contracted in Greece. Jacobson had proved himself capable of handling very difficult situations. Schwartz saw that he needed an exceptional man to head the office in Prague as the number of Jewish refuges kept growing in Czechoslovakia.

Israel Gaynor Jacobson was born in Buffalo, New York on May 12, 1892 and grew up in a hostile anti-Jewish environment. He reversed his first and middle name. He was born as Israel Gaynor Jacobson but later changed it to Gaynor Israel Jacobson.

Gaynor Israel Jacobson, JDC director in Prague

He had a strong background in social work and joined the JDC in 1944. Schwartz soon sent him to Italy to handle the special refugee problems in Italy. Jacobson accepted the post of Prague JDC Director and arrived there in April 1946.[31] Jacobson spoke several languages, notably Hebrew and Yiddish. He met with Brichah and Mossad officials in Prague who had their offices in the same building as the JDC.[32] He then began a series of meetings with key contacts in the Czech capital, including Jan Masaryk, Czech Foreign Minister, Zdenek Toman, head of

31 Szulc, Alliance, p. 131
32 Jozefova street, number 7, old city of Prague.

state security and Klement Gottwald, leader of the Czechoslovak Communist Party. The JDC knew that Masaryk was particularly friendly to the Jewish people. In 1940 when a Czechoslovak Government-in-Exile was established in Britain, Masaryk was appointed Foreign Minister. He remained Foreign Minister following the liberation of Czechoslovakia as part of the multi-party, communist-dominated National Front government. The Communists under Klement Gottwald saw their position strengthened after the 1946 elections but Masaryk stayed on as Foreign Minister. Shortly after the Communists took over Masaryk supposedly committed suicide by walking out of his office window.

The Czech relationships would become critical to the establishment of the State of Israel. In 1948 Czechoslovakia sold arms to Israel during the Arab–Israeli War. Masaryk would sign the first contract on January 14, 1948.

When they first met, Jacobson thanked Masaryk profusely for the help that Czechoslovakia was extending to the Polish Jewish refugees and for the assistance to the various Jewish social agencies that dealt with the Czech Jewish survivors. Masaryk told Jacobson that he should also meet Toman, head of security at the Ministry of Interior, regarding Jewish matters. Jacobson did not know at the time that Toman was Jewish (very few people in Czechoslovakia knew this fact).

Jan Masaryk, Czech Foreign Minister

Asher Zelig-Zdenek Goldberger Toman

According to author Tad Szulc, Masaryk even called Toman to tell him that Jacobson would visit him.[33] Toman received Jacobson in his office. Jacobson began to explain the Jewish situation in Europe and especially in Czechoslovakia. The two men hit it off, both coming from similar backgrounds although different countries. Both had experienced vicious anti-Semitism growing up. Toman promised to help and assured Jacobson that Polish Jewish refugees would continue to cross Czechoslovakia as long as he was Chief of Security.[34]

Toman, born Asher Zelig Goldberger, was the son of David and Rosalia Goldberger. Born March 2, 1909 in Sobrance (now part of Slovakia), he finished elementary school in Sobrance and high school in Uzhhorod. He entered the law faculty of Charles University in Prague in the winter term of 1927-1928 and graduated with a law degree in 1933. Toman joined the Communist Party at the university. He married Pesla Gutman on January 26, 1935, in Lodz, Poland and spent the war years in England where he was a member of the Czech government-in-exile. He returned to liberated Czechoslovakia, headed the State Security Office and was a member of the Czech Repatriation Commission. Toman helped the JDC and the Brichah organization transport thousands of Polish, Hungarian, Romanian, Czech, Slovak, Ukrainian and Baltic Jews across

---

33 Bricha. Martin Smok, Martin. Toman confirmed in an interview that he received such a call from Masaryk.
34 Szulc, Alliance, p. 158

Czechoslovakia to the DP camps in Germany, Austria and Italy. Toman officially stated that he helped 250,000 Jews reach safety. In 1948 that number reached about 300,000. In 1948 Toman was arrested but fled to West Germany, then to London and later to Venezuela where he joined the family business, Gexim, established by his brother Armin Goldberger. On June 23, 1949, he was condemned to death in absentia and lost all his property. Toman's appeal to the Czech Supreme court was rejected on April 3, 1950. His wife supposedly committed suicide on May 8, 1948 and his young son, Ivan Toman, disappeared forever.

Jacobson also made connections with Minister of Interior Vaclav Nosek, Minister of Welfare and Labor Nejedly and other Czech political leaders. These new relationships were soon tested when Yochanan Cohen, an active Palestinian Brichah leader was sent to Poland to help run the Polish Brichah. He led a group of Jews out of Poland through Czechoslovakia.[35] Their papers stated they were Austrian citizens returning home from captivity. At the Czech town of Moravska-Ostrava, the entire group of Jews was arrested and thrown in jail on suspicion of being Austrian Nazis. The Czech Chief of Police was not well disposed to Austrians or Germans and took a dim view of the group. The Jewish refugees were locked up in jail and allowed no telephone calls or notes to the outside. Then Cohen ordered someone in the group to play sick. The man was taken to an infirmary where by chance he met a Jewish doctor. He told the doctor their story and begged him to help. The doctor apparently informed the Jewish community of the situation, since the head of the community presented himself the next day at the local police station and asked the authorities to allow him to speak to the arrested Jews. He soon convinced the police that the arrested people were Polish Jews. The next day they received packages of food from the small Jewish community of Ostrava. The community also informed the JDC office in Prague of the situation. Jacobson, heard the news and immediately called Toman for help. The group was freed and headed to Austria as planned.

On another occasion, Yochanan Cohen crossed the Polish-Czech border with a transport of Polish Jews. They had a collective pass, forged in Krakow by the Polish Brichah, stating that they were Greek prisoners of war heading home. The Polish border guards ignored the group as did the Czech border guards. Suddenly a Soviet officer attached to the Czech border patrol asked Cohen, the leader of the group, to say something in Greek. Cohen would later write, "I kept my cool and said 'Itgadal

35 Yochanan Cohen, Brichah-Poland report, Yad Vashem, Jerusalem.

veitkadash shmei rabba,' the officer replied 'amen.'" Apparently the Soviet officer was Jewish and recognized the Aramaic words that open the "Kaddish" prayer for the deceased. He even said "amen," indicating that he was familiar with the prayer and the usual response to the prayer. The group continued its illegal journey.

Anti-Jewish pogroms occurred not only in Poland but also in Slovakia. The first pogrom took place in Kosice on May 3, 1945, later in the summer in Presov and in Toplcany on September 24, 1945. Pogroms continued to plague Slovakia until 1948. The causes of the pogroms varied from place to place but always revolved around the idea of Jews trying to control the place or Jews operating a black market. The Slovak pogroms never reached the intensity of the Polish pogroms but it is estimated that 36 Jews were killed and about 100 injured in the various attacks against Jews in Slovakia following the war.[36] Prior to the war the Jewish population of Slovakia numbered about 77,000; following the war there were about 33,000 and the number steadily declined.[37]

The Jewish population, especially the youth, saw no future in Slovakia and, seeing the constant transports of Jews out of Poland, joined the exodus. Most of the transports that left Poland crossed the border and reached the camps at Nachod and Broumov in Czechoslovakia. Here the refugees rested and were then shipped to Bratislava where they crossed to Austria or were sent across Czechoslovakia to the West German border at the hamlet of Asch. German Brichah members took the transports and directed them to the DP camps, mainly in the American zone of occupation. The Bratislava transports crossed the Austrian border and were escorted by the Austrian Brichah to the DP camps in Austria. Most of the transports stayed a few days in Czechoslovakia and then left the country. The Nachod camp was the largest camp administered by the Brichah and as in other camps, the JDC provided food, medicine and clothing if needed. There was another, smaller camp located near the village of Broumov that also handled Jewish refugees from Poland.

With the increased flow of illegals, Jacobson increased the food stocks and facilities at the camps. Most transports avoided Prague, the Czech capital, for fear of attracting attention and publicity. The Brichah, the Czech government and the JDC wanted to avoid attention because British and American pressure was building to tightly close the borders.

---

36 Cichopek-Gajraj. Violence, p. 115
37 Cichopck-Gajraj, Violence, p. 230

The British Ambassador to Prague lodged many protests demanding the closure of the borders, but the Czechs procrastinated.

Children's transport from Poland arriving at the Nachod camp

Prague was the center of a well-equipped communication system that connected all Brichah offices throughout Europe and Palestine. The communication equipment had been brought to Prague with the permission of the government, that is, the secret service headed by Toman. The office and the entire Brichah organization in Czechoslovakia was headed by Moshe Govsman who worked in close cooperation with Jacobson as did Lev Argov in Bratislava. Both were Palestinian Brichah men familiar with Czechoslovakia.[38] **Lev Argov** was born in Czechoslovakia and spoke the language fluently. He left Czechoslovakia prior to World War II and settled in Palestine where he actively participated in military underground activities. He was also an expert in international finance and foreign currencies.

Britain and the United States saw that their protests against the open borders were not succeeding, so they decided to use another tactic. They put pressure on UNRRA, which they controlled, to stop or effectively slow the reimbursement payments that Czechoslovakia was supposed to receive for its outlays of money for the Jewish transients. In talks with

---

38 Szulc. .Alliance, p.139

the Czechs, Elan Rees, local UNRRA chief, had intimated that UNRRA would assume most of the costs of transportation, temporary lodging and food for the transient Jewish refugees. But there was obvious discrimination. The UNRRA office readily paid transportation bills and other expenses for the transport of non-Jewish refugees while payment for transport of Jews dragged on. UNRRA officials easily determined which was which. Almost all the passengers on transports originating at the Polish borders heading toward Austria or Germany were Jewish. The Czechs were shocked when they learned that UNRRA refused to pay bills related to the transport of the Jewish refugees. The non-payment of bills increased the expenses of the Czech government.

Toman, as Czech Deputy Interior Minister was in charge of the borders, and insisted that the transports of illegal Jews continue even as more bills were presented to UNRRA. But as trains of Jewish refugees rolled across Czechoslovakia, the costs continued to climb, with no reimbursements forthcoming. The fact that UNRRA received the bills did not mean all the bills were paid. UNRRA decided which bills to pay and the Czech government frequently received less than it spent.

In an interview with author Tad Szulc, Toman said, "Had a non-Jew occupied my post, he would have definitely stopped the trains and other expenses until payment was made."[39] The fact that transportation costs and other expenses soared did not seem to bother Toman. As he said, as long as he was in power, Czechoslovakia would continue to provide transportation for the Jewish refugees.

The British and American campaign indirectly exploited this state of affairs through press connections. Some Czech newspapers and radio programs began to discuss the fact that UNRRA was not paying for the refugees and the expenses were being shouldered by the Czech government that could ill afford them. These discussions received a tremendous boost when Mary Gibbons, deputy assistant director of UNRRA operations for Europe, arrived in Prague. On July 7, 1946, three days after the pogrom in Kielce, Poland, she publicly stated that UNRRA would not pay for Jewish Polish refugees who crossed Czechoslovakia, since they had already been repatriated to their homes following the war[40]. She continued to repeat this statement throughout Czechoslovakia until July 14, 1946, when she left the country.

---

[39] Szulc. Alliance p.158
[40] Jacobson letter to JDC office in New York of August 26, 1946

According to the JDC's Gaynor Jacobson, Gibbons repeated the same statements over and over, namely that the repatriated Jews of Poland from the Soviet Union had been repatriated at UNRRA cost, therefore there was no reason to pay for them to move again. This implied that the Jews were taking advantage of UNRRA. The fact that they were running for their lives did not matter to Gibbons. In every meeting with Czech ministers, high officials and the press she repeated that her organization would not pay for Jewish transients.[41]

The publicized statements by Mary Gibbons of UNRRA had one objective, to force Czechoslovakia to close its borders and not permit Jewish refugees to transit the country. Britain believed it had to stop the illegal ships with Jewish refugees that were embarrassing it throughout the world, especially in the United States. The photographs showing British soldiers manhandling Shoah survivors undermined world public confidence in Britain's ability to control and rule Palestine.

Gibbons was not concerned with UNRRA but rather with British foreign policy. The Czech press and many government officials saw one thing, Czechoslovakia would have to pay large amounts of money that it did not have. Czech cabinet ministers began to discuss the situation and a decision was made to close the border. The Czech and Polish governments closed the Czech-Polish borders[42].

The theme espoused by Gibbons and the British and American embassies was seized upon by the local press. The country was just starting to find some traction after years of Nazi occupation. The Czech economy was struggling, the government nearly bankrupt, and unemployment was high. The Czech people were opposed to the use of the little money they had going to help Jewish refugees

The Kielce pogrom in Poland changed everything. Thousands of Jews began to move to the closed Czech-Polish borders. Confrontations between refugees and the authorities began. The General Secretary of the Czechoslovak Communist Party, Rudolf Slansky, visited the border and witnessed such a confrontation. Both governments were being strongly criticized for persecuting Jewish Shoah survivors. International Jewish organizations lodged protests in Czechoslovakia and Poland, accusing the countries of inhuman behavior. The free press showed photographs of the events. The Czech government met and discussed the situation.

---

[41] Jacobson letter to JDC office in New York of August 26, 1946
[42] Jacobson letter to JDC office in New York of August 26, 1946

The foreign minister, Masaryk, led the fight for opening the borders. He was about to leave for New York to attend the U.N. General Assembly and try to get a loan for Czechoslovakia. He knew that opened borders would jeopardize his chances of getting the loan. The cabinet ordered the Czech borders opened to Jewish transients from Poland. Several specifications were added including the requirement that the transports must leave Czechoslovakia within 48 hours of arrival, and no transient would ever receive a permit to stay in Czechoslovakia.

The Polish government was also under heavy pressure to act following the pogrom, for its international standing was at its lowest point. The cabinet met and made a dramatic decision to let all Jews leave Poland illegally. The decision served two purposes: get rid of as many Jews as possible and in doing so disarm the anti-government forces that kept insisting that Poland was controlled by Jews. The massive departing Jewish exodus would be proof that Poland was in Polish hands.

Itzhak (Antek) Zuckerman

The Polish government ordered Marshal Marian Spychalski, the Polish deputy minister of defense, to conduct secret negotiations with **Itzhak Zuckerman,** one of the leaders of the 1943 Warsaw Ghetto uprising and currently an active member of the Central Committee of Polish Jews. The two worked out a secret agreement that was to commence on July 27, 1946, and end about February 1947, and would not be made public by either party. The agreement restricted emigration only to Jews, who also were forbidden to take gold, foreign currency or personal papers when they left Poland.

Brichah - Hebrew for Escape or Flight

Marshal Marian Spychalski (center)

All travel arrangements were the responsibility of the Polish Brichah, which would also handle any and all other problems, including medical attention, food and clothing. Neither the Polish government nor any other Polish officials were to be involved in this modern exodus. Lastly, Marshal Spychalski verbally informed Zuckerman that the agreement only applied to the Polish-Czech borders.

While Zuckerman agreed to this last condition, he was distressed. The Brichah had long been making good use of the short but troublesome journey to the Polish-German border crossing at the port city of Szczecin (Stettin). The crossing point was troublesome due to Polish anti-Semitic attacks on Jews along the road and the Soviets manning checkpoints along this route. The Soviets frequently stopped and searched and sometimes arrested the Jewish refugees, handing them to the Polish authorities where they faced jail. Now the Polish government had told Zuckerman this shortcut was off limits. While Zuckerman understood the reasoning – the Poles wanted to keep the Jewish exit route a secret from both the Soviets and the British – he also knew the Soviets were aware that Jews were leaving Poland, although not the extraordinary numbers. The British would have been livid, knowing that many of the fleeing Jews would try to sneak through the blockade around Palestine. And the Poles had another reason not to upset the British. When the Polish government fled Warsaw in 1939 in the face of the Nazi invasion, they took Polish gold reserves with them, depositing them in British banks. And the gold reserves were still in London. Britain was in no hurry to return the gold and had used pretext after pretext to delay shipping the precious metal home. While the decision to let most of the Polish Jews leave was quickly turning into a matter of survival for the Polish government, the Poles had no intention of giving the British cause to keep Polish gold any longer than necessary. The Brichah agreed to funnel the massive exodus across the different borders points along the Polish-Czech border, notably the village of Nachod.

The Brichah was also determined to use the Szczecin (Stettin) crossing point whenever the need arose, regardless of the dangers. In 1946 alone, the Brichah led nearly 24,000 Polish Jewish refugees across the Szczecin border point.[43]

The Village of Nachod on the Czech side of the Czech-Polish border

The Brichah had another trick: it mingled Jewish refugees on trains carrying German citizens being deported from German areas that had been given to Poland at the Potsdam Conference held in Berlin from July 17 to August 2, 1945. These trains went from Poland directly into Germany. Once the trains stopped in Germany, the Jews were gathered up by Brichah guides and ushered to one of the DP camps in the American zone.

After the agreement with Marshal Spychalski was finalized, Zuckerman brought the document to the Central Committee of Polish Jews for approval. As usual, there was disagreement among the Jewish factions: the Communist and Bundist members vociferously objected to

---

43 Cohen report, p.465

the terms. The Jewish Communists were steadily gaining strength in the Central Committee; their allies and the Bundists were also opposed to Jews leaving Poland despite all the real dangers that the Jews faced there. The Jewish Communists and Bundists were determined to build a socialist utopia even though this option or any option that called for remaining in Poland was rejected by most Jewish survivors. The Polish Jewish Communists continued objecting to Jewish emigration from Poland. They believed in a new socialist society where everyone would be equal, and argued that Jews should stay and help with the historic effort. While the actual number of Jewish communists was small, they were very vocal, influential and had the support of the Polish Communist Party. The Jewish faction of the committee took the matter all the way up to the Polish Central Committee of the Communist Party. Much to the dismay of these Jewish Communists, they were informed that the top officials of the Communist Party agreed with the terms struck between Spychalski and Zuckerman. After that the Jewish Communists raised no more objections.

The Bund had been one of the largest and best organized Jewish worker organizations in pre-war Poland. Marxist-Socialist in ideology, the Bund was anchored in a firm belief in a Yiddish-speaking cultural autonomy. Vehemently opposed to Zionism, the Bund demanded that Jews fight for their rights where they lived and continued to adhere to this view even after the war. But when the Spychalski-Zuckerman agreement was brought for a vote at the Central Committee of the Polish Jews, the Bund members were outvoted.

With the way cleared the question of funding became crucial. The Brichah appealed to the Polish branch of the JDC to finance the legal transport of thousands of Jews out of Poland. **William Bein**, the new head of the JDC office in Warsaw, assumed the office following the tragic death of Guzik in a plane accident. The JDC was already paying the Brichah's expenses to sneak Jews out of Poland. By the time of the Spychalski-Zuckerman agreement, thousands of Jews had already crossed the Czech-Polish borders, 5,000 in 1945 alone, and that number was dwarfed by the number of Jews crossing in 1946. Bein informed Joseph Schwartz, the JDC head in Paris, of the rapid increase in refugees illegally leaving Poland, now mostly across the Czech border.

Jews from Poland crossing the Polish-Czech border during the winter while Czech and Polish border guards exchange some friendly words.

Schwartz answered by sending massive shipments of food, clothing and medical supplies to transit camps in Czechoslovakia where the Polish Jewish refugees stopped briefly on their way to the DP camps in Germany and Austria. The reception camps along the Czech borders were enlarged and stocked with provisions for the Jews arriving from Poland.

Thousands of Polish Jews crossed the Polish-Czech borders at Klodzko, Walbrzych, Katowice, Krosno and Nowy Sacz. The Association of Polish Jewish Religious Communities actively encouraged Jews to leave Poland. Chief Jewish Chaplain of the Polish Army, Colonel Rabbi David Kahana, who was also the head of the Union of Rabbis in liberated Poland, urged all Polish rabbis to help the Polish Jews crossing the Polish-Czech borders.

Jews crossing the Polish-Czech border in broad daylight.

Polish border guard officers with Polish Brichah officials

The JDC offices in Czechoslovakia and in Poland were placed on a military footing to cope with the impending mass movements. The Brichah mobilized all its forces to deal with the transports. The Brichah staff in Czechoslovakia expanded to 150 people from a small staff of about two dozen people.[44]

---

44 Israel Ministry of Defense, p. 49

Jews crossed the Polish-Czech borders prior to the agreement but the numbers were relatively small. In May 1946, 3,052 Polish Jews crossed illegally to Czechoslovakia, in June 1946, 8,000, in July 1946, 19,000. August 1946, 35,346 and in September 1946, 12,379 Jews crossed the border illegally.[45] For five months, 77,777 Polish Jews crossed the Czech –Polish border at a single place, Nachod. The camp was expanded and could handle up to 1,000 refugees for day or two. Of course, there were other crossing points in Czechoslovakia including Broumov where another temporary refugee camp existed. Both camps provided the refugees with a resting place, some food and some medical attention if needed prior to moving to the DP camps in Germany and Austria.

The Brichah and the JDC faced another serious problem, namely the Orthodox and the Hasidic Jews. Some of them had arrived with Brichah transports to Nachod or Broumov but then managed to travel to Prague. Others crossed the Polish-Czech borders with independent smugglers and reached Prague.[46] Their attire made them visible in Prague, which was off limits to Jewish refugees in transit because the Czech government did not want to publicize the transient activities. It also did not want to brazenly antagonize Britain and the United States. Many Orthodox Jews did not want to go to Palestine and assumed that the JDC had visas for the United States. The JDC supported them but had no visas to distribute. The Czech government began to pressure the JDC to remove the Jews from Prague. The JDC and the Brichah did not want to antagonize the Czech authorities and began to encourage the Jews to leave Prague. The JDC social services officer in Prague, Florence Jacobson, the wife of Gaynor Jacobson, talked to these Jews and explained the situation. Various compromises were made that resulted in the departure of most religious transients. Some went to the DP camps while others went to Italy, France, and the United States.[47]

The mass exodus of Polish Jews rapidly started to decline in November 1946 when only 2,545 Jews crossed into Czechoslovakia, and 1,987 Jews crossed the border in December 1946.[48] In January 1947, 1,029 Jews crossed and in February 1947 only 1,700 Jews crossed the Czech borders. The Stettin crossing point was closed. Yet there were still Jews sitting in Poland with packed suitcases. Reports began to reach

---

45 Bauer, Yehuda. Flight and Rescue: Bricha. New York: Random House,1970, p. 204
46 Szulc, Alliance, p. 163
47 Szulc, Alliance, p. 164
48 Bauer, Flight, p.287

them that the DP camps were overcrowded and there were only limited possibilities available to reach Palestine or the United States. So, they decided to sit and wait in Poland where security conditions began to improve. The Polish borders were closed at the end of February in accordance with the Spychalski- Zuckerman agreement. The January elections of 1947 gave the Polish government an absolute majority in parliament.[49] The government used all of its powers to crush the anti-government forces in the country. Public order was slowly re-established. The Jews felt a bit safer and hoped to be able to leave Poland directly without the need to smuggle themselves across borders.

The Brichah continued to organize transports of Jews from Poland and other areas and to send to Czechoslovakia. Most of the transports consisted of young people willing to endure hardship. During the entire year of 1947, only 9,315 Jews crossed the Czech-Polish borders.[50] Gone were the days of massive transports of Jews from Poland. The Brichah apparatus slowly decreased in size as did the JDC in Czechoslovakia. Both organizations played very important roles in transferring masses of Jews from Eastern Europe where they faced daily dangers to the DP camps in Germany and Austria. Both organizations worked together and established a force that would soon show its strength in the fight against Britain and in the establishment of the State of Israel.

List of Cechoslovak Bricha Agents

Last Name	First Name	Code name	G	Area of Operation
AMSTERDAM	Shimon		M	Czechoslo
ARGOV	Lev		M	Czechoslo
ASSA	Lea		F	Czechoslo
ASSA	Aaron		M	Czechoslo
BALTAN	Chaim		M	Czechoslo
BEN HALOM	Rafi	Fridel	M	Czechoslo
BEN NATHAN	Asher	Arthur	M	Czechoslo
BEN ZVI	Isser		M	Czechoslo
BRONSTEIN	Munia		M	Czechoslo
BRONSTEIN	Paula		F	Czechoslo
DAN	Yossef	Freilichman	M	Czechoslo
ELIASH		killed in action	M	Czechoslo
FRANK	Ernest -Ehrai		M	Czechoslo
FRIDMAN	Yaacov	Janek	M	Czechoslo

49 Bauer, Flight, p.327
50 Bauer, Flight, p. 289

Brichah - Hebrew for Escape or Flight

FRIDMAN	Nati		M	Czechoslo
FRIDMAN	Fredo		M	Czechoslo
FUCHS	Miriam		F	Czechoslo
GAFNI	Elchanan		M	Czechoslo
GIBMAN	Moshe		M	Czechoslo
GOTESMAN	Awraham		M	Czechoslo
GOVSMAN	Moshe		M	Czechoslo
GROSS	Moshe		M	Czechoslo
HERBST	Itzhak	Mimush	M	Czechoslo
HIRSHBERTG	Heniek		M	Czechoslo
HOOTER	Michael		M	Czechoslo
JUCHT	Tzipora		F	Czechoslo
JUCHT	Meir		M	Czechoslo
KIHEN	Shlomo		M	Czechoslo
KORN	Frida		F	Czechoslo
LANDAU	Ze'ev	Buba	M	Czechoslo
LANDAU	Bubu		M	Czechoslo
MARKUS	Yossef		M	Czechoslo
MENACHEM	Sharon		M	Czechoslo
NEUFELD	Akiva	Noy	M	Czechoslo
NEULANDER	Sylvia		F	Czechoslo
NUSSENBLAT	Hannah	Hanka	F	Czechoslo
OFFER	aaron		M	Czechoslo
PEARLS	Yaacov		M	Czechoslo
POSLANTZ	Yossef		M	Czechoslo
PRINTZIG	Victor		M	Czechoslo
RABINOWITZ	Zelig		M	Czechoslo
RAJCHMAN	Alexander	Shani	M	Czechoslo
RAKOWER	Shalom		M	Czechoslo
SELA	Itzhak		M	Czechoslo
SHMULEVITCH	Tushia		F	Czechoslo
SHTEINMAN	Jozek		M	Czechoslo
SHTEINMAN	Moshe		M	Czechoslo
SHWORDT	Leibush		M	Czechoslo
WANG	Dorka		F	Czechoslo
WANG	David		M	Czechoslo
WEISS	Hella		F	Czechoslo
ZISKIND	Shlomo		M	Czechoslo

Brichah - Hebrew for Escape or Flight

Chapter IV
Jewish Survivors In The Camps

With the end of the war there were about 80,000 Jewish Shoah survivors in the German and Austrian labor and concentration camps compared to about 10 million non-Jewish refugees[51]. The Allies adopted a policy of letting UNRRA (the United Nations Relief and Rehabilitation Administration) handle all problems relating to refugees. The organization had been created specifically to handle refugee issues. UNRRA proceeded to send refugees home or to their last address prior to being sent to Germany by the Nazis. The exception were the sick refugees. The refugee evacuation proceeded smoothly until politics entered the picture. Many camps that had large Polish populations were administered by the Polish Army and the Polish Government-in-exile, mainly in the British zone of occupation in Germany. The exiled government did everything in its power to block the return of Poles to their homeland now controlled by a predominantly communist government. The British government backed the Polish exile government as did the United States, to some extent. As a consequence, many Poles refused to return home. Many Hungarians, Ukrainians and Baltic refugees also refused to return home. Conflicts soon began in the various camps between the various nationalities, especially Poles and Ukrainians. The Polish administration insisted that the Ukrainians who were born within the Polish borders prior to the September 1939 war were Polish citizens. The Ukrainians rejected the Polish demands. Tensions escalated and fights broke out so the decision was made to create separate national camps. The Jews also wanted their own camps but the Allies, especially the British administration, at first refused to recognize the Jews as a national group. The Allies told the Jews that they were Poles or Hungarians according to the place of their birth or last residence prior to the war. The Jews refused to be part of the Polish or Hungarian camps and eventually Jewish camps were created with the assistance and guidance of American Jewish military chaplains, particularly Rabbi Abraham Klausner.

---

[51] Bauer, Flight, p.51

Rabbi Abraham Klausner in uniform

Abraham Judah Klausner was born in Memphis, Tennessee, on April 27, 1915, one of five children of Joseph Klausner, a Hungarian immigrant who owned a dry goods store, and Tillie Binstalk Klausner, an Austrian immigrant. He was raised in Denver, Colorado, graduated from the University of Denver in 1938 and ordained as a Reform rabbi at Hebrew Union College in 1941. Following ordination, Klausner joined the army and served as a chaplain at the Lawson General Hospital in Atlanta, Georgia.

Klausner eventually shipped out to Germany and was assigned to join the 116th Evacuation Hospital, which had just entered Dachau. The 116th arrived at Dachau, which was 10 miles northwest of Munich, in May 1945, just days after the camp was liberated. Rabbi Eli Bohnen was the first Jewish U.S. Army military chaplain to enter the camp. His unit remained only a short time at the camp. Rabbi Klausner arrived soon after. Most of the Jewish survivors found comfort in the fact that his military insignias showed the tablets of the commandments indicating that he was Jewish. Klausner helped to organize the camp and established a list of all of its Jewish survivors. He named the list the "shearit ha'pleita" or surviving remnant. The list contained 32,000 names and was posted in all of the camps in the American zone in Germany. He continued to publish lists of survivors of other camps. He also worked very hard at providing the Jewish survivors with kosher food, beds and medical needs.

On July 1, 1945, at the Feldafing Displaced Persons camp near Dachau, Klausner and Zalman Grinberg, a survivor of Dachau, established the Central Committee of the Liberated Jews in the U.S. Zone of Germany as the official representative body of the Jewish DPs. The purpose of the Central Committee was to champion the interests of the Jewish DPs and to draw attention to their plight. Klausner was horrified by the fact that the survivors were still living in the camps in much the same conditions as they had under the Nazis. He wrote letters of protest to his army superiors and included detailed reports about the camp conditions. Klausner also wrote to various Jewish organizations in the United States, which he felt were not doing all that they could to help the survivors. Klausner did whatever he felt was necessary to get the Jewish DPs what they needed including setting up Jewish hospitals and procuring clothes, food and medical supplies. While he did a great deal of good, his actions often put him at odds with the Army, the Red Cross, the UNRRA and various Jewish organizations. He also guided **Earl G. Harrison**, dean of the University of Pennsylvania Law School and U.S. Representative to the Intergovernmental Committee on Refugees, who arrived in Germany in July 1945 to investigate conditions in the DP camps.

Rabbi Philip Bernstein was another Reform rabbi who helped the Jewish Shoah survivors in Germany and Austria. He served as the Adviser on Jewish Affairs to the Commander of the U.S. Forces in Europe between May 1946 and August 1947. Born in Rochester, New York, Bernstein was ordained in the first class of rabbis at the Jewish Institute of Religion in 1926. He went on to become rabbi of Temple Brith Kodesh in Rochester.

During World War II the Jewish Welfare Board appointed him Executive Director of the Committee on Army and Navy Religious Activities. During his fifteen months of service under Generals Joseph McNarney and Lucius Clay, Bernstein labored to smooth relations between the American military and Jewish survivors, to improve the living standards of Jewish DPs and to provide educational, vocational and employment opportunities for them in Germany while they awaited immigration elsewhere. He also worked to gain official American recognition for their representative body, the Central Committee of the Liberated Jews in the U.S. Zone of Germany. Bernstein's most notable challenge and achievement during his tenure as Jewish Adviser was assisting the mass movement of Jews from Eastern Europe into the American zones of occupation and helping to dissuade the U.S. Army from closing the borders during the period of the mass migration of Polish Jews after the Kielce pogrom of July 1946.

Rabbi Philip Bernstein

Following his return to the U.S. in the summer of 1947, Bernstein served as President of the Central Conference of American Rabbis and later as Chairman of the American Israel Public Affairs Committee. Most Jews refused to return to their native homes and preferred to stay in the camps because they knew their families had been murdered and their homes destroyed.

Shimon Lang, born in Zmigrod, Poland, was a typical Jewish Shoah survivor. He was liberated by the Soviet army at the Theresienstadt concentration camp on May 10, 1945. He told an interviewer at Yad Vashem: "I remember the day of liberation. I was liberated on Saturday, May 10, 1945. Some inmates who were strong left the camp and started to enter German homes. Around the concentration camp there was a large population that provided the logistical support for the camp. These homes were attacked by the camp inmates. They took whatever food or goods they saw. They brought the stuff back to the camp. I was too weak to move but I decided that I must get something or I would starve. So next morning, I left the camp that was surrounded by Russian soldiers with rifles. I saw a German carrying a sack and I grabbed a corner of the sack. There began a tug of war. The German finally let go and left. I dragged the sack with all my energy to the road. I opened the sack and saw pictures of the man's wife.

490 911

```
L A N G          Simon

  .4.40            Zmigrod

1. .40 verhaftet in Zmigrod
                  ZAL
1. .42          "  Plaszow
10. . 4          KZ Theresienstadt

  9.5.45

    DP. .   Landsberg a. Lech


BLEA,  Mus.
```

German record of Shimon Lang's activities during World War II

I left the sack and went to a few houses where I found a small bag of sugar, a loaf of bread and a can of meat. I had no opener but banged the can until it split at the top. I made a sandwich and sprinkled the sugar on top of it. I did not eat too much and started to walk back to the camp but I did not feel good. I continued to walk and reached my barracks whereupon I collapsed. I do not know what happened nor how long I was unconscious. After a few days, I returned to my bed. Most of the inmates were gone. I rested on my bed. Two male nurses came looking for me. Outside were dead bodies all over the place.

Shimon Lang, a native of Zmigrod who survived the Shoah

Many of them died of dysentery. One of the nurses brought me a glass of water with a biscuit. I remained in bed. Then the Russians entered the camp and began to make order. They separated the sick from the dead. They spread sheets on the beds like in a hospital. No food was given except for tea. A few days later they began to distribute biscuits that were hardened. I started to work in the kitchen of the camp and slowly recuperated my strength. I remained in Theresienstadt about a month and a half. There was one Jew in the camp who began to organize a group of Jewish survivors that would go to Palestine. The camp administration had a policy of urging all the survivors to return to their native lands. The camp administration told us that we must return home and then we can go to Palestine. But we knew what it meant to return to Poland. I worked in Plaszow along the rail lines and saw the transports of Jews that were heading to Treblinka death camp."

"I did not want to return to Poland and I did not return," Lang continued. "I tried to influence all the Jewish survivors not to return to Poland where they would be killed. We were about 12 survivors. We decided not to return to Poland. I knew of a case where a survivor went to Poland and was killed by neighbors. The Russians decided to close the camp. We were placed aboard a truck and started to travel. We traveled for hours and reached the Italian border. To enter Palestine, we needed certificates that we did not have. We therefore traveled back to Vienna, Austria, where there were many Ukrainians. We continued to travel until we reached the City of Landsberg in the American military zone of Germany. There we met Dr. Greengrass who assigned us to rooms. We were six men in a room with bunk beds. We arrived at the Landsberg D.P. camp in June 1945."

"In Landsberg there was a Jewish Polish hospital that had several good professors. One of them examined me and told me that I would need surgery and to return on a particular day. The professor made all the preparations. I appeared before the surgeons and they told me that they were doubtful whether the surgery would succeed. I told them that I was a sole survivor and nobody would shed tears if I did not emerge from the operation. They proceeded with the surgery and I remained bedridden for a long time. A German woman nursed me for a month. I remained in the hospital for about eight or nine months. I could have left the hospital earlier but the place where I lived was not to my liking so I stayed at the hospital. I left the hospital and started working in a tailor shop. Following the surgery I was very weak and it took me many months to recuperate. I continued to work at the shop and learned to become a good worker. In 1946 I met my wife and married. We gave birth to a son and later to a daughter in Landsberg. We finally left the Landsberg D.P. camp and reached Israel.[52]"

Mordechai Lustig of Nowy Sacz, Poland, was another Jewish survivor who refused to go home to Poland. This is what he stated: "At about 10 A.M. on May 6, 1945, the American Army entered the Ebensee concentration camp located in Austria and began to restore order. The night before and in the morning, serious disorders took place in the camp. The inmates rampaged throughout the camp and settled scores with the remaining staff of the camp. The Americans ordered all inmates, including the disabled, to assemble at the square and to align according to nationalities. Each group, such as Jews, Poles, Frenchmen, Russians, Czechs, stood with their co-nationals. I now saw the Jewish survivors at the camp, particularly the Jews of Sandz.

---

[52] Interview of Shimon Lang by William Leibner

Brichah - Hebrew for Escape or Flight

Mordechai Lustig with his concentration camp cap
following his liberation on May 6, 1945.

They were:

- Chune Grinberg
- Moshe Laor
- Mendel Brown
- Shimon Brown
- Max Neuman
- Itzik Goldberg
- Shlomo Goldberg
- Kuba Fuhrer
- David Markus
- Shmuel Salomon
- Mendel Aftergut
- Mosdhe Chayes
- Nehemia Sheingit
- Markus Fridenbach
- Moshe Osteryoung

- Romek Gut-Hollander
- Asher Brandstern
- Chune Elzner
- Shimon Folkman
- Shlomek Wolf
- Mordechai Lustig
- Benyamin Hausenshtock
- Lulek Bittersfeld and father

I later discovered that Lulek Bittersfeld and his father were also liberated but were at the hospital in Ebensee where they were treated for typhus."

"Following the American roll call," Lustig said, "we all ran to the S.S. warehouses looking for food. We found small quantities of sugar and imitation coffee. We returned to the main camp and American soldiers invited us to join them in the hunt for S.S. men who had run the camp. Indeed, some of the guards were caught. One S.S. man was brought to the gate of the camp despite the fact that he had already managed to change clothes. He was recognized by one of the camp inmates. The inmates decided to kill him on the spot. They stretched him out on a board near the gate and everybody began to hit him until he died. A sign was written that read "Heil Hitler." The sign was placed in his hand and a bayonet was placed in the other hand."

"The Americans began to organize a kitchen to cook food for the inmates. The soup was loaded with solid foods and the inmates began to gorge themselves with the food. But they were no longer accustomed to such rich foods. Some inmates died since their intestines could not absorb the rich food. I was lucky that I took small portions and managed to digest them. I looked about and saw on top of the American tanks boxes of combat rations. I took some as did other inmates. We of course did not know what they contained. Romek Gut knew a bit of English and he read the content labels on the boxes and also the instructions on how to prepare the food. We organized a group that that began to prepare our meals for the day. In the following days, we continued to live off the combat rations that we removed from the tanks."

"The Americans forced the entire population of the township including the Mayor and other important officials of the nearby Ebensee city to march to the concentration camp to witness the horrible scenes of masses of dead, naked bodies scattered all over the place. They started to dig mass graves and carried the bodies and buried them outside the camp. The Americans brought nurses from the hospital of the nearby city of Shteinkugel who began to care for the sick inmates. Some of the inmates who were afflicted with typhus or other serious diseases were taken to the hospital while others began to be treated on the spot."

"A few of the Sandz survivors organized themselves into a small group that functioned as a unit. I took upon myself the position of cook and began to prepare the meals. Other members began to search the area for food. I cooked many soups and other items to help build the strength of the survivors. We then moved as a group to the Polish section of the camp. There were many civilian Polish citizens in the camp. They were brought to work mainly in agriculture. Of course there were also many Polish inmates who survived the war in the camp. We all began to travel in all directions to see the area. Once, my friend and I reached the city of Wels near Linz where the American military police arrested us. We had no papers or identification. We looked suspicious or perhaps they did not like us or our clothing. We wore 'Hitler Jugend' or Nazi youth clothing. We spent the night in jail and the next morning were freed by the officer who might have been Jewish. We returned to the camp and I went to the office to get some identification." I was issued a temporary identification that stated that I was an inmate of the camp."

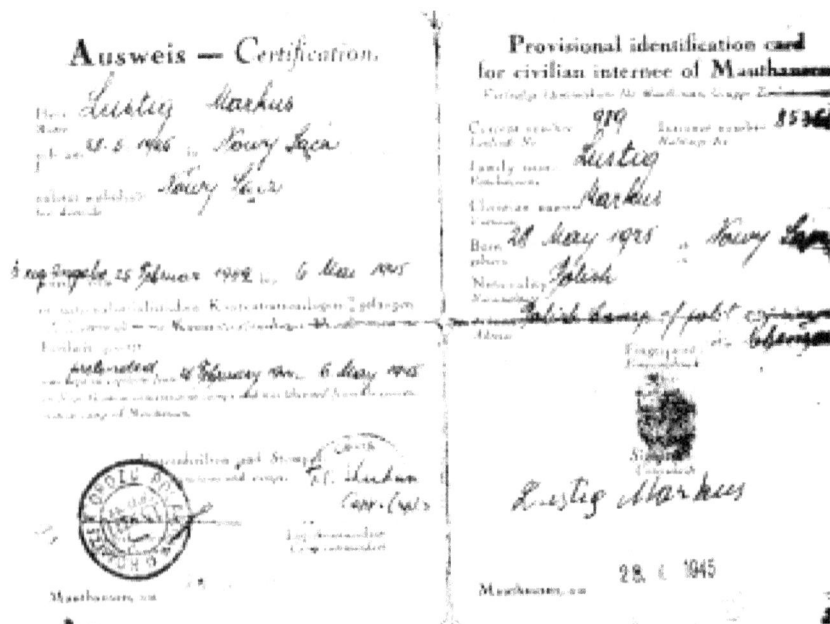

Identification paper stating that Mordechai Lustig was
an inmate of the Mauthousen concentration camp.

"A short period of time elapsed and Jewish soldiers from the Palestinian Jewish Brigade arrived at the camp. We did not believe our eyes when we saw the shoulder patches with the word Palestine and the Star of David. They talked to us in Yiddish and urged us to register to go to Palestine. They promised to help us get to Palestine. They left the camp and soon those who had signed up to go to Palestine received packages from the Red Cross. I had signed my name and picked up my package. The Jewish soldiers returned to their base in Italy."

"One day, the brigade soldiers showed up and told us to mount the trucks. I did not feel like going to Palestine and went to the men's room until the Jewish brigade left with some of the Jewish survivors. I was never a Zionist and I came from a very religious and Hasidic background that was opposed to Zionism. Palestine did not appeal to me. I wanted to live; I had suffered enough during the war. I was not going to a forsaken desert place to waste my life. I was not the only surviving Jew to remain in the camp although my name was recorded as wanting to go to Palestine."

"Romek Gut, Kuba Fuhrer, myself and two Poles from Warsaw, Poland, decided to head back to Poland. There were no regular trains or buses. The few transportation lines were reserved for military personnel. So we decided to hitchhike through the villages and small towns of the area. Wherever we reached, we went to the local chief and presented our identifications and asked for sleeping accommodations and food coupons. Most of them obliged. I had two identity cards: one in the name of Markus Lustig and the other one in the name of Markus Kannengisser. In our wanderings, we reached the hamlet of Ried where we met some of the inmates of the Schindler camp. The latter took over a house that contained a restaurant. The place belonged to a Nazi. The survivors opened the restaurant and it soon became a center of lively encounters between the survivors and the local girls. The American military police soon closed the place for violating the non-fraternization order of the American army. This order prohibited the mingling of the American soldiers with the local population. We spent one night at the place and continued our journey to Mimach, then to Asbach. Finally we reached the town of Braunau where we stayed at the local school. There was a nearby restaurant where we were able to eat, since we had food coupons. We remained a few days at the place. Romek Gut, Kuba Fuhrer and the two Poles decided to head to Poland. I decided to return to the Ebensee camp. I had no wish to return to Poland at the time."

*Mordechai Lustig, in the white t-shirt on the extreme right,
sailing to Israel with other Jewish volunteers.*

"I returned to the Ebensee camp and rested for a while. I then decided to travel to Linz, Austria, where they opened a new camp for Jewish refugees called Hart, located in Leonding. There they provided rooms to every three refugees and also food. I was also informed that being a camp survivor, I was entitled to replace my shoes and clothing. Indeed, my clothing needed replacement. I was given new shoes and new clothing; my appearance changed for the better. I also received a package with goodies from the Red Cross. Having time on my hands, I promenaded and walked about the city of Linz, which was very attractive. I eventually left for Israel[53]".

Other Jewish Shoah survivors headed back to Poland, including **Alexander Bialywlos**. He was born in Krosno and survived the war. He was liberated at the Gruennitz-Bruessau camp, better known as Schindler's camp, in Czechoslovakia on May 8, 1945. He was issued an identity paper stating that he was liberated from the camp. The document was written in Czech and German. "With a bottle of water, a bread and a piece of cloth," Bialywlos remembered, "I set out to the nearby railway station. I had no money. A train arrived and I boarded it. I took several trains since many of the bridges were damaged. Finally, I reached Prague."

---

[53] Extensive interview of Mordechai Lustig by William Leibner

Alexander Bialywlos

"At the Prague station, there was a stand of the American Red Cross that distributed hot soup. I rushed over and received some soup. The station was mobbed with refugees. Then a train arrived heading for Poland. I boarded it and reached Krakow and found the Jewish community center that assisted me with some money, food and information. I was told not to return to Krosno since some Jews were killed there by Polish opponents of the present government, but I continued my trip and finally reached Krosno. I recognized the city but not the people. No Jews in sight. I started to inquire and was told that there was a Jewish woman in town by the name of Mania Kalb. She survived the war with her little daughter. Her tiny apartment became the reception center for the few Jewish survivors that would come to the city."

"There was no reception office in the city for returning Jewish or non-Jewish survivors. No information, no financial aid, no assistance with locating a job. Anti-Semitic hatred directed at the Jew was everywhere. To earn a few zlotys, I began to sell cigarettes on the black market. I was disgusted with my situation and a bit hopeless when a cousin arrived from the Landsberg D.P. camp in Germany. While talking about the perished families, he unpacked his suitcase loaded with goodies and cigarettes, a real fortune in Poland of the day. We sat and talked. I gave him a picture of the situation in Krosno. He told me not to waste my time in Poland where there was nothing for me and to return to the Landsberg DP camp in Germany with him. I still had my liberation identity paper issued at the camp. I sold my belongings and I returned to Germany where later I resumed my studies and became Alexander White, formerly Bialywlos, M.D. I settled in the USA[54].

The returning Jewish Shoah survivors from the labor and concentration camps did not receive a warm welcome. Most of their homes were occupied by other people. In many instances, the homes were destroyed and the businesses shattered. The local population was suspicious, cold and hostile. Jewish refugees who had hidden during the war found themselves knocking at the doors to their old homes only to be met, many times, with a punch in the face. Many Polish citizens occupied Jewish homes, often using illegal Nazi documents, and refused to acknowledge any Jewish claim to the properties. Finding nothing left for them, the survivors milled around the city looking for shelter, food, even a bit of bread. During this period attacks against these Jewish survivors were a daily occurrence. It is estimated that between 1944 and 1946, 650 to 1,200 Jews were murdered in Poland[55].

Poland was in the midst of a violent wave of anti-Semitism that increased in intensity with the mass arrival of Polish Jews who were in the Soviet Union during the war. Attacks against single Jews on trains was very common. Pogroms occurred as early June 9, 1945, in Lublin. Three days later a pogrom took place in Rzeszow and later in Przemysl.

All this agitation was of course fueled by the Polish government-in-exile in order to undermine the present government in Warsaw. The country was on the verge of civil war as the rural areas were ruled by nationalist right wing elements while the government controlled the big cities. The nationalist forces pointed to the few Jews holding cabinet posts such as Jakob Berman, something unheard of in Poland before World War II, as proof that the Jews controlled Poland. These Jews were of course members of the Communist Party, so therefore all Jews, especially those who returned from the Soviet Union, were communists. The Polish masses bought these stories, which led to minor anti-Jewish incidents throughout Poland.

---

[54]White, Alexander. , Be a Mensch, A Legacy of the Holocaust USA, pp.138-143
[55] Cichopek-Gajraj. Violence, p.116

Yechiel Proper, the son of Arieh Proper of Sanok. This important and kind man was murdered August 17, 1945 or the 8th day of the Jewish month of Elul in the year Tashav or 5706.

Resentment was rapidly building against the Polish government. For the first time, Jews were in positions of influence and power. Many Poles, who had no love for Jews before the war, were now incensed that Jews had high positions in government. Polish Primate, Cardinal August Hlond, condemned the murder of the Jews, but he denied the racist nature of these crimes. "Army Krajowa" (home army), was the largest para-military underground organization in Poland during the war. The group was extremely nationalistic, anti-communist and anti-Semitic. Jews who joined with them during the war hid their Jewish identity. When the war ended, the Army Krajowa did not stop its para-military activities but continued to harass both the Polish government and any Jewish survivors it came across. This militia considered the communists the enemy of Poland, and the Jews part of the communist plan to take over the country

Anti-Semitic acts against Jews continued to plague the Jewish community and reached its zenith with the deadly Kielce pogrom that took place on July 4, 1946[56]. The surviving Jews in Kielce were accused of killing a Christian child for the blood needed to bake matzot, the unleavened bread Jews use during the Passover holiday. This holiday usually occurs in March or April and the event took place in July. This "blood-libel" was readily accepted by the Polish masses, who attacked the homes inhabited by the Jews and then rampaged through the streets, killing any Jews they found in the city. The mob was joined by members of the Polish police and other Polish security forces, even though these forces all had to be members of the Communist Party in order to get and keep their jobs. The Polish government had to rush to the city of Kielce special troops to re-establish order at gun point. Forty-two Jews were killed and 39 Jews were injured[57]. A mass funeral was held for the victims in Kielce. The news of the pogrom spread throughout the world. The Jewish community in Poland decided to leave Poland by all means, regardless of the dangers that awaited them. The fact that police and security forces joined the mob told the Jews that they had no safety in Poland regardless of what the central government said. Cardinal Sapieha reportedly said that the Jews had brought the violence on themselves. The Jews found themselves caught in a political game where the stakes were life and death. Many Jews had hesitated to leave and face the dangers of a perilous journey to an uncertain destination. This pogrom

---

[56] Cichopek-Gajraj., Violence, p.116
[57] Cichopek-Gajraj. Violence, p.117

broke the bond between Poland and the Jews. By the thousands they would flee the country within the coming months.

The burial of the Jewish pogrom victims in Kielce Poland.

Brichah · Hebrew for Escape or Flight

Chapter VI
Eastern Czechoslovakia Or Subcarpathian Rus

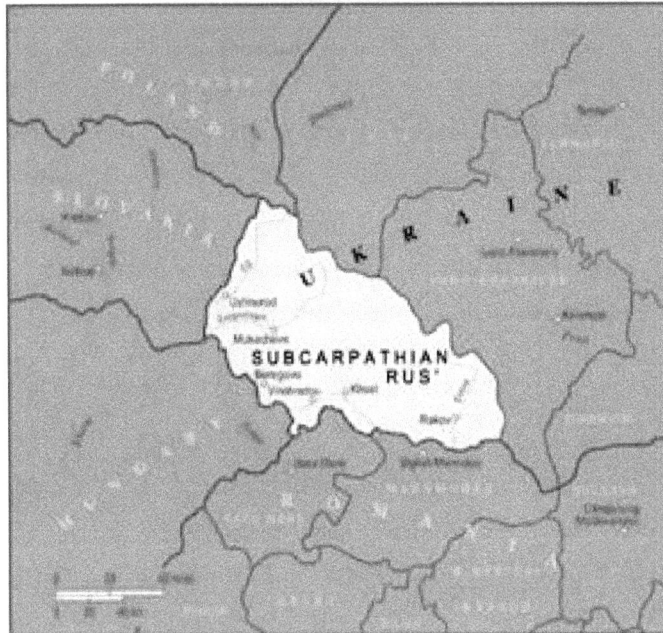

The area lighter area was called the Subcarpathian Rus.
The area was annexed by the Soviet Union following World War II.

The region that was known as Subcarpathian Rus lies in present-day Ukraine and is now known as Zakarpatska Ukrajina. The area became part of Czechoslovakia following World War I and remained Czech until Czechoslovakia was dismembered by Hitler in March 1939. Then the Hungarians annexed the area.

The first Jews likely settled in the area during the Turkish occupation of Hungary (1526–1686); they were probably of Sephardic origin. Later, a tiny stream of Moravian and Bohemian Jews arrived via the northern Slovak counties. The major influx of Jews, however, occurred in the late eighteenth and early nineteenth centuries, and consisted of migrants wandering southward from Galicia. The newcomers were welcomed by Magyar magnates, in particular by the Schönborn dynasty, which owned much land in the area. The Jewish population rapidly increased: in 1840 there were 21,640 Jews, a number that rose by 1880 to 83,076; by 1921 to 93,008; and by 1941 to 162,065 Jews. The population growth after the mid-nineteenth century can be attributed primarily to natural increase; the region had one of the highest fertility rates of European Jewry. Most of the Jewish population was very religious and the Hasidic movement was very popular among the Jews in the area. Neolog (Liberal) Judaism appeared in Ungvár (Uzhgorod. Uzhhorod) and Máramarossziget (Sighet

97

Marmației) but was small in numbers. Zionism also made its appearance, especially among the youth.

The area was poor and over populated. Many Jewish inhabitants were unemployed and sometimes homeless. Those gainfully employed included manual laborers in forestry who worked as lumberjacks, in agriculture and in artisan shops. Jews engaged in banking, wholesale trade, estate management and industry, especially timber.

During the existence of the Czechoslovak Republic, Jews could assert Jewish nationality and enjoyed all political freedoms. In 1930 the Czech government conducted a nationwide census that gave the inhabitants of the country a choice to state their cultural and linguistic preferences. Of course, they were all citizens of Czechoslovakia. The residents chose their preferences, including Czech, Slovak, German, Hungarian, Jewish, Ukrainian and Russian. A sizable portion of the Jewish population, including the family of writer Franz Kafka, chose the German culture in which they were raised. Some Jews chose the Hungarian culture, especially in Slovakia, and some Jews selected the Yiddish culture, especially in the Subcarpathian region.

With the dismemberment of Czechoslovakia, the Hungarians seized the Subcarpathian region and began the persecution of Jews. Jews who did not have proper legal Czechoslovakian papers were harassed even if they had lived in the area for generations. Starting in late July, in just a few weeks, the Hungarian authorities transports approximately 17,000 Jews across state borders to areas occupied by German troops. In late August the majority of these people (around 15,000) were machine-gunned into mass graves by SS units in the outskirts of Kaments-Podolisk.[58]

Young Jews were drafted into labor battalions where they would perish later on the Eastern front. Jewish companies were "arayanized" or seized and given to Hungarians. The Jewish population was slowly pauperized. Then the Germans invaded Hungary and rounded up the Jews of Hungary and the Subcarpathian region and deported them to Auschwitz between April and July 1944. Most of the deported Jews were murdered.

Soviet troops liberated the Subcarpathian region in the fall of 1944 and immediately annexed the area to the Soviet Union. The borders were closed to the outside world, and international aid organizations such as

---

[58] Robert Rozett, Conscripted Slaves, Yad Vashem Jerusalem, p.26

the Red Cross, the JDC and even UNRRA were not permitted to operate there. Nobody could leave the Subcarpathian region except those who were Czech, Slovak, Hungarian or German citizens. Citizenship was determined by the birthplace or cultural preference sheet that each person signed in the census of 1930. Jews who selected the Yiddish culture were not permitted to leave the area. The surviving Shoah Jews felt trapped and began to look for ways to enter Czechoslovakia. The Czech Brichah and the JDC helped these survivors.

*A typical roundup of Jews in Hungarian-held areas
prior to their deportation to the gas chambers in Poland.*

Jews Escape

William Leibner, author of this book remembered illegally crossing the Polish-Czech border and reaching the city of Brno by train. His group of illegal Polish Jewish refugees was joined by another group, supposedly from Poland also. But their Yiddish was not similar to Polish or Ukrainian Yiddish. Leibner asked his father, Jakob, about the strange speech patterns and was told that the Jews were from Czechoslovakia. The group actually consisted of Subcarpathian Jews who were smuggled out of the area under false Polish papers. On reaching Prague, the Subcarpathian Jews were immediately sent by the Brichah to the Czech-German border to reach safety in one of the German DP camps.

The Soviet authorities were aware of Jews disappearing from the Subcarpathian area and decided to act. They began to pressure the Czechoslovak police to expel all Soviet citizens from the country. The Czech police had no desire to comply with this request even though it was repeated several times. The Soviets decided to take control and ordered the Soviet NKVD or secret police to prepare an extensive dragnet to seize all Soviet citizens in Czechoslovakia, mainly Jewish citizens from Subcarpathia, and deport them to the Soviet Union. Zdenek Toman, head of Czech secret service, got wind of the plan and decided to act. He sent a letter to the Berman family to visit his office in Prague.

Nicholas and Gisele Berman knew Toman and his family. Gisele Berman was born in Sobrance as was Toman. Both went to the local school and later met in Uzhhorod, the provincial capital of the Subcarpathian area. Nicholas Berman was born in Uzhhorod and met Toman at the local high school. Nicholas and Gisele Berman married prior to the war. Both were deported and barely managed to survive. Gisele Berman returned to liberated Sobrance but found no surviving family and the few Jews there did not welcome her. She decided to move to Uzhhorod where there were more Jews. She also needed to recuperate and restore her health. She kept searching for family, mainly for her husband.

Aranka Goldberger, sister of Toman, also had returned from the death camps but found no survivors. Aranka Goldberger was born as Aurelie Goldberger on April 8, 1918 in Sobrance. She survived the Sipa Riga camp and Stutthof concentration camps.[59] She was liberated by the Soviet Army, reached Sobrance but found none of her family, so she too moved on to Uzhhorod.

Gisele Berman soon received the news that her husband, Nicholas Berman, had survived the Shoah but was gravely ill in a hospital.[60] She began to search desperately for transportation to Prague but none was available. She then met Aranka Goldberger and told her the problem. Aranka informed Gisele that her brother, Zdenek Toman, was sending a car to bring her to Prague. She offered Gisele a ride that was immediately accepted. The two women drove to the hospital and located Nicholas. He needed medication that the hospital did not have, but was obtained with the help of Toman and his sister. Nicholas slowly recovered and the couple settled in the City of Decin in Czechoslovakia near the German

---

59 William Leibner interview with Anna Neufeld, friend of the Goldberger family.
60 Berman, Gisele. My Third Life, USA, p.95

border.[61]   The city attracted many Jews from the Subcarpathian area. Life in Decin was better than in many other places but there were terrible food shortages. Gisele returned to visit Sobrance where a small Jewish community had begun to function. With the help of the JDC, the Jewish community would reach about 200 members.[62]

The Uzhhorod synagogue

The great majority of the Jewish survivors were from the district and not from the city proper, according to Anna Neufeld.[63] Most of the Jews left the city in 1949 and settled in Israel. Gisele also visited Uzhhorod and saw a small Jewish community that struggled to exist within the Soviet economy. Most of the Jews of the Subcarpathian area would leave the region with the help of the Brichah. It is estimated that between 6,000-10,000 Jews were smuggled out of the Subcarpathian area.[64] The Brichah and the JDC were deeply involved in this dangerous game but managed to get most of these Jews out of the area and into Czechoslovakia, whereupon most of them left the country under Brichah guidance.

---

61 Ibid., p.95
62 Leibner interview with Neufeld
63 Leibner interview with Neufeld
64 Szulc, Alliance, p. 150

Jewish transients waiting for the train in Bratislava, now in Slovakia, to take them to the DP camps beyond Czech borders.

Zdenek Toman was also very involved in these operations and managed to save a large number of Jews like the Berman family. The Berman's received an invitation from Toman and were afraid to open it. The letter merely stated that Toman wanted to see them in his office at their earliest convenience. The name of Toman was feared throughout Czechoslovakia. Few people had met him but his name and his office were enough to scare any citizen. Toman received the Berman's and told them that they had to leave Czechoslovakia if they wanted to live. He let them know that the Soviet secret police would soon begin to round up all Soviet citizens in Czechoslovakia, including Nicholas Berman who was born in Uzhhorod, and deport them to the Soviet Union. Toman further stated that he would not be able to protect the Berman's if they were arrested and urged them to leave immediately. They started to look for relatives in the United States who could send the necessary papers. The Berman's warned other Jews and they too began to make plans for a hasty departure. Toman also informed Jacobson of the impending Soviet police action. The Soviet secret police soon visited the JDC offices in Czechoslovakia and various Jewish aid offices but did not find many Soviet citizens.

The entire operation produced little for the Russians. The Berman's managed to reach the United States along with many Subcarpathian Jews. Others reached Britain and the DP camps in Germany and Austria. The Soviet police knew that somebody had leaked the information but did not pursue the matter.

Brichah - Hebrew for Escape or Flight

Chapter VII
The Brichah In Hungary

Map of Hungary after World War II

According to the 1910 census, the number of Jews in Hungary was 911,227, or 4.99% of the 18,264,533 people living in Hungary, (in addition, there were 21,231 Jews in the autonomous Croatia-Slavonia). This was a 28.7% increase since the 1890 census even though 324,000 Jews left Hungary for the United States between 1888 and 1901 and only a 0.3% increase (from 4.7%) in the overall population of Hungary. At the time, the Jewish natural growth rate was higher than the Christian community. The majority of the Jewish population of Hungary (75.7%) reported Hungarian as their primary language, so were counted as ethnically Hungarian in the census. Yiddish speakers were counted as ethnically German.

The population of Budapest included 203,000 Jews or 23% of the city population. This community had established numerous religious and educational institutions. Jews dominated the business area. Merchants, artisans, bakers, printers and innkeepers were heavily represented by Jews. Twenty percent of high school students were Jewish.

Interior of the Neologue Dohany Street Synagogue, Pest, Hungary.
This is the second largest synagogue in the world.
(The largest is the reform Temple Emanuel in New York City.)

Hungarian Jewry was divided among three religious groups, the Neolog group similar to the Reform movement in the US, the Orthodox group and the Traditionalist group. The Neolog movement was strong in Budapest, the capital, and in the south and west of Hungary. The Orthodox movement was strong in the north and west of the country. The Traditionalist synagogue was the smallest movement.

The Austro-Hungarian Empire was dissolved after World War I during which about 10,000 Hungarian Jews lost their lives on the battlefield. Hungary lost a great deal of land and people following the war. A communist regime headed by Bela Kun, a Hungarian Jew, seized power. It was soon overthrown by fascist elements that exacted a heavy price from the Jewish community. It is estimated that about 3,000 Jews were killed by the fascist forces. By 1920 the political situation stabilized and violence abated, but anti-Jewish sentiments did not wane. Anti-Jewish laws and regulations were enacted similar to the ones passed in Germany. For instance, enrollment of Jews in institutions of higher learning was restricted to five percent. Jewish reaction was timid. The Zionist movements in Hungary were very small and limited to some youth groups. Assimilation was very popular among the Jews and conversions to Christianity were increasing. Jews were restricted in how they could earn money and pauperization became widespread. Hungary joined the Axis powers (Germany, Austria and Italy) and thus annexed parts of Slovakia, Transylvania, Yugoslavia and Sub-Carpathian Ruthenia; most of these areas belonged to Hungary before World War I. By mid-1941, the annexation increased "Great Hungary's" Jewish population to 800,000.

The decimation of Hungarian Jews began in 1941. Jews who could not prove Hungarian citizenship were sent to the area of Kamieniec-Podolski, Poland where the Germans killed them. It is estimated that between July 15 and August 12, 1941 about 20,000 Jews were killed. In the massacres of Újvidék (Novi Sad) and villages nearby, 2,550–2,850 Serbs, 700–1,250 Jews and 60–130 others were murdered by the Hungarian Army and "Csendőrség" (Gendarmerie) in January 1942. Those responsible, Ferenc Feketehalmy-Czeydner, József Zöldy and others were put on trial in 1943 in Budapest and sentenced. Some of the murderers escaped to Germany.

During World War II, Jews were called up to serve in unarmed "labour service" units that repaired bombed railroads, built airports or cleared minefields at the front. Approximately 42,000 Jewish forced laborers were killed on the Eastern front, another several thousand forced laborers died in the copper mine of Bor, Serbia. Hungary behaved badly towards its Jewish population, especially towards the drafted Hungarian Jews. But the Hungarian Prime Minister, Miklós Kállay, refused to send the Hungarian Jews to the death camps in Poland. The Germans applied pressure but Hungary refused to cooperate. This situation lasted until March 19, 1944, when the Germans occupied Hungary. Miklós Kállay was dismissed and Döme Sztójay, a rabid anti-Semite, was installed as prime minister on March 23, 1944.

SS Obersturmbannführer Adolf Eichmann soon arrived in Budapest with 20 officers and a staff of 100, including drivers, cooks, etc. He immediately began plans to deport all Hungarian Jews. In May 1944, the first trains started to roll to Auschwitz. By July 9, 437, 402 Jews had been deported, according to the official German reports of Reich Plenipotentiary in Hungary Edmund Veesenmayer.1 One hundred and forty-seven trains were sent to Auschwitz, where 90% of the people were exterminated on arrival. Each day 12,000 Jews were delivered to Auschwitz, among them the future writer and Nobel Prize-winner Elie Wiesel, age 15 at the time.

Adolf Eichmann at his trial in Jerusalem

Elie Wiesel

Elie Wiesel was born in Sighet, a Romanian *shtetl*, September 30, 1928 to an Orthodox Jewish family. His parents, Shlomo and Sarah, owned a grocery store in the village. He had two older sisters, Hilda and Bea, and a younger sister, Tsiporah. When he was three years old, Wiesel began attending a "Heder" or Jewish school where he learned Hebrew, Bible, and eventually Talmud. His thinking was influenced by his maternal grandfather who was a prominent Hasid. Hasidut amongst Jews was prevalent in the area. The entire region was soon turned over to Hungary thus Wiesel became a Hungarian citizen without leaving his apartment.

Hungarian Jewish women and children from Carpatho-Ruthenia
after their arrival at the Auschwitz death camp (May/ June 1944).
Photo from the Auschwitz Album.

Most Hungarian Jews were deported from the provinces starting in May 1944, except for the Jews of Budapest. Eichmann had planned for them to be deported in August 1944, but the Hungarian government bowed to international political pressure. When the Germans cracked down further in Hungary, the Budapest Jews were also sent to Auschwitz. Members of the Hungarian Zionist youth movement smuggled around 4,000 Hungarian Jews into Romania. Some Jews escaped to Budapest, where there were already many illegal Polish and Slovakian Jews. The Zionists organized relief efforts and provided fake passports, food, clothing and places to hide. Two famous Palestinian paratroopers Hannah Senesh and Peretz Goldstein, tried to reach Hungarian Jewry but were caught and jailed by the Hungarians.

Two well-known individuals involved in saving Hungary's Jews were Charles Lutz, a Swiss diplomat in Hungary, and Raoul Wallenberg, secretary of the Swedish Legation in Budapest. The deportation of Budapest's Jews began in October 1944. The majority of the Budapest

Jews were sent to a central ghetto, while some managed to live in "protected ghettos" in quarters secured by various neutral states. Many Budapest Jews were forced on death marches to Austria and it is estimated that about 98,000 Jews from Budapest lost their lives in these marches by January 1945.

Brichah agents in Hungary. From right to left; Mordechai Rosman, Mordechai M., Zelig Rabinowitz, Rachel G., Moshe Laufer, and Naftali Kratzmer

At the end of the war, the Hungarian Jewish community consisted of about 200,000 people, 150,000 in Budapest and 50,000 throughout the country. 50,000 Jews were elderly and sick people who needed immediate help.[65] Hungary, unlike Poland and Czechoslovakia, did not permit Jews to leave the country. The JDC was the only relief organization permitted to operate in Hungary; even UNRRA was forbidden to enter Hungary.[66] Mordechai Rosman was sent from Poland by Abba Kovner to Hungary to assume the leadership of the Brichah in Hungary.[67] There he met Yoel Palgi, a Palestinian Jewish parachutist who helped the various Zionist youth movements in Hungary. The Brichah helped transport Polish Jewish refugees in Hungary to Romania or Austria. Many youth groups were sent to Brichah camps where they were trained to fight while they waited to go to Palestine. The JDC paid for these camps as well as for the various Zionist youth activities. As in other countries, the JDC also

---

65 Szulc, Alliance, p,177
66 Ibid., p.177
67 Bauer, Flight. p.156

provided food for elderly people and opened three hospitals for sick people. Hungarian authorities watched the JDC very closely. The Brichah managed to transport Jews out of Budapest by train via Sopron, Hungary, to Wiener Neustadt in Austria.[68] Due to a careless mistake, several Hungarian fascists joined a transport of Jews leaving Hungary. The Brichah agents were supposed to carefully check each group, but for some reason this did not happen. The Hungarian army decided to check the Jewish transport and found the two Hungarian fascists who were trying to leave the country. A scuffle occurred and the Hungarian army decided to ban all train transports of Jewish refugees. The Brichah leaders were arrested and interrogated until payment was made for their release. The Hungarians always demanded money for any legal infractions.

Hungarian Zionist youth group on route to DP camps in Germany.

Some Hungarian Jews, especially Transylvanian Jewish Shoah survivors, headed for Romania since they had nothing to return to after the war.[69] Initially after the war, Hungarian Jews left for Romania or Austria but this movement declined with time. Hungary became basically a transit place for Jewish Shoah survivors who came from Romania and headed to Austria. Many of these Jews were actually Polish Jews who went to Romania in the hope of heading to Palestine but that door was closed. They were joined by Romanian, Moldavian and Transylvanian Jews. It is estimated that from the end of the war to the end of 1946,

68 Ibid., 165
69 Bauer, Flight, 153

110

about 18,000 Hungarian Jews left their country via Austria and Yugoslavia.[70] Toward the end of 1946, few Hungarian Jews left the country. The economic situation in Hungary improved and Jews saw an opportunity to live in peace. The Communist Party gained more power, especially in Budapest where Zoltan Vas, mayor of the city, greatly restricted the activities of the Brichah. The idea of spending time in a DP camp became less and less appealing to Hungarian Jews. Still, about 18,000 Romanian Jews transited Hungary on their way to Austria.

Yona Rosen surrounded by the secretaries of the Brichah office in Budapest, Hungary. Notice sign at the entrance: Jewish Agency for Palestine

Partial list of Brichah agents in Hungary

Name	First	Code name	G	Country
ALEXANDER	Mathan	Dr.	M	Hungary
ALFI	Moshe	Pil	M	Hungary
ALON	Moshe	Haupt	M	Hungary
AYALON	Itzhak		M	Hungary
BILITZER	Asonihu	Reigush	M	Hungary
BLATBERG			M	Hungary
BREITBARD	Moshe		M	Hungary
BREITBERG	Moshe		M	Hungary
DAN	Sheike		M	Hungary
DORON	Amir		M	Hungary
EOZEN	Yona		M	Hungary
FORRER	Moshe		M	Hungary
GANTZ	Hannah		F	Hungary
GEIR	Albert	Dr.	M	Hungary

70 Bauer p.295

GLATBERG	Israel		M	Hungary
GLICK	Moshe		M	Hungary
GRINWALD	David	Tzutzi	M	Hungary
GROSSMAN	Alexander		M	Hungary
HAFT	Shlomo		M	Hungary
HARRY	Yehudit		F	Hungary
KAMAI	Shlomo		M	Hungary
KATZ	Moshe		M	Hungary
KISH	Kathleen		F	Hungary
KOMIN	Eliezer		M	Hungary
KOPSTEIN	Evri		M	Hungary
KOTZER	Zvi	Peitzek	M	Hungary
KRATZMER	Naftali		M	Hungary
LAUFER	Rachel G.		F	Hungary
LAUFER	Moshe		M	Hungary
LEVI	Yehuda	Pitzi	M	Hungary
LIVINTHEIM	Shmuel		M	Hungary
MEIR	Moshkowitz	Janek	M	Hungary
MELETZ AUGEN	Miriam		F	Hungary
MIRON	Yaacov	Polek	M	Hungary
PALGI	Yoel		M	Hungary
PFEIFER	Yehuda		M	Hungary
RABINOWITZ	Zelig		M	Hungary
REIZMAN	Yossi		M	Hungary
RETZMAN	Yossef		M	Hungary
ROSENBAUM	Pinhas	Tibor	M	Hungary
ROSENBERG	Raphael	xxx	M	Hungary
ROZEN	Yona		M	Hungary
ROZEN	Meno		M	Hungary
ROZMAN	Mordechai		M	Hungary
ROZMAN	M.		M	Hungary
SABO	Zeev	Willie	M	Hungary
SHACHAR	Mordechai	Muka	M	Hungary
SHALMON	Mihai		M	Hungary
STEIN	Eliezer		M	Hungary
TALMI	Yehuda	Arieh	M	Hungary
VARDI	Yaakov		M	Hungary
WEISS	Chaim		M	Hungary

Chapter VIII
Yugoslavia

*Map of former Yugoslavia now divided into several
independent states and autonomous areas.*

Yugoslavia was ideally suited for the Brichah since it provided many routes for transporting Jews out of Eastern Europe. At first it was hoped that the routes would lead to Greece and onward to Palestine. But Britain had great influence in Greece and made sure that Greek ports were closed to Brichah agents. Since the Brichah was prevented from moving south it turned west to Italy or north to Austria.

Yugoslavia had a Jewish population of about 80,000 Jews prior to the war. Just 14,000 Yugoslav Jews survived the war. About 4,572 recorded Yugoslav Jews fought with the partisans and some reached high positions within the ranks of the partisan army of Marshal Tito, leader of the Yugoslav Communist party and military commander of all partisan forces in the country. He welcomed the Palestinian parachutists and aided their efforts.

113

Josip Broz Tito

Yugoslav partisans with Jewish parachutists from Palestine 1944

Following the war, the surviving Yugoslav Jews returned home and started to rebuild their lives. Jewish communities began to function again including Zionist youth groups who would become instrumental in Brichah efforts.

Meanwhile thousands of Jewish refugees were stuck in Romania since Romanian ports were closed to the Brichah. Kovner discussed the problem with his assistants and they decided to launch exploratory missions to neighboring countries. As mentioned earlier, one of the roads led to Budapest in Hungary. In April of 1945 Kovner sent a group of partisans headed by **Mula Ben Haim** to Yugoslavia[71]. They arrived in Belgrade and immediately began to make contacts with local organizations. A smaller group led by Pinhas Zeitag reached Split in May and met up with soldiers of the Jewish Brigade stationed in Treviso, Italy, next to the Yugoslav border. The linking of European Jewry with the Palestinians was vital to the Brichah efforts. The Yugoslav Brichah had established a new route for the Jewish refugees stuck in Romania. Papers were forged to the effect that the carriers of these identity papers were repatriated to their homeland. The route began in Arad or Timisoara, Romania headed to Belgrade, or Zagreb, Yugoslavia and then to Trieste, Italy[72]. Even the British embassy accepted the documents as authentic and allowed entry to Palestine for 100 Jewish refugees. Yugoslav authorities soon realized the repatriation papers were not legitimate but decided to ignore them.

Mula Ben Haim, head of Yugoslav Brichah

The Brichah now had two routes that enabled them to transport the Jews refugees from Romania. The Hungarian route was the best organized since it relied on the Hungarian Zionist youth groups who had great success moving Jews towards Italy and Austria. But many Jews, particularly those coming from Russia, preferred the Yugoslav road since it offered safety from Soviet control.

---

71 Bauer, Flight, p.40.
72 Ibid., p.41

The Yugoslav route was used extensively by Jewish Brigade representatives who came from Italy to Bucharest, Romania to discuss ways of improving the movements of Jewish refugees to Italy. Slowly the number of Jewish refugees climbed to 70,000[73]. The survivors were quartered in Italian DP camps supported and maintained by the JDC.

Mula Ben Haim's fake papers in Yugoslavia.

Ben Haim established excellent contacts with the Jewish community in Belgrade who introduced him to high ranking officials in the government. The Brichah office even received a partial official standing regarding matters of emigration to Palestine. The Yugoslav route was used extensively by the Brichah and Kovner himself used it to reach Italy. Very few Jewish refugees remained in Yugoslavia, most of them continued their journey to Palestine while some managed to reach other countries. Yugoslavia was yet another country that actively helped the mass exodus of Jews from Eastern Europe to Central Europe. The British government pressured these governments and countries to stop the flow of Jews. Britain knew that most of the Shoah survivors were trying to get to Palestine. But Britain was losing power and the Jews who had survived Hitler and Stalin were now fighting hard for their future. Many countries preferred to let them go and the Jews left en masse facing an unknown destiny.

73Israel Defense. p.102

Partial list of Yugoslav Brichah Agents

Name	First	Code name	G	Country
BABETLERDER	Itzhak	Jacek	M	Yugoslavia
BEN HAIM	Mula		M	Yugoslavia
BEN-HAIM	Rivkah		F	Yugoslavia
BEN-YAIRI	Yaacov		M	Yugoslavia
DAN	Shaike		M	Yugoslavia
DAN	Eva		F	Yugoslavia
GOLDSTEIN	Benyamin		M	Yugoslavia
HERSHKOWITZ	Zvi		M	Yugoslavia
WEISS	Masha		F	Yugoslavia
WERNIK	Natke		M	Yugoslavia
WIERNIK	Itzhak		M	Yugoslavia
ZEITAG	Pinhas		M	Yugoslavia
ZILBER	David		M	Yugoslavia

Chapter IX
Britain at War with the Jews

In 1930 Britain introduced limitations on the number of Jews entering Palestine. From then on one had to obtain a certificate of entrance granted on the basis of certain qualifications notably financial or skills. The system was steadily tightened and the number of certificates reduced. The number of Jewish applicants increased each day with Hitler's rise to power in Germany. In 1936, 60,000 Jews reached the shores of Palestine. Palestinian Arabs protested and an Arab revolt began that lasted until 1939. Britain decided to further reduce the number of Jews entering Palestine and to militarily crush the Arab revolt. Both policies succeeded. The Arab revolt was slowly squashed and the number of Jews entering Palestine dwindled with the passage of the *"White Paper"*, which restricted Jewish immigration to 75,000 for five years and said that any new immigration would have to be approved by the Arab majority. The gates of Palestine were closed to the thousands of Jews who would have found a safe haven from the death camps of Europe.

The Jewish Agency of Palestine went along with the British policies until adoption of the *"White Paper"*. This was the breaking point between Britain and Jewish Palestine. Already in 1934, the "Halutz" or Zionist pioneer organization in Poland had successfully sent 350 passengers to Palestine illegally on the ship *Vellos*. The Jewish Agency had opposed the move and made sure that such operations were stopped. The *Vellos* passengers were helped by the Haganah or Palestinian Jewish underground as a one-time event. The Revisionist Zionist movement under the leadership of Ze'ev Jabotinsky ignored the British rules and began to organize illegal ships that sailed to Palestine with Jewish passengers. These operations tended to be small because of a lack of funds. At first small boats like *Af Al P* or *Dor* were used but with time larger vessels like *Patria* with 850 passengers in 1939 were used[74.] With publication of the Britain's *"White Paper"* the Jewish Agency created an office called "Mossad l'Aliyah Bet" to handle illegal immigration to Palestine[75]. More illegal ships began to reach Palestine with Jewish immigrants but the British Navy was there to greet them.

The British were well informed of the Jewish situation in Palestine and expected some reactions to their policy of preventing Jews from

---

74 Arens, Moshe. Flags Over the Ghetto of Warsaw, USA: Gefen Publishing House,, P.80
75 Szulc, Alliance p29

immigrating. The Royal Navy was already partially mobilized due to the war-threatening situation in Europe. The Navy and the Royal Air Force were ordered to patrol the Mediterranean Sea and intercept illegal ships with Jews. [76] British agents in Mediterranean ports were ordered to be on the lookout for the ships. Even the Foreign Office began to apply pressure on Romania to stop the flow of Jews to the Romanian ports where they embarked on boats heading to Palestine. As mentioned earlier, the British were very successful in stifling the illegal aliyah. Some illegal ships still managed to leave Europe but had tragic consequences, notably the *Patria* and the *Struma*. The *Patria* was blown up by the Haganah on November 25, 1940 to stop it from taking illegal Jewish immigrants to the island of Mauritius. The explosion sunk the boat within minutes and resulted in the estimated death of 267 people[77]. As written about in Chapter II, the *Struma* had a tragic end which caused a temporary stop to the illegal aliyah since the risks were so grave.

With the liberation of Italy from the Germans, the Mossad renewed the illegal shipping of Jewish Holocaust survivors to Palestine. The Royal Navy and Air Force chased the ships throughout the Mediterranean Sea, seized most of them, and sent the passengers to detention camps on the island of Cyprus. The British foreign office applied pressure to all the countries notably Italy, France and Greece, to stop illegal ships from leaving their ports[78].

With the end of the war, the Jewish Shoah survivors refused to cooperate with Britain. The hundreds of thousands of Jewish survivors and Jewish refugees who had fled the Nazi horrors and the anti-Semitic pogroms in Eastern Europe were determined to reach Palestine. Most of them had no place to go and only Jewish Palestine wanted them. Even after the atrocities of WWII became evident, Britain still stubbornly prevented the Jews from entering Palestine, devoting considerable military resources to stopping illegal ships. Britain already had approximately 50,000 soldiers in Palestine to control the situation and prevent illegal refugees from entering the country. Since 1945 Britain had lost 223 soldiers fighting the Jewish underground in Palestine with 478 wounded.

---

76 Zertel, Idith. From Catastrophe to Power, Holocaust Survivors and the Emergence of Israel. University of California Press, P.20

77 San Francisco Jewish Community Publications Inc. JWeekly.com 2 "Deaths of 260 in 1940 ship explosion commemorated". 14 December 2001. Retrieved 25 May 2013.

78 Kochavi, Post, p.40

In spite of these actions the ships kept coming, mostly from Italian ports. The British tried to pressure the Italian government to close the borders and to patrol the shores of the Adriatic Sea. The Italian government was happy to see refugees leave the country and did not care to help the British. The Italians did not want to take drastic action against Jewish refugees fearing American public opinion. Britain also appealed to France and Greece but the pleas proved fruitless since the governments of these countries had other more important pressing problems.

The British foreign office stepped up the pressure and imposed a blackout on Jewish news throughout Europe. British Jewish social services were prevented from assisting Jewish Holocaust survivors in the British zone of occupied Germany. Rabbi Herzog was also kept out. The British foreign minister kept repeating the story -- there was no Jewish problem in Europe therefore no need to discuss Palestine.

Ernest Bevin, British foreign minister admitted that there were refugees in Europe but said they were nationals of various European countries notably Poles, not Jewish refugees. Bevin urged all refugees including the Jewish refugees to return to their native countries. But the Holocaust survivors were determined to break the British blockade. They enlisted the help of American public opinion that supported a Jewish homeland in Palestine. Americans demanded President Truman take action on behalf of the Shoah refugees. The reasoning was clear; countries including the US, did not want to admit large numbers of Jewish refugees, but Palestine did want them. Britain refused to budge assuming the US was posturing for its public. The State Department and the Pentagon assured Britain that the US would support the British position.

But President Truman knew that he had to take a stand and was in favor of Britain slightly opening the gates of Palestine. Immigration to Palestine was becoming an issue between England and the US. Truman felt that he must give something to his Jewish constituents who were demanding action. As mentioned earlier, American Jewish soldiers and chaplains were writing home about the terrible conditions of the Jewish Shoah survivors. This became the most important topic of conversation at Jewish community centers and temples. During the war, the Jewish organizations were promised that that the situation in Europe would be seen to once the war was over. They now demanded action.

Brichah - Hebrew for Escape or Flight

Earl Harrison Dean of the Pennsylvania University Law School

Truman then decided to investigate the situation of the refugee camps in the American occupation zones in Europe. He appointed Earl Harrison, Dean of the Pennsylvania University Law School and former Commissioner of Immigration, to investigate the DP situation. Harrison submitted his first impressions at the end of July 1945 and the final report to the president on August 24, 1945. His findings were very critical and accused the United States Army of inhuman conduct towards Jewish DPs. The report stated that the survivors were still fenced in by barbed wire and guarded by soldiers. Many of them were still wearing the rags from the camps. The report also suggested that 100,000 Jewish DPs should be permitted to go to Palestine. The president ordered the military to take steps to implement the recommendations in the Harrison report. General Eisenhower, supreme allied commander issued specific orders to the military establishment in the American zones to implement the recommendations notably the establishment of separate Jewish DP camps, removal of barbed wire, soldiers, and the establishment of elected representation in the camps. Most military commanders implemented the recommendations. President Truman seriously considered Harrison's recommendation to send some Jewish DPs to Palestine and the US. The British refused to listen and insisted on continuing their policy of no Jewish emigration to Palestine.

Some American officers resented the new policies including General George Patton, Commander of the Third Army, who decided to take steps to stop the flow of Jewish refugees to his sector which extended into Czechoslovakia near Pilsen. The Karlov camp, an UNRRA refugee camp, was located in this zone. The Brichah began using Karlov as a staging point to smuggle Jewish refugees in transit from Czechoslovakia to the American zone in Germany. In the spring of 1945, three transports totaling about 600 Jewish refugees arrived from Czechoslovakia and entered the Karlov camp and were registered by the camp officials. But Patton ordered his men to round up the new arrivals, put them back on a train, and send them out of the American zone back into Czechoslovakia. (See New York Post Oct 2, 1945 and New York Post October 7, 1945.) The screaming headlines of the New York Post told the story of Jewish Shoah survivors being forcibly removed by American soldiers.

President Truman was furious. He had already signed the Harrison Report that called for the improved treatment of Jewish survivors in the DP Camps in Germany and Austria. He and Eisenhower were deeply embarrassed by the incident.

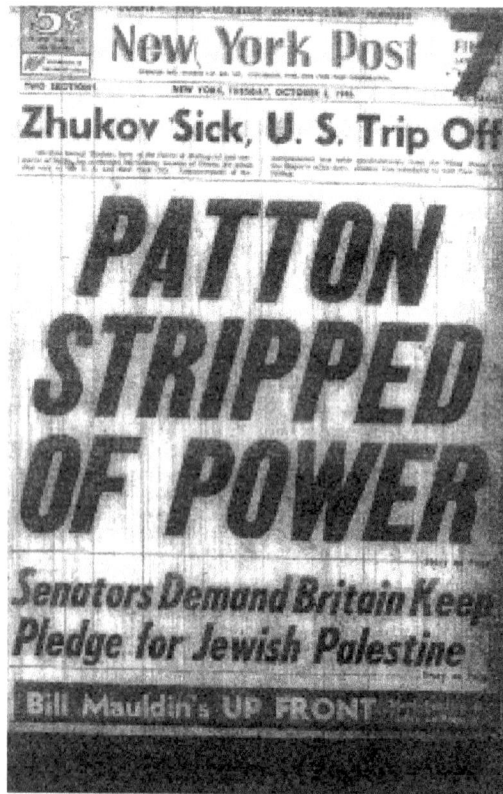

York Post headline on October 2, 1945

New York Post front page dated October 2, 1945

Here is a typical article about the event:

"Patton Turned Back 600 Jews Fleeing Terror in Poland"

by Pat Frank

Pilsen, Czechoslovakia, Oct. 2- At the order of Gen. Patton, 600 Polish Jews who hoped they had reached asylum in the U.S. zone from an anti-Semitic wave of terror sweeping their homeland, were forcibly returned to that country, this correspondent established today.

A Munich cable on Sept 21 reported that 600 Jews who had escaped from Poland had arrived via Prague at the Pilsen reception camp a month before. Interrogated by American officers, they sought to pass themselves off as German Jews desiring to return to Munich. Their faulty German, however, gave them away, after which "an American general," the cable stated, ordered them all returned to Poland. The anti-Semitic terror in Poland was attested to by Jews who have escaped to the American zone.

Ike's Policy Ignored

At least 3,000 Polish Jews have reached the U.S zone. What happened to the 600 who believed they had found refuge at Camp Karlov, the United Nations' displaced persons center here, is another story. The tale is nearly as shocking as what happened to them when they were returned from Nazi concentration camps to their homes in Poland. Gen. Patton's 22d Corps, stationed in the U.S. zone in Czechoslovakia, violated the oft-repeated policy of Gen. Eisenhower- that refugees or persecuted peoples who do not desire to return to their homelands, or whose lives would be endangered in so doing, would not be returned by force. Furthermore, it is to be noted that Jews alone were singled out for forcible return. The Jews began crowding into Camp Karlov around the middle of August. Three trains, each carrying 175, arrived at the Pilsen railway station, temporary American zone in Czechoslovakia. Others afoot sought refuge here after trudging through the Russian zone in Czechoslovakia. The top authorities of the 22d Corps requested permission to ship these Jews to Germany where special camps for Jews were being erected. But Gen. Patton's headquarters ordered them shipped back to Czechoslovakia. It is somewhat complicated to trace the exact responsibility for this order since the DP officers then in charge of Camp Karlov have been redeployed. However, the officers now in charge say that Gen. Patton's 3d Army headquarters ordered the Jews returned because "there wasn't room for any more Jews in Germany, where the camps are already overcrowded" and "the trains that brought those Jews entered our zone without proper authority." To this correspondent, enlisted men at Camp Karlov described the pitiful scenes that ensued when the 600 Jews were loaded aboard trucks, on Aug, 24, and taken to the Pilsen railroad station. The women among them fought bitterly, screaming and kicking.

We Had To Use Force

The military detachment found itself unable to cope with the situation and asked assistance. The 8th Armored Division sent troops with rifles, machine-guns and armored vehicles. Pvt. Edward Heilbrun, of Chicago, who is Jewish and who helped to load the hapless, protesting Jews aboard the trucks, told me: "My job was sickening. Men threw themselves on their knees in front of me, tore open their shirts, and screamed, 'Kill me now!' They would say, 'You might just as well kill me now. I am dead anyway if I go back to Poland.' "They kept jumping off the trucks. And we had to use force." There was more trouble at the railroad station where the troops were forced to jam the 600 Jews aboard a train.

After the train started, the trouble continued, according to witnesses. Men threw themselves from the moving train. Troops fired in the air attempting to frighten them into remaining on the train. Where the train was routed, after leaving the American zone, is still a mystery. One woman who was scheduled to return to Poland did not have to go. Luba Zindel of Kracow, was having a baby at the hospital when the train departed. I talked to her at Camp Karlov. This is her story: With her husband and an earlier child, she had spent three years in the Nazi concentration camp at Lublin. After the Russians captured that city, the family was released. They returned to their home in Kracow on June 20 1945. On the first Saturday in August, while the family was attending services, the synagogue was attacked and stormed by uniformed AK troopers. "They were shouting, she told me, that we had committed ritual murders. They began firing at us and beating us. My husband was sitting beside me. He fell down on his face full of bullets." The widow was among those selected by the Jewish Committee in Krakow to be given a chance to escape to Czechoslovakia. She arrived here aboard the first of three trains".

The train with the Jewish refugees was forced to leave the American enclave and crossed the Czech border. It was stopped and the passengers were removed by the Czech Brichah to temporary shelters where they were fed and rested. All the refugees would again cross the border but in smaller groups led by the Brichah. General Patton was of course dismissed from his post and no further attempts would be made by the American army to stop Jewish refugees entering the American zones. Zdenek Toman was very pleased with the results since he could continue to permit Jewish refugees to cross Czechoslovakia.

All these American activities surrounding Jewish refugees drove Britain mad. They looked for ways to reduce the American preoccupation with the Jewish refugees. The British continued to repeat their claims that there were no Jewish refugees, only former nationals of European countries. On instruction from London, the British military authorities in their zones of occupation refused to recognize the representative of the Jewish DPs in the Bergen-Belsen camp, Josef Rosensaft. He was elected on April 17, 1945, two days after the camp was liberated. Bergen Belsen was the largest Jewish DP camp in the British zone in Germany with about 10,346 Jewish refugees. The entire Jewish DP population in the British German zone was 12,232 and this number hardly changed. Even British Jewish social services were not permitted to enter DP camps in the British zones.

The British government was determined to hide the Jewish problem in Europe by any and all means. But Jewish refugees kept entering Germany and Austria and then headed to the Mediterranean ports where they boarded illegal ships to Palestine. The illegal fleet of the Brichah grew with the arrival of American ships and American crews notably the Exodus. These ships received wide coverage in the American press and created an anti-British climate. Although the British tried to stop the campaign by seizing the ships at sea and sending the passengers to the Cyprus detention camps, more ships continued to arrive. Press coverage intensified with screaming headlines and pictures of British soldiers mishandling Jewish Holocaust survivors.

Brichah - Hebrew for Escape or Flight

Britain was desperate and tried to paint the Jewish refugees as terrorists. British foreign policy directives bade their officials to promote wild stories about Soviet agents wearing Zionist clothing. The most publicized event was a press conference held by UNRRA Director of European Operations, Lieutenant-General Sir Fredrick Morgan, on January 3, 1946 in Frankfurt, Germany. The general stated that "he was not impressed by all the talk about pogroms within Poland". Furthermore, he stated that "a Jewish secret force is organizing the exodus of Jews from Europe and added that Jews fleeing from Poland to Berlin were well dressed, well-fed, rosy-cheeked and have plenty of money". There were elements of truth in these words namely the Brichah refugee smuggling operations, but the crude anti-Semitic representations created a storm in the Jewish world, especially in the US, the main financial backer of UNRRA. Of course, the general, who was ostensibly in charge of helping poor and destitute refugees, Jewish and non-Jewish, attempted to soften the impact of his crude statements by claiming he was misunderstood or misquoted or both. He was certainly understood as representing British foreign policy. But the American press was against Morgan and insisted on action. Fiorello La Guardia, head of UNRRA had no choice but to dismiss Morgan from his post. Morgan protested the dismissal. Bevin strongly backed Morgan. But the US did not want to create a greater gap than already existed between the two countries. La Guardia was forced to reinstate Morgan who continued to make embarrassing anti-Semitic statements to the detriment of UNRRA.

Lieutenant-General Sir Fredrick Morgan

GENERAL MORGAN REINSTATED

Post With UNRRA

LONDON, Jan. 30 (A.A.P.). The UNRRA office in Great Britain has announced that Lieutenant-General Sir Frederick Morgan has succeeded in his appeal against termination of his appointment as chief of UNRRA operations in Germany.

[Early in January General Morgan said at a Press conference that a secret Jewish organisation was promoting the exodus of thousands of Jews from Poland to the United States zone in Germany. After protests by Jewish organisations, UNRRA headquarters asked for his resignation. An investigation by the United States Third Army resulted in a report supporting General Morgan's statement.]

Morgan continued to make anti-Jewish comments. The British government ultimately dismissed him from this post after criticizing incompetence and corruption within UNRRA. The general claimed that UNRRA was diverting resources to Zionist causes.

American Jewish organizations were furious with Morgan's anti-Semitism and demanded his permanent dismissal. In London, British Jewry was also pressuring for his dismissal as well as an opening of access to the Jewish Shoah survivors in the British zone of occupation. The combined pressure forced the British authorities to ease up on their strict policies toward the Jewish refugees.

President Truman decided to appoint **Simon H. Rifkind**, a US District Court Judge for the Southern District of New York, as a civilian Special Advisor on Jewish Affairs in Europe. Judge Rifkind was sent to Europe in November 1945 to tour UNRRA facilities and prepare a report. Judge Rifkind was highly respected both by the army and many charitable organizations.

Brichah - Hebrew for Escape or Flight

Judge Simon Rifkind (on left)

When he first arrived Rifkind served under Allied Commander for the European Theater General Dwight D. Eisenhower, but "Ike" left his post a month after Rifkind arrived. Rifkind then served Eisenhower's replacement, General Joseph T. McNarney, remaining in Europe until March 1946.

Years later Judge Rifkind's son Robert said that the six-months his father had spent in Europe had made him much more of a cynic having witnessed first-hand the atrocities that the Germans had committed, and the unjust discrimination these same Jews who managed to survive were still suffering. According to Robert Rifkind, his father said that almost all the Jewish refugees he encountered wanted to go to Palestine. No where else.

Not long after Rifkind arrived in Europe, David Ben Gurion, Chairman of the Jewish Agency Executive, arrived from Jerusalem to visit the "saved remnants' of the Jewish people. He was greeted with great enthusiasm.

Rabbi Samuel Abramovitz, then a young man recently released from the U.S. Army, was volunteering with the JDC in a German DP camp. According to Abramovitz, who had a long distinguished career with the JDC, Ben Gurion was 'greeted like a king.' Crowds turned out waving flags and cheering.

The British and Americans tried hard to stop the flow of refugees through Czechoslovakia. The British ambassador to Prague, Philip Nichols, demanded that Czech borders be closed the day following the Kielce pogrom in Poland. He even insisted that Jacobson be expelled from Czechoslovakia[79]. The American ambassador to Prague, Lawrence Steinhardt, consistently pressured Czechoslovakia to close the borders to Polish Jewish refugees. The Czechs replied that only refugees with legal papers were permitted to travel through Czechoslovakia. Still the ambassador protested, he was urged to complain in writing which he did. The letter was received by Masaryk, who leaked a copy of the letter to Toman. Toman invited Steinhardt to his office and told him:"I (Toman) am going to send the National Guard and they will take you out of the office, and like a sack of potatoes we shall throw you out.[80]" Toman was furious that Steinhardt, a Jew, fought so hard against his own people in trouble. Furthermore, Steinhardt supposedly suggested that Toman be removed from his office since he was Jewish. This incensed Toman. The contents of the protest letter were published in Paris

Lawrence Steinhardt, USA ambassador to Prague

and created a sensation that embarrassed the President of the USA[81]. Even the Russian ambassador to Prague, Valery Zorin, told Gottwald that Czechoslovakia was permitting too many Polish Jews to cross the country. Gottwald called on Toman and showed him the letter. Toman managed to get himself off the hook by stating that he was fighting the Anglo-American Imperialistic plots aimed against the Communist world[82]. Zorin was not terribly pleased but he was busy planning to seize power in Czechoslovakia and wanted the Czech Communist party to be united and ready for action.

---

79 Szulc, Alliance, p.155
80 Szulc, Alliance, p.157
81 Szulc, Alliance, p.157.
82 Szulc, Alliance. P.155

Still the trains with illegal Jews continued to roll and Britain's relationship with the US worsened. Bevin decided to heal the rift by proposing the creation of a combined committee to study the entire problem and make binding recommendations. Truman accepted the proposal. The governments of Britain and the United States formed the Anglo-American Commission for Palestine to devise a policy that could be recommended regarding the immigration of Jews to Palestine. Other committees also examined the situation in Palestine, but this was the only committee that dealt with the conditions of the Jews left in Europe. The Commission consisted of six Americans and six British members. The findings were to be binding. Britain packed its delegation with supporters of British foreign policy and was certain that it would pick up some American votes so the British position would be always supported or at worst, there would be a tie within the Committee. The Commission visited the United States and London, Arab capitals and Palestine, and DP camps in Europe, where they questioned Jewish Holocaust survivors. Most of the survivors said they wanted to move to Palestine.

Ben Gurion (back row) beside Rabbi Herzog, at
Commission meeting on Mt. Scopus, Jerusalem

Professor Chaim Weitzman, head of the World Zionist organization and David Ben Gurion, head of the Jewish Agency in Palestine, addressed the Commission. Rabbi Herzog also testified, claiming that the new Jewish entity could absorb all the Jewish survivors in Europe. He also testified to what he had personally witnessed in the Italian DP camps. Rabbi Herzog was well prepared and eloquently presented his case with biblical quotations and references to Jewish history including the fact that Jews prayed three times a day to Zion.

The Commission's final report, issued in October 1946, recommended Jewish immigration of 100,000 refugees to Palestine. Britain rejected the findings, in spite of its commitments to abide by them. Bevin shamelessly dropped the report that he himself proposed in the waste basket. Truman was angry and felt a bit betrayed by his British ally. Britain continued to adhere to their policies as though nothing had happened, issuing only 1,500 certificates a month until the number would reach the original White Paper number of 75,000 immigrants. Most of those interred on Cyprus, received priority in getting certificates.

Brichah - Hebrew for Escape or Flight

Chapter X
Receiving and Transit Country-Austria

Map of Austria

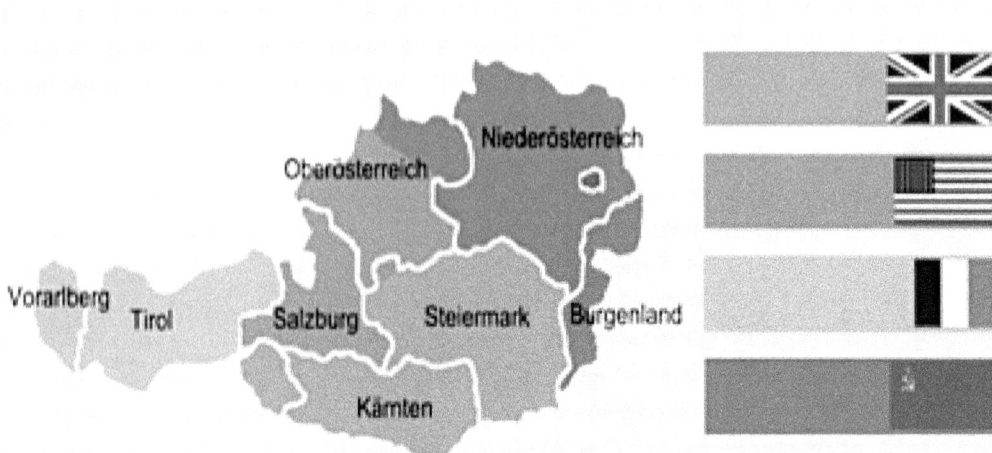

Austria was divided into four military allied zones.
Vienna, capital of Austria represented by a black dot, was also
divided into four zones but was located deep in the Soviet zone.

With the end of the war, there were about 50,000 Jewish concentration camp survivors in Germany and Austria[83]. It is estimated that there were about 10,000 in Austria[84]. Austria would become a Jewish transit station and about 180,000 Jewish refugees would transit this country on the way to Germany or Italy[85] [86]. Most of the Jews from France, Holland, Belgium, Germany, Hungary and Czechoslovakia returned to their native countries. Most of the Polish, Lithuanian and Ukrainian Jewish survivors refused to return to their native countries. This is what Mordechai Lustig, a native of Nowy Sacz, Poland, had to say following the liberation: "I was liberated at about 10 A.M. on May 6, 1945. The American army entered the Ebensee concentration camp in Austria and began to restore order. The night before and in the morning, serious disorders took place in the camp. Some of the inmates settled scores with the remaining Germans or their helpers in the camp."

Mordechai Lustig wearing his concentration camp hat following his liberation.

Lustig had no desire to return to Poland. He knew that most of his family had been killed and he had no inclination to visit his native city of Nowy Sacz.[87] He remained at the camp in Austria and began to recuperate. Slowly he started to visit the nearby villages and towns. Some of his friends returned to Poland but he refused to return. He even refused to join the Jewish Brigade that came to the camp to remove the Jewish inmates to Italy and then to Palestine.

---

83 Bauer, Flight, p.55
84 Schiff, David and Nathan, Asher Ben editors. Habricha. Israei Ministry of Defense, 1998, p.75.
85 Ibid p.75

87 William Leibner interview with Mordechai Lustig

"One day," Lustig said, "Jewish soldiers from the Jewish Brigade arrived at the camp. We did not believe our eyes when we saw the shoulder patches with the word "Palestine" and the Star of David. They talked to us in Yiddish and urged us to register to go to Palestine. They registered all the Jewish inmates that wanted to go to Palestine. They promised to help us get to Palestine. They then left our camp and soon those of us who had signed up to go to Palestine received packages from the Red Cross. I had signed the list and received a package."

The soldiers were stationed at the Treviso base, near the triangle where Italy, Yugoslavia and Austria meet. As the soldiers received passes to travel through the surrounding countries, they encountered more survivors, and many were faced for the first time with the harsh truth of the Nazi horrors in the concentration camps. Some of the soldiers, if they could, smuggled individual survivors to the brigade camp. There, in Yiddish, these survivors told their tragic tales, shocking their fellow Jews with news of the Nazi atrocities. The details of the locations of the concentration camps were passed onto Captain Aaron Ishai Hooter of the Jewish Brigade. He and Sergeant Mordechai Surkis worked together with the Haganah in Palestine. Hooter and some of his men and his staff set out from the British camp in Treviso in search of the Jewish survivors in the concentration camps in Austria and Germany. They soon found Jewish survivors at Bergen Belsen, Mauthausen, Ebensee and other liberated concentration camps that were now displaced person camps run by the United Nations Relief and Rehabilitation Administration.

When the Jewish soldiers reported the existence of Jewish survivors at the Ebensee concentration camp, the order was given to bring them to Italy. This was easier said than done since the Ebensee concentration camp was in the American military zone in Austria. The rescuers had to cross several military zones of occupation to get to the American zone in Austria. Many forged military papers had to be made before the rescue mission could start. The Jewish Brigade made all the preparations and one day the Jewish brigade reappeared at the Ebensee camp and invited all Jewish inmates to board trucks. The Jewish Brigade repeated these actions in other camps and removed many Jewish Shoah survivors to Italy. The Jewish Brigade extended help and assistance to those Jews who did not want to leave the camps.

Mordechai Lustig said "I did not feel like going to Palestine and went to the men's room until the Jewish Brigade left with some of the Jewish survivors. I was never a Zionist and I came from a very religious and

Hasidic background that was opposed to Zionism. Palestine did not appeal to me. I wanted to live; I had suffered enough during the war. I was not going to a forsaken desert place to waste my life. I was not the only surviving Jew to remain in the camp although my name was recorded as wanting to go to Palestine."[88]

Some Jews did return to Poland and at the Polish frontier were arrested for supposedly collaborating with the Germans during the war. They were arrested on the spot and sent to a special camp of hard labor. A few managed to escape and return to Austria and warn Jews not to dare to return to Poland.[89] A Jewish Shoah survivor naFromtchik returned to his Salzburg D.P. camp and this is what he had to say: "I have already come back from my Fatherland. There are hundreds, even thousands who, like myself, have felt for themselves what we can expect in our former homes."[90] These stories repeated themselves among the Jewish Shoah survivors and reinforced the decision not to return to the old home. Furthermore, the Jewish Brigade soldiers appeared in camps and urged the Jews to organize and form committees to defend their interests. The soldiers advised the survivors to ignore the Allied pressure to return to their former homes. The soldiers told them that thousands of Poles, Lithuanians and Hungarians had refused to return home. As a matter fact, the Polish government in London urged the Poles not to return to Poland. Britain and the United States had to accept this decision since the London Poles were allies. The Jewish soldiers pointed to the Polish refugees and told the Jewish survivors that they could do the same thing. With brigade assistance, the Jewish survivors began to demand Jewish camps or separate living quarters since the camps had many anti-Semitic elements.

As time passed, more and more former Jewish camp inmates began to return from their former homes to the former Austrian and German labor or concentration camps. Even non-camp residents began to reach the Austrian and German camps. The Jewish survivors, individually or in groups led by the Brichah, began to reach Bratislava, Czechoslovakia, from Poland, Ukraine and the Baltic countries. Previous chapters describe the ways used by the Brichah to get the people to Bratislava, Czechoslovakia. Now they led the Jewish refugees from Bratislava to Vienna across the Morava River. It is estimated that between 1945 and

---

88 Lustig, Mordechai, The Red Feathers, Published Israel, pp. 241-245
89 Bauer, Flight, p. 50
90 Ibid., p. 50

1949, about 130,000 Jewish refugees used this route.[91] Of course, there were other routes that were used by the refugees. The area was within the Soviet-occupied zone in Austria. The Soviets did not officially interfere with the movement of Jewish refugees. The latter headed to Vienna that was also divided into four occupation zones. The refugees headed to the American zone where the Rothschild Hospital was located.

Polish Jewish refugees arrived in Vienna after the war. They were sheltered at the Rothschild Hospital displaced persons camp. The hospital was located at Severingasse, in the IX district of Vienna.

The hospital was established by the famous Jewish banking family in Austria and served the Jewish community. It was designed to accommodate 600 people. The hospital was closed in 1942. At the end of the war, the place was in a shambles. Stanislaw Teicholz, a Jew from Lemberg, Poland, had survived the war, and then joined the Brichah where he was appointed to head the Rothschild Hospital refugee center in Vienna. The committee was granted the keys to the Rothschild Hospital.[92] Teicholz opened the place to all Jewish refugees in Vienna. He contacted the Joint Distribution Committee to help with food and

---

91 Thomas Albrich and and Ronald Zweig, Editors, Escape through Austria, published by Frank Cass, London 2002, pp. 8-11
92 Bauer, Flight, p.158

medical supplies to reopen the medical sections of the hospital. He also contacted UNRRA and the American army for help. The American army supported the move since Teicholz took the refugees off their hands. They even provided him with food for the refugees. The stream of Polish Jewish refugees kept increasing, especially after the pogrom in Kielce, Poland. The number of Jewish refugees who arrived at the camp frequently reached 8,000 people who had to be cared for. The overcrowding was beyond description and the Brichah tried to remove as many Jewish refugees, but the numbers kept growing by the day. The Brichah sent Asher Ben-Nathan (also known as Arthur Pier) from Palestine to take control of the Brichah in Vienna. Ben Nathan was a native of Vienna and very familiar with the city that he had left a few years earlier.

Stanislaw Teicholz
Head of the Rothschild Hospital transit camp in Vienna, Stanislaw Teicholz

Asher Ben-Natan was born Arthur Piernikartz in Vienna, Austria, on February 15, 1921. His father, Natan Piernikartz, operated a clothing business in the Austrian capital.[1] He attended a Hebrew high school and was a member of the Young Macabbi Zionist youth organisation. Following the Anschluss of Austria in 1938, Asher Ben-Natan fled Austria to Palestine. His family followed suit. After the end of the war in Europe, Ben-Natan was sent to Austria as head of the Brichah. As a cover, he also worked under the pseudonym Arthur Pier as a correspondent for news agencies.

Asher Ben-Natan, Brichah commnader in Vienna and Austria

In Vienna, a seemingly endless flood of Jewish survivors from Poland, then Romania, streamed in from Eastern Europe, overloading the established camps. The JDC helped transform the dilapidated Rothschild Hospital into a makeshift camp.

Ben-Nathan proceeded to negotiate with the UNRRA officials and the American officers about the need for more breathing space for the refugees where conditions were bad. He was successful and managed to locate several school buildings that were converted into transit camps. Here are the names of all the Jewish refugee camps in Vienna:

- **Rothschild Hospital,** Severingasse, Stadtteil Alsergrund, UNRRA camp 350, Durchgangslager, Wien IX

- **Rupertsusplätz,** Dombach, Stadheil Hemals, former school Wien XVII

- **Arzbergengasse No. 2** Stadteil Hemals, subcamp of Rothschild Hospital, former school Wien XVII

- **Alserbachstrasse** Stadteil Alsergrun transit camp Wien IX.

-

All of these reception centers were very crowded. Some of the refugees remained a day, some a few days and some still longer. The JDC and UNRRA provided food. The refugees could not stay in Vienna for an extended time since their places were needed for other refugees who were making their way to Vienna. The Brichah was also uncertain of Vienna, which was surrounded by Soviet forces on all sides. Nobody knew the Soviet intentions regarding the movement of Jewish refugees. After all, most of these refugees had come from areas controlled by the Soviet Union. Their attitude could change any moment; thus the need to ship the Jewish refugees out of Vienna as fast as possible. The Brichah organized train transports and shipped most of Vienna's Jewish refuges to Salzburg, which was located in the American zone of occupation in Austria,

Abba Weinstein was born in Lithuania. During the war he joined the partisans and distinguished himself. Following the war, he joined the Jewish Brigade and became very active in rescuing Jewish Shoah survivors. He was promoted to be in charge of the Brichah in the city of Salzburg.He once said :" I acted the Greek part and and knew two Greek words-*kalimera and dispera.* Then I was an Austrian refugee born in the British zone of occupation. Then I arrived at Salzburg and returned to be a Jew" [93]

---

93 Bauer, Flight, p. p.88

Abba Weinstein, later changed name to Gefen, Brichah commander in Salzburg

This quotation describes the various nationalities that the Lithuanian born Weinstein had to assume while in the Brichah.

Salzburg was a very important strategic Brichah center. From here, transports of Jewish refugees were sent to Germany, mainly to the American military zone, to Italy and to France. Transports arrived constantly from Vienna and had to be assigned to a refugee shelter. As the flow of refugees continued almost daily, the Brichah soon had to open more transit camps. The Brichah transported the Jewish refugees and the JDC and UNRRA fed them. The American military authorities in Austria always complained and protested about the large influx of Polish Jewish refugees to their zone of occupation and sometimes stopped transports from entering the American zone. The Brichah leaders then shifted the transport to another border point where the transport crossed the border.

List of Jewish transit camps in Salzburg.

Salzburg; DP Hosp. (U.S. zone) - In the town of Salzburg were a number of Jewish DP camps:

- **Riedenburg (Machne Yehuda)** on the "Neutorstrasse, Ecke Moosstrasse."
- **Camp Herzl** (Franz-Josefs-Kaserne) between Schrannengasse and Paris-London-Strasse.
- **Camp Mülln** 6 DP in Müllner Hauptstrasse 38.
- **Beth (Beit) Bialik** in the part of Salzburg called Maxglan.

140

Brichah - Hebrew for Escape or Flight

Beth Bialik 1946; source: Yad Vashem

Beth Bialik; kitchen staff; source: Yad Vashem

- Beth Trumpeldor **in the part of Salzburg, called Gnigl,** and
- New Palestine **(called later Parsch) in the Wiesbauerstrasse 9 in Salzburg-Parsch (Parsch is also the part of Salzburg)**

Other DP camps in the country (province) of Salzburg, outside the city of Salzburg, were called:

- **Puch bei Hallein** and
- Camp **"GIVAT AVODA"** (in the Wallnerkaserne) opened in summer 1946 in the small village called "Saalfelden" am Steinernen Meer.

There were also Jewish refugee centers in Linz, Insbruck and Graz. All received refugees from Vienna and then shipped them to their destinations. Most of the Jewish refugees were sent to Germany where there were many Jewish D.P. camps. Salzburg was near the German border. There were no Jewish refugee centers in the Soviet zone. The British zone in Austria had some refugee centers, but as mentioned before, Britain discouraged Jewish refugees from entering its zones in Austria and in Germany. The Brichah led Jewish refugee transports through the British zone in Austria to get to Italy. The British harassed the Brichah transports but they managed to transit the British zone on their way to Italy. There were also some small Jewish refugee centers in the French zone of Austria. All of these centers were integrated into a tight Brichah system of communication that was controlled from Vienna by Asher Ben-Nathan. He had a large force of agents at his disposal and managed to move thousands of Polish Jews and then Hungarian and Romanian Jews through Austria. The Brichah activities were also supported by American Jewish military personnel, that is, Jewish chaplains.

Convoy of Jewish refugees leaving Austria for the Italian border.
(Yad Vashem Archives).

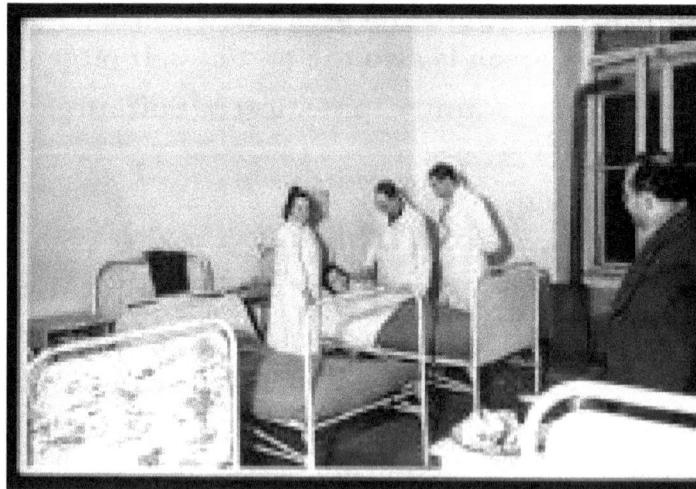

The Rothschild Hospital in Vienna provided medical care
to the many Jewish refugees who transited Austria.

The Austrian JDC had to restore the Rothschild medical facility that was closed in 1942 by the Nazi regime. Equipment and staff had to be brought from the United States. This was not the only hospital in Austria; there were other hospitals, clinics, infirmaries that provided medical aid to the Jewish survivors of the concentration camps and to the Jewish refugees who arrived from Eastern Europe. To provide for all these and other needs, the JDC had huge warehouses where the material arrived from the United States and was stocked for the needs of the Jewish population throughout Austria and Germany,

JDC supply officers and drivers with the fleet of trucks. The former airplane hangar served as one of JDC's 68 warehouses where supplies from overseas were stored before distribution to the camps. Hundreds of thousands of tons of food, clothing and amenities were distributed every month to camp residents to supplement their basic rations.

The Austrian JDC faced many problems due to the various military that divided the city of Vienna and the country of Austria into military zones. Each military zone was administratively independent and headed by military men. The JDC appointed officials in every section to expedite the smooth running of the organization. The Soviet sectors had no refugee centers and thus no JDC offices. The French zones had a few small Jewish refugee camps but were not very accommodating to new Jewish arrivals. The British zones did everything in their power to limit the arrival of newcomers in accordance with the British foreign policy that the Jews should stay in their places. The American zones had the largest number of Jewish refugee camps and facilities. The Brichah directed the flow of Jewish refugees to the American zones where they infiltrated the existing camps. Most of them remained in Austria for short periods of time. In 1947, the Austrian JDC finally managed to place all its activities under the leadership of Harold Trobe.

Trobe Harold

Harold Trobe was born in Pennsylvania and was a graduate of the Columbia University School of Social Work. He began his career with the Joint Distribution Committee in 1944. He was appointed director of operations in Lisbon, JDC's wartime base and a haven for refugees fleeing Nazi-occupied countries and seeking to emigrate to Palestine and the Americas. After liberation, Trobe was named JDC Country Director of Czechoslovakia, and charged with administering a welfare program for survivors. In 1946, he was assigned to supervise JDC activities for Jewish refugees and displaced persons in northern Italy. From 1947 to 1952, he served as Country Director for Austria.

The JDC was not the only organization to have administrative problems in Austria due to the various military zones. The Brichah also had many problems, especially in the British zone of Austria. The Brichah was closely watched by the British, who knew the aims of the Brichah, namely to bring Jews to Italy. These Jews had to cross the British sector of Austria. Constant new routes had to be found that required good coordination between the various Brichah sectors. The troubleshooter for the Brichah in Central Europe was Ehud Avriel, deputy Brichah commander and assistant to Surkis.

Ehud Avriel was born Georg Überall in Vienna, Austria, in 1917. Avriel was educated at a local gymnasium. He was a member of the Blue-White movement, and between 1938 and 1940 worked for the Youth Aliyah office in occupied Vienna. He immigrated to Mandatory Palestine in 1940 and settled in kibbutz Neot Mordechai. He joined the Haganah and was involved in the Rescue Committee assisting Jews to flee Europe.

Brichah - Hebrew for Escape or Flight

After the war he was sent to Europe where he joined the Brichah. He helped illegal Jewish immigration to Palestine. In 1946, he was sent to Czechoslovakia to purchase arms for the Jewish community.

Ehud Avriel

Partial list of Brichah Agents in Austria

Name	First	Code name	G	Country
ALON	Moshe		M	Austria
ALON-HAFT	Agnes		F	Austria
AUGOSHEWITZ	Dworah		F	Austria
AUGUSHEWITZ	Yehuda		M	Austria
BASHAN	Bronia		F	Austria
BASHAN	Eliezer	Leshek	M	Austria
BEILIN	Ada		F	Austria
BEILIN	Father		M	Austria
BEILIN	Mother		F	Austria
BEIN	Sali		F	Austria
BEN-ARI	Mordecha		M	Austria
BEN NACHUM	Daniel		M	Austria
BEN NATHAN	Asher		M	Austria
BEN NATHAN	Erica		F	Austria
BIRENBAUM	Shulek		M	Austria
BOIM	Shmuel		M	Austria
BOKIN	Michael		M	Austria
BOKON	Reuven		M	Austria
BOKON	Dov		M	Austria
BRESLAV	Mark	Arthur	M	Austria
DAGANI	David		M	Austria
DEKEL	Ephraim		M	Austria
DEKEL	Shoshana		F	Austria
EISENBERG	Murice		M	Austria
ERNHALT	Sarah		F	Austria
EVA			F	Austria
FARGERICHT	Awraham		M	Austria
FEINBAUM	Israel		M	Austria
FEINGOLD	Max		M	Austria
FELBS	Shmuel		M	Austria
FELDMAN	Mula		M	Austria
FICHMAN			M	Austria
FIVHMAN	Malczik		M	Austria
FLEKS	Mundek		M	Austria
FRED	Ori		M	Austria
FRIDRICH	Irena		F	Austria
FRUTER	Dov		M	Austria
GEFFEN	Abba		M	Austria
GEFFEN	Frida		F	Austria
GERMAN	Eisik		M	Austria
GERMAN	Hannah		M	Austria
GERSHONOWITZ	Nachum		M	Austria
GINGER	Marks		M	Austria
GIRA	Hela		F	Austria
GIRA	Awraham		M	Austria
GLASS	Pnina		F	Austria
GLICKER	Henia		F	Austria

Brichah - Hebrew for Escape or Flight

GOLDBERG	Yosef		M	Austria
GOLDMAN				Austria
GORKI	Shumek		M	Austria
GOTLIEB	Yosi		M	Austria
HAAS	Itzhak		M	Austria
HAFTEL	Gila		M	Austria
HALEVI	Sami		M	Austria
HARAMTI	Zvi		M	Austria
HARRARU	Tzemah		M	Austria
HERAL	David		M	Austria
HERSH	Awraham		M	Austria
HOINEBESKY	Bolek		M	Austria
ITZHAK	Michael		M	Austria
KAKGNON	Boris		M	Austria
KAMINSKY	Dov		M	Austria
KANTOR	Itzhak		M	Austria
KAPLAN	Sheldon	Army	M	Austria
KAUFMAN	Beti		F	Austria
KIWSKY	Antek		M	Austria
KLATZKOWSKY	Israel		M	Austria
KNIP	Victor		M	Austria
COHEN	Eugene	military chaplain	M	Austria
COHEN	Awraham		M	Austria
KOPPASH	Eliezer		M	Austria
KOPPELBERG	Pinhas		M	Austria
KROCHMAL	Max		M	Austria
LANGER	Itzhak		M	Austria
LAZNIK	Awraham		M	Austria
LEVI	Itzhak		M	Austria
MALACHI	Hanina		M	Austria
MALACHI	Hinda		F	Austria
MONIK	Meir		M	Austria
MORLI		Leutenant	M	Austria
MOWSKY	Awraham		M	Austria
MUNKACZ	Mordechai		M	Austria
NESTEL	Yurek		M	Austria
NOWINSKI	Stanley	Captain	M	Austria
OFFER	Yoav		M	Austria
OFFER	Hawa		F	Austria
OLMER	Itzhak		M	Austria
OSTREIL	Asher		M	Austria
PAAR	Esther		F	Austria
PINES	Zvika		M	Austria
POLIAKOFF	Dov		M	Austria
REVEL	Amos		M	Austria
ROITER	Moshe		M	Austria
ROIZ	Ephraim		M	Austria
RONAL-ROZEN	Ephraim		M	Austria
ROSENBERG	Sylvia		F	Austria

ROSENBERG	Yeshayahu		M	Austria
ROSENBLUM	Moshe		M	Austria
ROSENTZWEiG	Danu	Gidoni	M	Austria
ROSENTZWEiG	Rina		F	Austria
ROZMAN	Brak		M	Austria
RUDELNIK	Israel		M	Austria
SCONCEDEK	David		M	Austria
SHAVIT	Eliezer		M	Austria
SCHLINGER	Nathan		M	Austria
SHMUEL			M	Austria
SHMUTZ	Michael		M	Austria
SHOREMI	Beti		F	Austria
SHUSTER	Yaacov		M	Austria
SPERLER	Nuta		M	Austria
SURKIS	Mordechai		M	Austria
TALIA	Bela		F	Austria
TEICHOLTZ	Bronislaw		M	Austria
TORENSHREIBER	Moshe		M	Austria
TRAMBERG	Asher		M	Austria
TUR	Toniia		F	Austria
TZUTZIK	Meir		M	Austria
VAN ASSEN	Shlomo		M	Austria
WANGLISZEWSKY	Yuri		M	Austria
WEIGARTEN	Awraham		M	Austria
WEIGARTEN	Moshe		M	Austria
WEISS	Hela		F	Austria
WEISS	Jozek		M	Austria
WERBER	Itzhak		M	Austria
WIDRO	Abraham		M	Austria
WOLKOWITZ	Shlomo		M	Austria
ZANDBERG	Bolek		M	Austria
ZIBERT	Richard	Leutenant	M	Austria
ZRUBACHAK	Feivel		M	Austria

Chapter XI
Germany

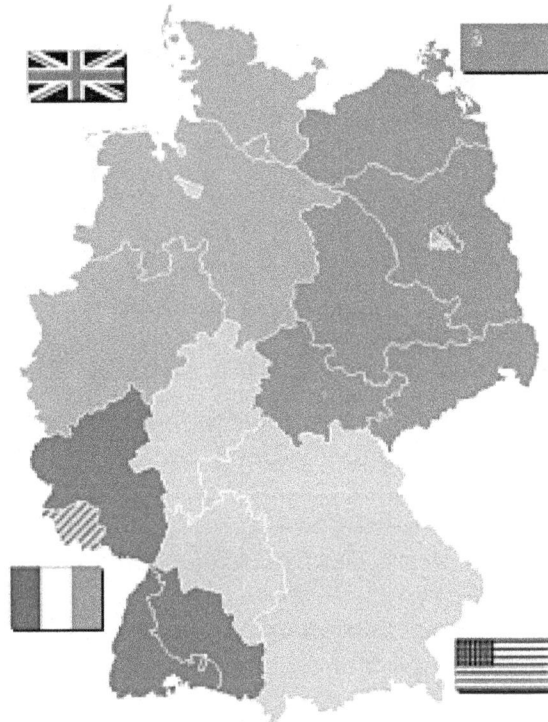

Map of occupied Germany

Germany was a divided country with millions of German and non-German refugees including forced laborers, volunteers, camp inmates and concentration camp survivors. The last group included Jewish Shoah survivors that were located in Ravensbruck, Theresienstadt, Bergen Belsen, Dachau, Allach and Ebensee concentrations camps.[94] The health conditions were appalling in most of these camps particularly Bergen Belsen where 13,000 inmates, mostly Jews, were on the verge of death. The situation at Dachau was not much better. The Americans and the British threw all their medical teams into the camps to help the inmates. They did a heroic job in spite of the fact that they had never encountered or dealt with such massive health problems. The biggest problem was what to do with all the refugees estimated at 10 million people, amongst whom were 80,000 surviving Jews[95]. The relatively small number of Jews seemed to be fairly unimportant.

---

94 Bauer, Flight, p.55.
95 Bauer, Flight, p.51

Bergen-Belsen concentration camp was liberated by the British in April 1945. The survivors immediately erected a memorial saying: "In memoriam to the 30,000 Jewish victims of war and starvation who fell during the regime of the German tyrants and the concentration camp of Bergen-Belsen." Joseph Rosensaft, chairman of the camp's Central Jewish Committee of Liberated Jews, later noted that JDC's representatives were the first to visit from the outside world, and that JDC staff brought survivors "warmth and encouragement from America." Germany, 1945 (Yad Vashem Archives)

As stated earlier, the Allies did not consider Jews as a nationality but classified them as nationals of the country where they lived or were born. Polish born Jews were assigned to Polish camps. This situation was highly flammable since most Polish born Jews refused to go back to Poland and refused any contact with Poland. Incidents began to flare up between Jews and other nationalities. Jewish inmates began to move to camps that had larger numbers of Jews. Feldafing DP camp in the US zone in Germany became the first Jewish camp after Hungarian refugees were sent to the Dachau DP camp and the Jews from Dachau were sent to Feldafing. The commandant of the camp was Lieutenant Irving Smith, a Jew[96]. Most of the Jewish survivors related with ease to Jewish soldiers or officers, especially chaplains that carried tablets of the commandments on their collars. The Jewish military men tried to understand and help the survivors with their problems. They frequently gave advice on how to avoid orders to return to their native country or mailed letters to relatives in the U.S., since there was no postal service immediately after the war. The Jewish chaplains helped the survivors organize to defend their interests.

---

96 Bauer, Flight, p.56

An emissary from Palestine speaking to residents of the
Feldafing DP camp in the American zone of Germany. (Yad Vashem Archives)

As mentioned earlier, Rabbi Abraham Klausner was very active in helping the survivors. He became a "father figure" for the more than 30,000 emaciated survivors found at the Dachau concentration camp near Munich, Germany. He also cared for thousands more left homeless in the various camps following the war as the victorious Allied Forces determined where they should go.

Rabbi Abraham Judah Klausner

At Dachau, survivors constantly asked whether he knew their relatives in the United States. He began to send letters to the US attempting to establish contact between survivors and their families. His lists of survivors were instrumental in reuniting people with what family they had left. He traveled throughout Bavaria looking for survivors, helping to reunite families and setting up a center for survivors at the Deutsches Museum in Munich. Rabbi Klausner traveled extensively throughout Bavaria and saw the terrible conditions of the Jewish DP's at most of the camps. There was overcrowding, inadequate food, poor shelter, a lack of clothing and medical supplies. Klausner realized that these problems were more than he alone could handle. He decided to enlist the DP's in the struggle for improvement of their living conditions. He urged Zalman Grinberg, a ghetto survivor and head of the Feldafing DP Jewish Council to launch the formation of a Central Committee that would represent all liberated Jews in Germany and Austria. Such an organization would speak louder than he himself.

Zalman Grinberg was born September 4, 1912 in Lithuania and was educated as a medical doctor with a specialty in radiology. He survived the Kovno ghetto and many camps. Towards the end of the war, he was imprisoned in the concentration camp at Dachau. At the end of the war he was living near the St. Ottilien monastery, near Dachau. He managed to set up a hospital at the monastery, recruiting nurses and physicians among the concentration camp survivors. The hospital was critical for the survivors many health needs. He then moved to the Feldafing DP camp where he assumed a leading role in the life of the community and met Rabbi Klausner. Grinberg was soon elected head of the Feldafing Jewish Council.

Zalman Grinberg

On July 1, 1945 at the Feldafing camp, Klausner and a survivor of Dachau, established the Central Committee of the Liberated Jews in the U.S. Zone of Germany as the official representative body of the Jewish DPs. The purpose of the Central Committee was to champion the interests of the Jewish DPs and to draw attention to their plight. Rabbi Klausner advised Grinberg and his aides to expand their efforts to include all liberated Jewish camps in Germany and Austria. Jewish leaders were invited to the Funk-Kaserne camp where a committee was created representing every Jewish camp in Germany and in Austria. Present at the meeting were Brichah officials, representatives of the Jewish Brigade, chaplains of the military forces, Zionists and representatives of all the DP camps. The assembly endorsed the creation of the Central Committee of the Liberated Jews in Germany and Austria. The general meeting elected Zalman Grinberg as chairman of the organization. Also elected were several deputy assistants including Samuel Gringauz.

The newly created body established its headquarters in Munich (located first at the Deutsches Museum and later at 3 Sieberstrasse) and set up seven sub-committees to formulate policy and coordinate activity in the areas of education, culture, religious affairs, clothing, nutrition, emigration and information. The Feldafing meeting was quickly followed by a conference in St. Ottilien on July 24. Its purpose was to expand the representative base of the Central Committee and to draw public attention to the plight of Jewish survivors in DP camps and put pressure on Britain to open Palestine to immigration.

The 94 delegates from German and Austrian camps issued a resolution demanding the abrogation of the British White Paper, which prevented them from leaving the camps and starting their lives afresh in their own homeland. In addition, they called for the recognition of the Jewish DPs as a distinct group meriting their own camps, in which they would govern themselves. The Central Committee failed in its attempt to incorporate the Jewish DPs of Austria and the British zone of Germany into their organizational structure. However, it continued to represent the largest group of Jewish DPs and eventually won recognition by the American Army of Occupation. In the five years of its existence, the Central Committee convened three formal congresses: Munich, January 27-29, 1946; Bad Reichenhall, February 25-28, 1947; and Bad Reichenhall, March 30-April 2, 1948. Grinberg served as the Chairman of the Central Committee from its inception until his immigration to Palestine in 1946. He was succeeded by his deputy, **David Treger** (another Kovno ghetto survivor), who was elected Chairman at both the second and third congresses.

The Central Committee was involved in every aspect of Jewish DP life, either independently or in conjunction with one or more of the Jewish welfare agencies operating in the area. Through its constituent departments the Central Committee played a central role in education, culture, and religion, as "the legal and democratic representation of the liberated Jews in the American zone."

David Treger, chairman of the Central Committee of Liberated Jews in Germany

General Joseph McNarney signs the charter of recognition of the Central Committee of Liberated Jews in Bavaria, whereby the American Army acknowledged the Central Committee as the official representative body of Jewish DPs in the American Zone of Germany.

The military commanders were not pleased with these new developments, especially the British commanders. They did everything in their power to sabotage the Central Committee and succeeded in detaching the British zone DP camps from the organization. Josef Rosensaft was the leader of the Jewish DP camp of Bergen-Belsen.

Josef Rosensaft was born January 15, 1911 in Będzin, Poland. He was the son of an affluent scrap-metal dealer. Before the war he was active in the Zionist Labor Movement. He was deported to Auschwitz in 1943 but escaped the transport by jumping into the Vistula River. He was injured by gunfire during the escape but walked back to Będzin, where he was captured again, given 250 lashes and confined to a chicken cage, before being sent to Auschwitz. He was confined at several other camps and finally reached Bergen-Belsen, where he was liberated on April 15, 1945. At the time he weighed just 76 pounds.

Josef Rosensaft at work in his office of Bergen-Belsen.

A born leader, he immediately began his campaign to be elected head of the Jewish council of the Bergen-Belsen camp. The British objected to the council and said that Rosensaft was a Polish citizen and must obey the Polish authorities that were present in the camp. The Polish Army that had been created in the Soviet Union and fought with Britain was stationed in Germany. This army obeyed the orders of the Polish government in London and not the orders of the current government in Warsaw. Officers of the Polish army were active in the camps that had large Polish populations. Rosensaft refused to acknowledge the Polish authorities and openly stated that he was no longer a Polish citizen. Most of the Jewish population of the camp supported Rosensaft and refused to cooperate with the Polish authorities. He effectively campaigned in Yiddish and used the Yiddish printed word in his election materials. He was elected head of the Jewish Council but the British authorities refused to acknowledge him. The Jewish camp survivors loved him and reelected him time and again. In spite of the British refusal to co-operate, he organized the few DP camps in their zone and established the Central Committee of Liberated Jews in the British Zone of Germany and served as chairman. He headed Bergen Belsen until it was closed, working closely with the Brichah, the JDC and the Jewish Brigade. The British watched him and his camp as they did all Jewish DP camps in their zone. They received orders not to permit new Jewish refugee arrivals to enter the British zone and were successful in containing the Jewish numbers in their camps. The Brichah avoided the British zone unless it was absolutely necessary.

The JDC was supplementing the food and medicine provided by UNRRA to Jewish camps, and entered Germany with an abundance of food, supplies and personnel, reaching every camp where there were Jewish Shoah survivors. Herbert Katzki was appointed head of the JDC in Germany.

A road marker in a German city indicates the direction to the office of the AJDC.

Herbert Katzki was born in Elizabeth, New Jersey, He joined the JDC in 1936 as Assistant to Executive Director Joseph Hyman and remained with the organization for 60 years. When World War II broke out, Katzki was sent to the JDC office in Amsterdam, then to Brussels, and finally to Paris, where he served as Secretary of EUREXCO (European Executive Council). Just days before the Nazis entered the city, Katzki sealed the office and fled to Bordeaux, and then to Lisbon, where JDC relocated its overseas headquarters. From there, Katzki returned to France to open a JDC office in Marseilles for assistance to Jewish refugees in unoccupied France. He remained there until December 1941, when the US entered the war, and returned to Lisbon the following year. In 1943, Katzki was drafted into the US Army, following his discharge, Katzki was appointed JDC Country Director for Germany, where he headed a vast program for survivors and displaced persons. Schools were organized for Jewish children who had little opportunity to attend school during the war. Cheders were established where Jewish children received a religious education. Some camps even had Yeshivas where older students resumed their interrupted studies. Most of the camps were autonomous to the extent that the residents elected their representatives who administered each camp. The camp council ran the police department, fire department, medical facilities and educational facilities.

The Pocking camp was immense. It was a former Luftwaffe air base and plane parts were still on the ground. Most of the people at the camp were Jewish and the predominant language was Yiddish, followed by Hungarian, Romanian and Polish. The streets had Hebrew names such as Rehov Herzl. Hebrew was the official language of the camp although few people knew it. Posters were printed in Hebrew and Yiddish. There was regular communication between the camps including sharing of camp published newspapers. JDC sponsored many sports activities to keep the youth active, including Hapoel Pocking, a soccer club that competed with Jewish clubs in other camps. Pocking also had an ORT training school where Jewish refugees were taught a variety of trades, based on the vocational organization started in Tsarist Russia. ORT spread throughout Europe and the Western world. The main office of the organization was forced to leave the Soviet Union ending up in Geneva, Switzerland. Following World War II, ORT established many schools in the Jewish DP camps. The first ORT school in Germany was opened in the Landsberg Jewish DP camp in 1945.

The population in Pocking was strongly Zionist oriented, with branches of all Zionist organizations represented. **Jacob Leibner**, father of the author of this book, was a member of the Hapoel Hamizrahi or religious Zionist party. He was in charge of collecting wood during the summer in order to provide the camp with heating material during the winter. While at the branch office of the local Hapoel Hamizrahi, he overheard that Rabbi Itzhak Halevi Herzog, chief rabbi of Palestine would be visiting some Jewish DP camps in the American zone in Germany. He quickly discovered the dates for the Rabbi's tour and decided to travel to the first camp where the Rabbi was expected to speak. Leibner was familiar with some of the UNRRA drivers who delivered wood to the camp and approached one with a proposition to take a day off with his truck. The driver agreed. One morning all the selected passengers met at a desolate place in the camp and boarded the truck. Leibner and his son

William, traveled together for several hours to the Neu Freimann camp near Munich where Herzog was scheduled to speak.

שעת לימון מלמדת עברית, ילדששט

The late Yehuda Leibner learning Hebrew at the Pocking Jewish primary school. The teacher was Mrs. Waldman. The Pocking camp located near Passau, was also referred to as the Waldstadt camp.

Jewish children receiving a religious education at the Pocking camp cheder.

They were not the only visitors at the camp, many other DP Jews wanted to hear the words of the spiritual leader of Palestine. There was great excitement in the camp as the residents awaited the Rabbi's talk. Leibner and his group were ushered to a large open area where the Rabbi and his entourage were already seated at the podium. Herzog was escorted by his son Jacob, and Rabbi Solomon Wohlgelernter, liaison officer between UNRRA and the American Vaad Hatzala organization. Vaad Hatzala was established in the US by Orthodox rabbis to help rabbis and yeshiva students in Europe. Leibner said that the rabbi spoke a "Heimishe" (down-to-earth) Yiddish, and always used the word "us" as though he were one of the refugees. Herzog was an excellent speaker and interjected biblical lines and quotations. His language was familiar to the crowd and they were enraptured by his words. The rabbi, more in his official role as Chief Rabbi of Palestine, assured the survivors that the Jewish community of Palestine had not forgotten them, and promised that their liberation was not far off. "Soon you will be living like free men in your own land, he told us. The rabbi assured us that our sufferings would soon end and we would soon abandon the cursed (German) soil where our people have suffered so much. He urged us to have hope and faith because our Geula (redemption) was not far off. We were very impressed by the Rabbi's words and headed to our awaiting truck that took us back to Pocking. Our driver was paid in packs of camel cigarettes obtained at the American military base. Cigarettes, especially American cigarettes, were frequently used as a means of payment instead of money."

The UNRRA drivers were frequently used by the Brichah to bring Jewish refugees from the border to the camps and also transported the potential refugees that were selected by the local Brichah officers for illegal aliyah to Palestine. Pocking not only had a Brichah office but also a Haganah recruiting office urging young Jews to join the Haganah training camps in Germany. The "Etzel" or Irgun Ha-Tzva'i Ha-Leumi or National Military Front also had an office. The NMF followed the Revisionist ideological party line of Ze'ev Jabotinsky.

All the major camps in the American zone in Germany and Austria had recruiting offices. The volunteers were usually sent to the Jewish Agency office in Munich where they underwent medical examinations and were sent to special camps to begin military training and to study Hebrew. The camps were disguised as regular DP camps and the recruits wore civilian clothes. The overall command of these training camps and recruiting offices were directed by Haganah officers who came especially from Palestine for this purpose. These officers worked closely with the Brichah and the Mossad.

Brichah - Hebrew for Escape or Flight

The Brichah and the Mossad constantly sent transports of Jewish DPs from the camps in Germany and Italy to embarkation points in Italy and France. These organizations received the wholehearted support of the Committee of Liberated Jews that represented all the American Jewish DP camps in Germany and Austria. The Jews hated Germany for obvious reasons but were forced to stay on German soil and jumped at any chance to leave, legally or illegally. The American army was also happy to see Jewish DPs leave their zones--less people to feed and care for. Besides, the illegal departures were the only positive action that took place in the camps. Most countries including the US granted few admission papers to the Jewish camp residents. Between the end of 1945 and July 1, 1948, it is estimated that 12,649 Jews were admitted from the camps to the USA[97]. The number of Jews kept increasing in the U.S .zones and soon reached the figure of about 250, 000. The number of Jewish DPs in the British zones hardly changed from the end of the war. The Brichah in Germany was mostly run by former Palestinian Jewish soldiers, mainly Jewish Brigade soldiers. The Brichah was well organized in the German American sector and received full cooperation from the JDC. Some 70,860 Jewish refugees arrived in Germany between June 1945 and the end of October 1946. By the end of 1946, there were 140,000 Jewish refugees in Germany[98]. The Jews were distributed amongst 57 DP camps, 15 special children homes, 39 agricultural training farms and 25 hospitals and sanatoriums[99].

The number of Jews kept growing until Poland closed the Polish-Czech borders in accordance with the previously mentioned Spychalski – Zuckerman agreement. The Brichah activities in Poland declined to a trickle in 1947 and by 1948 a total of 2000 Jews crossed illegally into Czechoslovakia and onward to Germany[100]. The Brichah in Poland came to an end, besides the Polish government was granting visas that enabled Jews to leave the country legally. The European Brichah shifted its emphasis from Poland and Czechoslovakia to Germany, Austria and Italy. The Brichah was very active in Germany in all military zones. It was solely focused on transporting Jews from Poland, Czechoslovakia and Austria to the DP camps in Germany.

---

97 Bauer, Flight, p.205
98 Bauer, Flight, p.274
99 Ibid., p.274
100 Ibid., p.290

JJewish DP camps in Germany, Austria and Italy.

A particular problem was the accumulation of Jewish refugees in Berlin, located in the Russian zone. The Polish Jews came by foot, truck, and train to Berlin where the DP committee received them. But the Brichah had to get them out of Berlin to make room for other Jews, especially children. The British commanders refused to help and the

Brichah - Hebrew for Escape or Flight

Brichah had to circumvent the British zone to reach the American zone where they were received. The flow of Jewish refuges came mainly from the city of Stettin or Szczecin. The former residents of the port city had left it or were chased out by the Poles and the city was practically deserted. The Polish government encouraged all repatriated Poles from Russia to settle in the city. The Jewish population soon reached 20,000 people[101], and was the largest Brichah group in any one place. Yaacov Erner, nicknamed Tulek, headed the Stettin group, and was later assisted by Mordechai Mittelman, a Palestinian who had been imprisoned by the Soviets for Zionist activities. They organized the transports of Polish Jews to Berlin. There was competition by private smugglers but the Brichah dominated the field. Stettin was also a center for the expelled German residents in Poland who waited for trains that would take them to Germany. The Brichah decided to infiltrate the trains by providing Jews with forged papers saying they were former German citizens returning home. The scheme worked and thousands of Polish Jews reached Germany. The activities of the Brichah were frequently dangerous and one of the agents named Yossef Nissenbaum was killed in the line of duty by Russian soldiers.

The Brichah agent Moshe Zonenshein was killed in a car accident crossing the Alps. (Yad Vashem Archives)

In addition to Berlin, there were Jews at other centers and borders waiting to be transported to the DP camps in Germany. This was an enormous task that involved thousands of Jewish refugees who had to be allocated living quarters, food, medicines and other life necessities. Once

101 Ibid.p.233

settled in a camp, the refugees were registered with the UNRRA offices. The next step would be transport an embarkation port to Palestine. The immense organizational challenges were carried out with great precision. For instance, in the case of the *Exodus 1947* ship, within a period of two weeks approximately 4,500 Jews were dispatched from the DP camps in Germany to the area of Marseilles in France, without legal papers or proper border crossing authorizations, where they boarded the ship with their Brichah guides.

For the complex task of transporting so many refugees, the Brichah needed a fleet of trucks and drivers and a large amount of gas that had to be purchased on the black market for dollars or bartered for American goods like Camel cigarettes, Hershey chocolates or nylon stockings. The Brichah frequently borrowed trucks and their drivers from the UNRRA or JDC. Some drivers earned sums of money but the Brichah did not care as long as the refugees were moved to the right place at the right time. The Brichah in Germany also had its own trucks purchased by the Jewish Agency that were driven by Brichah volunteers.

Brichah agents in the Foehrenwald DP camp prior to leaving the camp with their escorts for Marselles, France. From left to right; David Schechter-Bral, Gary, Chaim Ben-Uri, Meir Port, Ephraim Dekel, and Zivia Hershkowitz. (Yad Vashem Archives)

Brichah - Hebrew for Escape or Flight

*A group of Brichah drivers. From left to right; Zvi Steiglitz, Shimon Pritzki,
David Reich, Itzhak Werber, Teichner, Israel Steiglitz (Yad Vashem Archives)*

*The Hebrew slogan of the Brichah reads: "Between Mountains and Borders,
in starless nights, we will lead Jewish convoys". Pictures of the
Bad Reichenhall Brichah members*

Brichah Agents in Germany

Name	First	Code name	G	Country
AKSELROD	Batia		M	Germ
ASHKENAZI	Sonia		M	Germ
BEN ARI	Chaim	Wilner	M	Germ
ELLER	Misha		M	Germ
FEINMAN	Gideon		M	Germ
FISHMAN	Burka		M	Germ
FIZICKY	Shimon		M	Germ
FORT	Meir		M	Germ
FRANK	Ernest	Ephraim	M	Germ
FRIDMAN	Israel		M	Germ
KAMINSKY	Dov		M	Germ
KRYSTAL	Moshe		M	Germ
LANDSBERG	Itzhak		M	Germ
LANDSBERG	Ida		M	Germ
LINIWSKY	David		M	Germ
LISS	Zelig		M	Germ
MILHAUSEN	Lucian		M	Germ
MILHAUSEN	Michel		M	Germ
MIZRITZER	Abrasha		M	Germ
MIZRITZKY	Rachel		M	Germ
NISSENBAUM	Yossef	Killed	M	Germ
PERLES	Shalom		M	Germ
PERLES	Yaacov		M	Germ
RAM	Itzhak	Peretz	M	Germ
RHEINHAL	Max		M	Germ
RITTER	Willi		M	Germ
ROGER			M	Germ
SCHECHTER	Zeev		M	Germ
SCHECHTER	Tzizik		M	Germ
SHALOM			M	Germ
SHEINBERG	Baruch		M	Germ
SHEINBERG	Genia		M	Germ
SHIKLER	Mordechai		M	Germ
SHNITZER	Moshe		M	Germ

Brichah - Hebrew for Escape or Flight

STEIGLITZ	Israel		M	Germ
STEINFELD	Zeev		M	Germ
STOCKLITZK	Itzhak		M	Germ
TEICHNER	Mundek		M	Germ
WAKS	Sheptel		M	Germ
WEGEN	Itzhak		M	Germ
WEINSTEIN	Amnon	Grisha	M	Germ
WERBER	Itzhak		M	Germ
WIDRY	Abraham		M	Germ
WROBEL	Pessah		M	Germ
ZONENSHEIN	Itzhak		M	Germ

Chapter XII
Italy

Map of Italy

Most of Italy was liberated by the British 8th Army under the leadership of Field Marshall Bernard Montgomery. Many of his soldiers were Palestinian Jews. The Jewish community in Palestine had volunteered to fight the Nazis as early as 1940. Over 5,000 Jewish volunteers from Palestine were organized into three infantry battalions, officially named the Jewish Infantry Brigade Group, established in late 1944 under the command of a career Jewish army officer, Brigadier Ernest F. Benjamin. The Haganah, the Jewish underground army in Palestine, ordered many Haganah men to volunteer for this brigade. These "volunteers" formed Haganah cells within the Brigade, and took orders directly from Haganah headquarters in Palestine.

The Jewish Brigade was deployed in Italy. As the British troops fought their way from Southern to Northern Italy, the Palestinian Haganah gave the order to the Jewish Brigade to be on the lookout for Italian Jewish survivors. Italy had a Jewish population of about 46,000 Jews prior to World War II. It is estimated that about 30,000 Italian Jews and 6,000 non-Italian Jews survived the war in Italy.[102] These survivors, seeing the Star of David on the Jewish Brigade soldiers' shoulders, came out of hiding, ragged, hungry and desperate. The Jewish soldiers provided help and began to organize support systems, everything from small dispensaries to soup kitchens, all using British supplies and facilities. As was mentioned before, many survivors were not Italian Jews and were now classified as DPs and placed in camps under UNRRA administration.

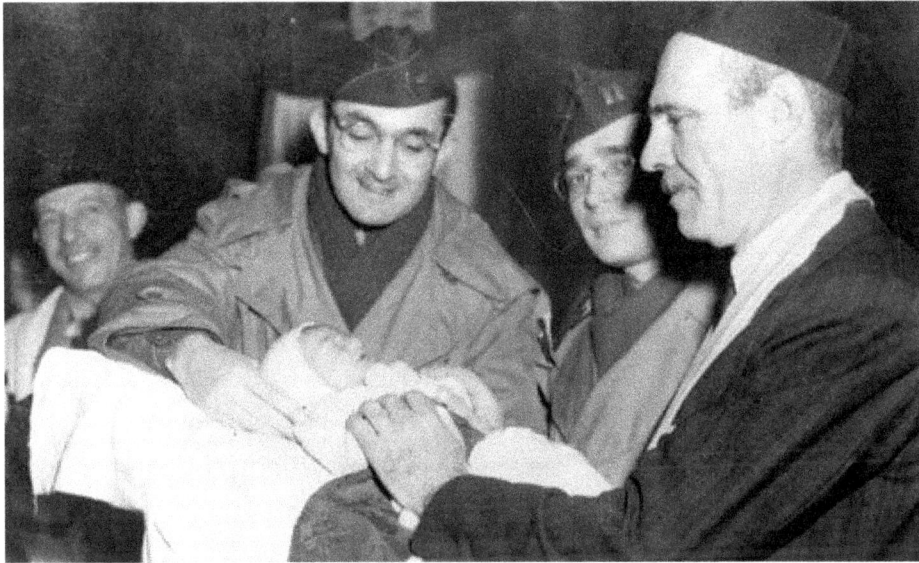

Cinecittá Jewish refugee camp in Rome, Italy. Circumcision ceremony of a non-Italian Jewish boy. Holding the child is Reuben B. Resnik, director of the JDC in Italy in 1945. (Yad Vashem Archives)

The Jewish Brigade kept a close watch over the Jewish refugees and helped the Italian Jews to reestablish their communities. The Palestinian Haganah now ordered the Brigade to move Jewish refugees from Northern Italy to the South where they would be able to board ships and head to Palestine. The Brigade was helped in this endeavor by the Mossad office headed by Shaul Avigur, whose activities have already been described. The two organizations began to work hand in hand, soon joined by the Brichah.

Shaul Avigur, head of the Mossad or illegal aliyah to Palestine.

The Mossad was a secret organization created by the Jewish Agency. Its head, Avigur, was born in Russia and brought to Palestine as a child. He devoted himself to military matters and joined the Haganah at an early age. He was given full command of the Mossad organization and personally selected agents who were sent to Europe to smuggle Jews to Palestine illegally.[103] Avigur established an effective organization that worked with the Brichah, the JDC and the Jewish Brigade.

Yehuda Arazi, Mossad representative in Italy

---

103 Zertal, Power: pp.40-49.

All the groups went into high gear with the arrival in Europe of **Yehuda Arazi,** dressed as a Polish pilot, smuggled first out of Palestine to Egypt, and then to Italy. The Polish-born Arazi had been appointed head of the Mossad in Italy and soon had a stream of small boats transporting Jews from Italy to Palestine.[104] Often the British Navy ignored these small boats. On the way back to Italy they often transported weapons for the Haganah and various communication experts and military leaders who were needed by the Mossad and the Brichah in Europe. An effective communication network, mentioned earlier, was established between the Mossad and Brichah offices throughout Europe, notably in Prague in the community building. The main base operated in Palestine.[105]

Shimshon Lang in British uniform

The Mossad and Brichah offices throughout Europe continued to work closely with the Jewish Brigade, the local JDC, the Jewish Agency of Palestine and the various local Zionist groups. From the end of the war until 1947, nearly 50,000 Jewish refugees had entered Italy. Italy with its long coastal shores and many ports offered an ideal place to hide the illegal ships that would be boarded by Jewish refugees brought from nearby Italian Jewish DP camps. Similar camps also existed in France, notably around the port of Marseilles. Many of these refugees made it to Palestine while, as mentioned before, others were intercepted by the British navy at sea and sent to British detention camps in Cyprus.

---

104 Szulc, Alliance. p.90-91
105 Szulc, Alliance.,p.91

These detentions did not deter Arazi from continuing his work. The Mossad office in Italy greatly expanded its activities, relying heavily on the Jewish Brigade and Jewish soldiers in the British Army like **Shimshon Lang**, one of the 300 drivers in the 462nd General Transport Battalion of the British 8th Army. Lang's story is typical of the Palestinian Jews. Lang had escaped Poland for Palestine in 1939 on an illegal ship.[106] The ship was stopped by the British Navy and Lang was given a choice, spend the next few years in an internment camp or join the British Army. He chose the latter, and served until 1946. In an interview, Lang said "My unit delivered supplies to the army units from the coastal areas in Southern Italy, and on the return journey loaded the trucks with refugees.[107] I spoke to the young skeletal survivors in Yiddish and saw myself as one of them that happened to have escaped Hitler's death squad nets just in time. They represented to me the survivors of my family that perished in the Holocaust. No British Army rule could stop me from extending help to my surviving brethren. I was not alone with these thoughts, others felt the same way. We translated the ideas into reality by transporting the surviving Jews from Austrian and German DP camps to Italy and then to Palestine. We used empty shipping containers or extra military uniforms to hide the refugees at border crossings." According to Lang, not only trucking units were involved in this movement of Jewish refugees. Ambulances and maintenance vehicles were also used to smuggle survivors from the former concentration camps in Austria and Germany to Italy. Most of the Jewish volunteers for the British forces in Palestine were similar to Shimon Lang; born in Europe and barely escaped to Palestine.

When Jewish survivors were discovered in former concentration camps by Brigade soldiers Arazi worked quickly to remove them to Italy. Leo Rosner, a Jewish survivor of Mauthausen said, "We were several hundred Jewish survivors in the concentration camp of Mauthausen with no place to go except to return to Poland and most of us did not feel like going to Poland.[108] Suddenly an army truck appeared with Star of David markings. At first we did not believe our eyes. We were certain that we were the only Jews left and suddenly we see other Jews and fighting Jews. The truck was immediately surrounded by Jewish survivors; they kissed and hugged the soldiers. They exchanged greetings and stories.

---

106 Leibner interview with the late Shimshon Lang
107 Ibid.
108 Rosner, Leo, The Holocaust Remembered. USA, 1998, p.97-100

Most of the Jewish soldiers spoke Yiddish as well as the survivors, so communication was easily established. A few days later, more Jewish soldiers appeared. About two weeks later, a convoy of trucks arrived near the camp at night and we were instructed to leave the camp one at a time so as not to arouse suspicion. Most of the Jewish survivors left the Mauthausen concentration camp", Rosner continued, "and headed to the large convoy of trucks. Once we were loaded on the trucks, Jewish soldiers placed empty oil barrels and boxes of ammunition to block the view of the inside of the trucks. The soldiers then covered the trucks and we moved. We traveled towards the Italian border for hours. We crossed into Italy escorted by military police provided by the Jewish Brigade, ultimately reaching the Brigade headquarters in Treviso."[109] Our presence at the base was highly illegal since it was an army base. The Jewish soldiers smuggled us into the nearby Modena Jewish DP camp in Italy."[110]

The Brichah transports left the region of Munich
and headed south to Austria and to Italy

109 Ibid.,
110 Ibid.,

This large and complex operation was not Arazi's only activity in Italy on behalf of the Mossad. Similar operations, rescuing Jews from Austria and Germany, were constantly carried out. Jewish Brigade soldiers provided the backbone of these operations, aided by Jewish partisans and discharged Jewish soldiers from the Polish and Soviet armies. Large illegal ships with Jewish survivors headed to the shores of Palestine. As with other countries, the British applied heavy pressure on Italy to stop the entry of Jews through the northern border and to control the shores. British agents picked up news that a large convoy of Jewish refugees would be heading to the small port of La Spezia in Italy where they were to board two illegal ships, the Fede and the Fenice, heading to Palestine. The British purposefully misinformed the Italian police that a large group of Italian fascists would be heading to La Spezia to board the ships. The Italians were told the ships would then head for Spain where the supposed Italian fascists could not be touched by Italian justice. Italian police and security forces were rushed to the entrance of the small port city.

On April 4, 1946, a convoy of 38 British Army trucks appeared.[111] The Italian police stopped the convoy and began to search the trucks. Most of the drivers were soldiers of the Jewish Brigade or other Palestinian units within the British army. Two of the Jewish Brigade soldiers, dressed in their military uniforms, stepped forward and surrendered on condition that the waiting Holocaust survivors be permitted to board the ship since they had no other place to stay. The Italian police quickly realized that they had been set up and permitted the Jewish refugees to board the vessels. Immediately, the Jews renamed the ships. The *Fede,* with 675 Jewish refugees aboard*,* was renamed the *Dov Hoz..* The *Fenice*, with 339 aboard, was renamed the *Eliyahu Golomb.* These two illegal vessels were left moored to the pier, guarded by Italian police.

The next day Josef de Paz presented himself to the police of La Spezia and asked to join the Jewish survivors heading to Palestine. The request was granted. Most of the Mossad and Brichah agents aboard the ships recognized de Paz as Mossad's Italian chief Yehuda Arazi who immediately took command of the ships. Arazi began to broadcast appeals for help. The appeals were picked up by the Italian press and the news soon made international headlines. The Jewish passengers aboard the two ships went on a hunger strike and threatened to sink the ship if

---

[111] Zertal, Power, p.28

anyone attempted to board the vessel. Meanwhile, embarrassed by the events, the British insisted that the Italians remove the Jews. But the Italians refused. The struggle lasted nearly 30 days, until May 8, 1946, when the Jewish refugees were finally permitted to sail for Palestine.

Unnoticed by the Italians and the British, Arazi managed to slip off the ship before it sailed, disappearing quickly into the Italian countryside. The Jewish Brigade drivers who had been caught by the Italians faced military court proceedings. Realizing the extent of the Jewish Brigade's involvement in the affair, in July 1945, the British government decided to relocate most of the Jewish Brigade units to Belgium and the Netherlands. Shimshon Lang's trucking battalion was dismantled completely and he was shipped back to Palestine. In an audacious move, some of the Jewish Brigade soldiers gave their uniforms to illegal Jewish refugees, who were then unknowingly sent to Palestine as part of the British Army units. Other Jewish Brigade soldiers who were mustered out of the British Army in Europe joined the Mossad or the Brichah and played a vital role helping Jewish refugees reach Palestine.

The JDC had the responsibility of providing the Jewish refugees with their basic needs. JDC director Jacob Trobe insisted that no JDC official be involved in the actual border crossings so that nobody could accuse the organization of acting illegally. But he insisted that all help be given to the Jewish refugees once they crossed into Italy.[112] The new JDC director in Rome, **Ruben Resnik**, did not approve of this policy and tried to change it. Arazi stopped him and instead insisted that all help be given to Jews attempting to leave for Palestine regardless of how the British or Italian officials felt about it. The Italian government did not want to admit to the country how many Jewish refugees were coming from Germany. Italy claimed that it was a poor and devastated country. Arazi claimed that the Jewish refugees did not compete with Italians for jobs and would all leave Italy. Arazi and the Brichah continued to bring more Jews to Italy and played about with the statistics in the Italian DP camps, not reporting deaths or numbers of people who left the camps.

Arazi's activities in Italy irritated Resnik, who insisted on doing everything legally. Resnik believed that the JDC's only function was to help the local Jewish community reestablish itself. This was the traditional function of the organization. But everything had changed following the war. There were thousands of Jewish refugees in Austria,

---

112 Israel Defense Ministry, p.22

Germany and Italy who were not citizens of these countries and did not want to remain there. They were desperate to leave and many wanted to go to Palestine. The Mossad, the Brichah and the Jewish Brigade gave them hope. Resnik did not understand the situation; or was afraid to act. The refugees were thankful for all assistance they received but were interested in solutions the JDC did not have. Joseph Schwartz, European director of the JDC, saw the reality and tried to guide Resnik to adopt a more conciliatory approach to Arazi and his supporters, who were not interested in legalities but in hard action. Schwartz even sent Gaynor Jacobson to Italy to help Resnik. Jacobson was sent to Southern Italy where most of the illegal shipping to Palestine took place and immediately established good relations with the Brichah, the Jewish Brigade, and the Mossad. He helped them as much as he could without involving the JDC in illegal activities, providing extra food rations for those departing for Palestine. He also gave support to the Italian Jewish communities. Resnik resented Jacobson's popularity and began to exercise his power as JDC director in Italy. Jacobson resigned from his post in Italy but was quickly sent to Greece by Schwartz who had been impressed with Jacobson's performance.

Arazi frequently resorted to illegal activities that Resnik could not abide, such as forged documents, bribes and other shady tactics to facilitate the movement of the refugees. Resnik refused to cooperate, creating tension between the two men, and their organizations. Protests to Arazi were ignored. Arazi turned to the Jewish leaders in Palestine, saying, in effect, get Resnik off my back. In turn, the Jewish Agency pressured the JDC headquarters in New York to remove Resnik from his position in Rome. Even Jewish leaders from the DP camps pressured the JDC to remove Resnik. He tried to ride out the wave of discontent, but the problems grew daily and he faced a lack of cooperation on many fronts. Schwartz finally eased Resnik out and brought in Charles Passman to head the Rome office.

Charles Passman was born in Lithuania and brought to the United States at the age of 12 He later settled in Palestine, became involved with the JDC and was appointed to head the small JDC. He spoke Hebrew, Yiddish and English and able to smooth things between the many Jewish organizations in Italy including the DPs. He was also experienced in dealing with the British in Palestine, which helped him handle British military officials in Italy.

Brichah - Hebrew for Escape or Flight

Passman Charles

The Italians were slow to implement their government's orders to comply with British requests to close the borders. In fact, the Italian police often notified the Brichah when British patrols were checking the roads. The refugees usually assembled at the Bad Reichenhall or Leipheim DP camps where they were prepared for the long journey to Italy. The Brichah used side roads and small paths across the Alps; even the Brenner Pass was used to enter Northern Italy. Then most refugees would be transported south where Brichah boats would appear and take them aboard for the trip to Palestine.

Ships that left Italy for Palestine included:

- August 28, 1945, the Italian fishing vessel *Dalin* left Italy carrying 35 immigrants and landed at Caesarea, Palestine.

- September 4, 1945, the *Natan* left Italy carrying 79 immigrants and landed in Palestine. On its return trip to Italy, it carried seamen and radio operators from the Palmach and Jewish Agency emissaries to Italy.

- September 9, 1945, the *Gabriela* left Italy carrying 40 passengers and arrived in Palestine.

- September 17, 1945, the *Peter* left Italy carrying 168 immigrants and landed in Palestine.

- October 1, 1945, the *Natan* again left Italy and landed in Palestine

- October 22, the *Natan* left Italy and landed in Palestine with 174 passengers.

- November 23, 1945, the *Berl Katznelson*, carrying 220 Jewish refugees to Palestine

- December 14, 1945, the *Hannah Senesh*, carrying 252 passengers, to Palestine.

Brichah - Hebrew for Escape or Flight

From the summer of 1945 to May 1948 when the State of Israel was established, 69,878 Jewish refugees boarded Brichah ships and headed to Palestine.[113] Just in 1946, 22 illegal ships left Europe mostly from Italy. As mentioned earlier, most of the Brichah ships were intercepted and the passengers sent to Cyprus. Before long, the British were tasked with feeding and maintaining a Jewish population of close to 50,000 on the island. Over 1,600 Jews drowned at sea. Only a few thousand actually entered Palestine. The Brichah was well aware that most of the illegal ships would be intercepted but were determined to test British rule in Palestine and wanted desperately to keep Palestine in the headlines. Correspondents such as I.F. Stone were invited to go aboard the illegal ships and publish their observations, especially in the American press. The violent confrontations between the illegal passengers and the British troops made Britain lose public opinion in the world. British Foreign Secretary Ernest Bevin led Britain to a confrontation with the United States that he was bound to lose. The United States could not support British policies in Palestine despite secret promises from the State Department. American Jews and non-Jews demanded action and President Truman had no choice in the matter. Bevin was so obsessed with the Jews that he continued the confrontation even though the United Nations had already decided to partition Palestine. Brichah ships continued to be intercepted practically on the verge of the establishment of the State of Israel.

List of illegal ships:

- January 17, 1946, the *Enzo Sereni* carrying 908 passengers, intercepted.
- On March 13, 1946, the schooner *Winga,* carrying 248 passengers, was intercepted.
- On March 27, 1946, the steamer *Tel Hai,* carrying 736 passengers, was intercepted.
- On May 13, 1946 the ship *Max Nordau,* carrying 1,754 immigrants, was intercepted
- On May 13, 1946, the *Dov Hos* (675 passengers) landed with permits.
- On May 13, 1946 *Eliyahu Golomb* (735 passengers) landed with permits. Both ships were involved in the La Spezia case.
- On June 8, 1946, the *Haviva Reik,* carrying 462 passengers, was intercepted.

---

113 Bauer, Flight,p.281

Brichah - Hebrew for Escape or Flight

- On August 11, 1946, the *Yagur*, carrying 758 passengers, was intercepted.

- On August 12, 1946, the *Henrietta Szold,* carrying 536 passengers, was intercepted.

- On August 13, 1946, the *Katriel Jaffewith* 604 passengers was intercepted.

- On August 13, 1946, the *Twenty Three* with 790 passengers was intercepted.

- On August 16, 1946, the yawl *Amiram Shochat*, carrying 183 passengers, landed in Palestine.

- On September 2, 1946, the *Dov Hos,* this time named the *Arba Cheruyot,* carrying 1,024 passengers, was intercepted.

- On September 22, 1946, the brigantine *Palmach,* 611 passengers, was intercepted.

- On October 20, 1946, the *Eliahu Golomb,* renamed the *Braha Fuld,* carrying 806 passengers, was intercepted.

- On October 19, 1946 the *Latrun* (1,279 passengers), was intercepted.

- On November 9, 1946, the *HaKedosha* (600 passengers), foundered in a gale and sank. The passengers were rescued by the Knesset Israel. The Knesset Israel, carrying a total of 3,845 passengers, was intercepted.

- On December 5, 1946, the *Rafiah* (785 passengers), was wrecked on Syrina Island in bad weather. The survivors were rescued by two Royal Navy and one Greek warship, and were taken to Cyprus. Women and children were taken to Palestine.[11]

- On February 9, 1947, the wooden brigantine *Lanegev* (647 passengers) was intercepted.

- On February 17, 1947, the steamer *HaMapil HaAlmoni* (807 passengers) was intercepted.

- On February 27, 1947, the *Haim Arlosoroff* (1,378 passengers) was intercepted.

- On March 9, 1947, the *Ben Hecht* (597 passengers) was intercepted.

- On March 12, 1947 the *Shabtai Luzinsky* (823 passengers) landed in Palestine.

- On March 30, 1947. the *Moledet* (1,588 passengers) developed a list and suffered engine failure some 50 miles outside Palestinian waters and issued an SOS. Passengers were transferred to the destroyers *HMS Haydon* and *HMS Charity,* minesweeper *HMS Octavia* and frigate *HMS St Brides Bay,* and the Royal Navy towed *Moledet* to Haifa.

- On April 13, 1947, the *Theodor Herzl* (2,641 passengers) was intercepted.
- On April 23, 1947, the *Shear Yashuv* (768 passengers) was intercepted.
- On May 17, 1947, the *Hatikva* (1,414 passengers) was intercepted.
- On May 23, 1947, the *Mordei Hagetaot,* carrying 1,457 immigrants, was intercepted.
- On May 31, 1947, the Haganah ship *Yehuda Halevy,* carrying 399 immigrants, was intercepted.
- On July 28, 1947, the 14 *Halalei Gesher Haziv,* carrying 685, was intercepted.
- On July 28, 1947, the *Shivat Zion,* carrying 411 Jews, was intercepted.
- On September 27, 1947, the *Af Al Pi Chen* (434 passengers), was intercepted.
- On October 2, 1947, the *Medinat HaYehudim* (2,664 passengers) was intercepted.
- On October 2, 1947, the *Geulah,* with 1,385 passengers, was intercepted.
- November 15, 1947, the *Peter,* renamed the *Aliyah* and carrying 182 passengers, landed.
- November 16, 1947, the *Kadima,* carrying 794 immigrants, was intercepted.
- December 4, 1947, the *HaPortzim* with 167 passengers landed in Palestine.
- December 22, 1947, the *Lo Fafchidunu* (884 passengers) was intercepted.
- December 28, 1947, the 29 *BeNovember* (680 passengers) was intercepted.
- January 1, 1948, the *HaUmot HaMeuhadot* (537 passengers) landed.
- January 1, 1948, the *Atzmaut* (7,612 passengers) was intercepted.
- January 1, 1948, the *Kibbutz Galuyot* (7,557 passengers) was intercepted.
- January 31, 1948, the 35 *Giborei Kfar Etzion* (280 passengers) was intercepted.
- February 12, 1948, the *Yerushalayim Hanezura* (679 passengers) was intercepted.

Brichah - Hebrew for Escape or Flight

- February 20, 1948, the *Lekommemiyut* (696 passengers) was intercepted.
- On February 28, 1948, the *Bonim v'Lochamim*, formerly the *Enzo Sereni*, (982 passengers) was intercepted.
- On March 29, 1948, the *Yehiam* (771 passengers) was intercepted.
- On April 12, 1948, the *Tirat Zvi* (817 passengers) was intercepted.
- On April 24, 1948, the *Mishmar HaEmek* (782 passengers) was intercepted.
- On April 26, 1948, the *Nakhson* (553 passengers) was intercepted.

PARTIAL LIST OF BRICHAH AGENTS IN ITALY

Surname	First name	Nickname	G	Country
BAR-SHATZ	Itzhak	Izir		Italy
BARZILAI	Moshe	Miki	M	Italy
BEREL			M	Italy
CHAIM	Shipper		M	Italy
CHAIM	Spekulant		M	Italy
CHAIMOWITZ	Issachar		M	Italy
COHEN	Zvi		M	Italy
ENGELMAN	Rivkah		F	Italy
ENGELMAN	Moshe		M	Italy
ENGELMAN	Nechama		F	Italy
ERAN	Yochanan	Tibi	M	Italy
HAREL	Yossi	Hamburger	M	Italy
HERMAN	Gabriel		M	Italy
HIRT	Lisha		F	Italy
KANTONI	Vitoria	Goldman		Italy
KARMIN	Yossef			Italy
KOROCH	Benyamin		M	Italy
LEWKOWITZ	Jonasa		F	Italy
LEWKOWITZ	Brunek		M	Italy
LILO			M	Italy
LOIUSH			M	Italy
LOR	Daniel	Lichtenstein	M	Italy
LUTEN	Shimshon		M	Italy
MARCIN	Mrs		F	Italy

MICHAEL			M	Italy
MILGROM	Genia		F	Italy
MILOSH			M	Italy
NEUMARK	Helena		M	Italy
NEUMARK	Israel		M	Italy
NUSBAUM	Otek		M	Italy
NUSTBAUM	Genia		F	Italy
ORI	Chaim		M	Italy
PICHOWITZ	Tziporah		F	Italy
PICHOWITZ	Jorek		M	Italy
RUBINSTEIN	Lea	Reifman	F	Italy
SELA	Michael		M	Italy
SHWEITZER	Ori		M	Italy
STERN	Nachum		M	Italy
STERN	Eisik		M	Italy
STERN	Yossef	doctor	M	Italy
SURKIS	Mordechai		M	Italy
TANKIST			M	Italy
TITO				Italy
TRICHTER	Poldi		M	Italy
WEINSTEIN	Yossel	Turek	M	Italy
YUCHERSON	Boris		M	Italy

Chapter XIII
France

MAP OF FRANCE

With the liberation of France, the country's civil administration began to function again. Elements that had co-operated with the Germans were dismissed or jailed. France under Charles de Gaulle refused to allow refugee camps to be created and also would not permit UNRRA to operate there. The French government rapidly expedited the return of refugees in France to their countries of origin. Unlike many other countries, France did not have slave labor or concentration camps with one exception.

On April 21, 1941, near the village of Struthof, the Nazis opened the only concentration camp in France, Natzweiler, located in the province of Alsace. Its annexes, scattered over the 2 sides of the Rhine, made up a network of close to 70 camps. Of the nearly 52,000 detainees of KL-Natzweiler, about 35,000 did not go through the central camp. A labor camp supporting the Nazi war industry, it was also used for medical experiments by Nazi professors from the Reich University of Strasbourg. From 1941 to 1945, the KL-Natzweiler was one of the most murderous camps of the Nazi system. Nearly 22,000 deportees died there. On

November 23, 1944, the Allies discovered the site which had been evacuated by the Nazis on September 14.

Present-day view of Struthof Concentration Camp in Natzweiler, France

Jewish Shoah survivors began to arrive in France following the end of the war mainly from Germany and Austria. French Jewish survivors included those from labor and concentration camps as well as those who had lived in hiding in the countryside during the war. The JDC built an extensive organization to help the French Jews as well as the newer illegal Jewish arrivals. It also supported orphanages, youth homes, and hospitals. The JDC also had to help Jews that fell by the wayside from the massive Brichah transports that arrived from Germany and headed south to Marseilles. Some travelers became sick while others had accidents that prevented them from continuing the journey. Still others decided to abandon the transports and remained in France. It is estimated that between 1945 and 1948 about 35,000 Jews reached France illegally. The JDC, the Mossad and Brichah agreed to let the local JDC handle these cases so they would not become a burden to the French government, which was dealing with serious post war problems. The JDC opened several offices in France where these illegal Jews received help and information on the condition that the individuals learn trades through the ORT training schools that were established throughout France.

Camp entrance of Struthof-Natzweiler concentration camp

The Mossad in France was headed by Shmarya Tzameret and Ze'ev Hadari.

Shmarya Tzameret, one of the chiefs of the Mossad in France

185

Brichah - Hebrew for Escape or Flight

Shmarya Tzameret, formerly Gelfand, was born October 17, 1910, in Cleveland, Ohio. Tzameret moved to Palestine in 1925, settled in Tel Aviv, and joined the Haganah and kibbutz movement. He was one of the founders of kibbutz Beit-Hashita that was established in 1936 and was one of the first members of the Mossad. His American passport enabled him to travel throughout Europe in the service of the Mossad. The British regularly followed him but he managed to elude them. He became one of the leaders of the Mossad in France following World War II, establishing his residence in Marseilles from where he directed the movement of Jewish refugees to the illegal boats.

Chateau Vouzon (owned by the French Rothschild family)
in Perigueux near Toulouse France was a home for Polish
Jewish children brought to France on their way to Palestine.

Ze'ev Hadari, formerly Pommerantz, was born in 1916 near Lodz, Poland. He came to Palestine in 1935 as a pioneer, joined the Haganah and was sent to Turkey by the Mossad during World War II to help rescue Jews in Europe. With the end of the war he was sent to Marseilles to head Mossad activities there. Marseilles became an important Mossad base since it had several ports and camps where Jewish refugees could await their ships. The camps were small but well supplied by the JDC and could absorb many refugees for short periods of time. The camps were off limits and self-sustained. When the Mossad office in Paris announced the arrival of an illegal ship to the shores of Marseilles, the

Brichah offices in Germany and Austria were ordered to send passengers who then crossed the French borders and arrived to the embarkation point. The Mossad worked closely with the local French police to expedite the departure of the so-called South American passengers. The police often checked their papers but not their authenticity. Sometimes the illegal ships needed repairs or alterations that were performed under cover in French ports, unlike Italian ports where Britain had large naval and military forces

The Mossad and Brichah communications system was very busy signaling orders to the various camps in Germany to send transports of Jewish refugees. The French police let the transports through since they had all kinds of group visas, mostly forged, stating that the passengers would leave France from the embarkation port. The French were sympathetic to the plight of the Jews and were also happy to see them leave. As in other countries, the British government tried to pressure France to take a firmer stand against the Jewish refugees, but the French paid only lip service to the requests.

Shlomo Korn described one of the camps near Marseilles, "I left Strasburg, France and reached Marseilles with several of my friends including David Danieli. A Mossad man picked us up at the railway station and we headed out of the city. We drove a while and reached the camp called the "Chateau". The place was once a nice place but now it was run down, the lawns were unkempt, the trees needed trimming. The place was owned by a French collaborator who supported the Germans in France. The place was requisitioned and the Mossad managed to obtain it and use it as an assembly point for Jewish refugees heading to Palestine."

"The rather large walled-in grounds of the estate consisted of five or six acres. The main building was a rambling, two-story house with large, high-ceilinged rooms. Except for a kitchen and supply room on the ground floor, most of the rooms were crowded with cots, dormitory style. As the weather was still warm, crude dining tables and benches occupied the yard outside the kitchen, and all meals were served outdoors. Grouped around the sides and front of the chateau were some fifteen Army tents, each crowded with cots. There were a number of Jewish refugees from the German DP camps awaiting to board the next illegal ship. They all spoke Yiddish and most of them were from Poland."

The small town of Salon de Provence, a small distance north of Marseilles was the center of Brichah and Mossad activities in the port areas. Three refugee camps were located nearby, the largest, called Daphna, was five kilometers from town. The camps were off limits to civilians and the French police kept the places isolated. Each camp was headed by Palestinian military men and were organized in military fashion and focused on preparing people for the long voyage ahead.

A view of Salon-de-Provence, with the church and clock tower

While at the camp, Shlomo Korn had a variety of jobs including stamping papers indicating that the bearers would be heading to South America, and stocking ships with food and supplies. His work was interrupted one day when he was ordered to board a truck heading to the Salon railroad station to meet Jewish DPs arriving from Germany. The refugees left the train and boarded the trucks that would take them to the various nearby camps. During the entire operation, the French police closed the area until the trucks left the station. The refugees might wait weeks for a boat to arrive. As mentioned earlier there was a lack of ships in postwar Europe and also a shortage of sailors. Not many sailors wanted to be stuck in a camp for weeks or months in Cyprus. The British had great leverage over ship owners who could be prevented from trading with the Empire. The Mossad was forced to look to America for ships and sailors.

Chapter XIV
American-Mossad Ships

The Wedgwood, the first American Mossad-Brichah ship to
carry illegal Jewish passengers from Europe to Palestine.

The Mossad was challenged to find ships and sailors not influenced by the British or the threat of the Cyprus camps. Few ships managed to bypass the Bsea blockade of Palestine. Shaul Avigur was determined to crack the blockade and flood the shores of Palestine with thousands of illegals. He needed larger and faster ships that could only be obtained in the United States. The Mossad decided to send Ze'ev (Danny) Schind to the United States.

189

Ze'ev (Danny) Schind

Ze'ev (Danny) Schind was born September 7, 1909, in Wilno, Poland (today Vilnius, Lithuania). He joined the Zionist youth movement and in 1929 went to Palestine where he joined the kibbutz Ayelet Hashahar. He became active in the Haganah, especially in shipping Jews illegally to Palestine. In 1941 he was sent to Turkey to try to connect with the Jewish communities under Nazi domination. With the end of the war, he was sent to the United States to establish an organization that would purchase ships and recruit crews for those ships.

He had the assistance of several American Jews, including Morris Grinberg who was involved in the shipping business.[114] The first two ships to be purchased were Canadian military corvettes, the *Beauharnois,* later renamed the *Wedgwood (*after Josiah Wedgwood, an ardent Zionist member of the British Parliament*)*, and the *Norsyd,* later renamed the *Haganah.* Now that Schind had ships, he started recruiting naval personnel. Some enlisted men came from the navy and had seen action during the war, others were members of the Zionist youth movement. All were told that they might wind up in Cyprus if intercepted by the British navy. But the idea of helping Jewish Shoah survivors in Europe was much more important to them.

---

114 Hochstein, Joseph M.and Greenfeld, Murray S. The Jews' Secret Fleet. Jerusalem: Gefen Publishing House Ltd., p.37

Brichah - Hebrew for Escape or Flight

The Wedgwood in Haifa as its illegal passenger's disembark under the watchful eyes of the British. (Yad Vashem Archives)

The *Wedgwood* underwent extensive repairs and changes during its trip from the United States to Europe. On June 18, 1946, it arrived at the port of Savona, Italy. At night the ship left for a sandy beach area where Brichah trucks brought 1,259 Jewish refugees from German DP camps who all boarded the vessel. The small *Wedgwood* crew of thirty Americans was responsible for keeping the large ship moving. The military and political commanders were Palestinian Jews referred as "Shu-shu boys", apparently derived from their constant Yiddish saying "sha" or "quiet." Most of the services aboard the vessel were carried out by the refugees themselves who were well organised

The British tried to stop the ship but the *Wedgwood* left port and headed to Palestine. The British had no trouble identifying this vessel, and it was waylaid on June 25th, when still about 75 miles from the shore of Palestine. Four British destroyers surrounded the vessel and accompanied her to the port of Haifa. An attempt was made by those on board to have the vessel captured outside the territorial waters of Palestine, so that there would be no grounds for its confiscation by the British. That attempt failed and another attempt was made to lower a launch to the water, in order to land 25 young men on the shore of Kiryat Chaim, but the launch was intercepted and the men were taken into custody. The Wedgewood was running out of gas, and finally surrendered to the British troops, who boarded the vessel on June 27th and turned it to the Haifa port. The passengers were disembarked and escorted to waiting British trucks. The crew disappeared as did the Haganah commanders aboard the ship. Some hid aboard the ship until the cleaning crews came aboard and brought them clothing that enabled them to mix with the cleaners and later disappear, while others melted into the crowd of refugees and were sent to Cyprus.

With this new effort, the British were faced with big, fast ships with American crews who were willing to defy the blockade and had no fear of internment; few expected to reach Palestine but they were determined to keep Palestine in the headlines. The British were furious, particularly with the obvious American involvement since most of the crew members were American citizens.

The situation in Palestine steadily deteriorated as military terrorist attacks against the mandatory administration became a weekly event. British Foreign Secretary Ernest Bevin managed to unite Palestinian Jewry against him with his anti-Jewish policies. Britain decided to restore order and on June 29, 1946 responded with the "Black Sabbath" or "Agatha" operation arresting and imprisoning about 2,700 Jewish leaders in Palestine. The British tried to break the Jewish Agency leadership but failed. The arrested Jewish leaders refused to talk to the mandate authorities. Terror attacks continued although on a smaller scale.

The second American Mossad ship, the Haganah, reached France in June of 1946 where the French Brichah loaded the boat with 1,000 Jewish refugees. On June 22, 1946, the Haganah, carrying 1.000 passengers, departed from France and transferred 1,108 of its passengers to the small steamer Biriah, west of the island of Crete. The Biriah was intercepted by HMS Virago on July 2, 1946. The Haganah picked up a new party of 2,678 refugees in Bakar, Yugoslavia, and set sail for Palestine on July 24th. The ship was found at sea with its engines broken down and no electrical power, and was towed to Haifa by HMS Venus. Its passengers were arrested and interned. The crew again disappeared.

The internment camps in Palestine were overflowing and Britain decided to send the illegal Jewish refugees to the island of Cyprus, knowing that the decision would provoke protests, especially in the

United States. On August 7, 1946, the British informed US officials of the decision by secret cable and stressed that the illegal voyages must be stopped. Instead, the Mossad-Brichah partnership increased the number of ships of all sizes creating more difficulties for the British.

The Haganah in the port of Haifa, Palestine

The next ship was the *Chaim Arlosoroff*, named after an important Zionist leader. **Chaim Arlosoroff** was born in Romny, Ukraine in 1899. He obtained a doctorate in economics at the University of Berlin and became a key leader of *Ha-Po'el ha-Tza'ir*, ("The Young Worker Party"), a political party which attracted many Jewish intellectuals. As a result of his party affiliation, Arlosoroff was appointed editor of *Die Arbeit*, and in 1919 published his treatise "Jewish People's Socialism", relating to a nationalistic hope for the Jewish people in Eretz Israel. At the age of 24 he served on the Zionist Action Committee and in 1926 represented the Jewish Agency for Palestine at the League of Nations in Geneva. Later he was named Political Director of the Jewish Agency for Palestine, a prominent position he filled until his assassination in 1933.

Chaim Arlosoroff

Arlosoroff successfully negotiated with the Nazis to allow Jews leaving Germany, who had money or assets, to deposit the money into a special account which the Jewish Agency for Palestine could use to purchase products and machinery in Germany and sell in Palestine. The proceeds were then turned over to the German Jews who settled in Palestine. About 60,000 German Jews came to Palestine and received some of their assets. This was an unusual effort which was attacked bitterly by the Revisionists and their leader Jabotinsky. Not long after the deal was negotiated, Chaim Arlosoroff was murdered in Tel Aviv. His death greatly aggravated political relations within the Zionist movement. The Revisionists were accused of the murder but no definite proof was found and all suspects were eventually released.

The *Ulua* OR *Chaim Arlosoroff* was purchased in Baltimore where it underwent extensive repairs. It had a crew of 27 men, with Eliyahu Eliav, a Palestinian Mossad commander, serving as military captain of the vessel. He was assisted by Nissim Levitan, Israel Auerbach and Zvi Katznelson, all Mossad agents. The ship headed to Trelleborg, Sweden, where 664 Jewish Shoah survivors, mostly girls, waited to go to Palestine. The ship experienced many problems but at the end of February reached the port of Metaponto, Italy, where 734 more illegal passengers boarded the ship, which then sailed toward Palestine. It was intercepted by British military vessels that pursued it to the shores of Palestine. The *Arlosoroff* crew managed to crash the ship on the rocks of Bet Galim, near Haifa. The event occurred opposite a British military base. All passengers were interned by the British.

The Chaim Arlosoroff being chased by British warships just before it crashed onto the Palestinian shores. British military waits on the shore.

Hillel Kook was born in Lithuania in 1915, the son of Rabbi Dov Kook and younger brother of Abraham Isaac Kook, the first Ashkenazi Chief Rabbi of the British Mandate in Palestine. In 1924, his family immigrated to Palestine, where his father became the first Chief Rabbi of Afula. Hillel Kook received a religious education at Yeshiva Merkaz HaRav established by his uncle, Rabbi Abraham Isaac Kook, and attended the Hebrew University. He joined the pre-state Jewish Haganah underground in 1930 and helped found the more militant Irgun, eventually becoming a member of the Irgun General Headquarters.

In 1937 Hillel Kook began his career as an international spokesperson for the Irgun and Revisionist Zionism, traveling to the US with Ze'ev Jabotinsky, where he took the name of Peter Bergson in order not to embarrass his rabbinical family in Palestine. In 1940 he became the head of the Irgun and the Zionist Revisionist mission in the United States. Kook warned the world about the fate of European Jewry and antagonized the American Jewish establishment. He bitterly attacked Britain for closing the gates to Palestine just at a moment when the Jews needed it most. Hillel Kook became Ben Hecht's mentor on Zionism.

Hillel Kook his assumed name Peter Bergson)

Ben Hecht

Ben Hecht was born in New York City in 1894, the son of Russian Jewish immigrants grew up in Racine, Wisconsin. His father, Joseph Hecht, worked in the garment industry. In 1910, at age 16, Hecht moved to Chicago and started a career in journalism, covering Berlin after World War I for the Chicago Daily News. While in Berlin he wrote his successful novel, *Erik Dorn* (1921). Hecht and fellow reporter, Charles MacArthur, collaborated on the well-known play, *The Front Page*, which was later made into a successful film. Hecht went on to write 35 books and some of the most entertaining screenplays and plays in America. Hecht was active in civil rights efforts but was never close to the Jewish community or the Zionist movement until he met Peter Bergson.

Hecht became a staunch Zionist and collected money for the Irgun in Palestine. Hecht introduced Kook to influential people in the United States. They formed the so-called "Bergson Group" that campaigned throughout the US to help the Jews in Europe and to open the gates of Palestine. With the end of the war, the Irgun in the US also wanted to help ship Jews from Europe to Palestine. They decided to honor Ben Hecht by naming an illegal ship in his name

With Ze'ev Schind's help the Revisionists managed to acquire the *Abril* on March 9, 1946. The *Abril* or Ben Hecht sailed for Port du Bouc, France and left France for Palestine on March 1, 1947. It was the only Revisionist illegal ship to leave the United States. Its decks were crammed with over 600 Holocaust survivors. Seven days later the Ben Hecht was spotted by British reconnaissance aircraft and soon after British destroyers intercepted the ship. It was boarded, impounded and towed to Haifa under British control. The refugees were sent to the prison camps in Cyprus. Most of the crew was arrested and sent to prison where they would face trials. It is not known why the crew did not disappear among the illegal refugees as was the case with other crews.

The Abril or Ben Hecht

The Hatikvah

The *Tradewinds* was built in Canada and served as an icebreaker and then as a Coast Guard cutter. It was moored in Miami and then in Baltimore, where it had extensive repairs, before sailing to Europe. It first stopped in the Azores and then proceeded to Lisbon where the Haganah Commander Yehoshua Baharav boarded the vessel. He was a Moshavnik from Palestine and an experienced blockade runner.

In April, 1947, the Tradewinds docked in Lisbon, Portugal, next to its sister ship, President Warfield or Exodus, for more refitting. When Portuguese police became suspicious of Yehoshua Baharav, the Mossad leAliyah Bet agent who directed the repairs, had him arrested. The Tradewinds then moved from Lisbon to Marseille, then to Port-de-Bouc, and finally to Portovenere, Italy, where 1,414 Jewish refugees waited to board the ship. Most of the passengers had just crossed the Alps under the guidance of the Brichah. Once loaded, the ship, now called *Hatikvah* or Hope, sailed for Palestine. A British reconnaissance aircraft spotted the Hatikvah approaching the coast of Palestine. On May 17, 1947, the ship was intercepted, rammed and captured by the destroyers HMS Venus and HMS Brissenden. Most of the passengers and crew were sent to Cyprus. Some of the crew members were detained in Haifa.

The Exodus

The President Warfield, named after the president of the Baltimore Steam Packet Company, began to sail in 1928. It was an excursion ship that saw action in World War II. Then it was sold several times until it reached the American Mossad, which rebuilt the ship in Baltimore. British officials in the United States tried to block the ship from sailing but all their efforts failed. The Warfield, under the command of Captain William C. Ash, left the port of Baltimore for the Azores. Stormy weather disabled the ship and it managed to reach the Norfolk harbor where serious repairs began. Finally the ship left and reached the Azores on April 5, 1947, where it obtained fuel and proceeded to Marseilles. The British Navy constantly shadowed the Warfield, which raced from port to port around Marseilles. The maneuvering was performed by a 23 year-old Palestinian captain, Itzhak Ahranovitch, who had acquired his sailing experience during World War II aboard British and Norwegian merchant ships. Meanwhile, the British embassy in France obtained legal papers that stopped the ship from leaving the port of Sete near Marseilles. The local Mossad commander, Shmarya Tzameret, tried unsuccessfully to bribe the guards to let the ship sail. While talks were taking place between French officials and the Mossad, eight trains brought thousands of Jewish refugees from DP camps in Germany to the port of Sete.115

---

115 Szulc, Alliance p.174

Brichah - Hebrew for Escape or Flight

When the Exodus entered the Mediterranean Sea, the Brichah was issued orders to dispatch Jewish refugees from the DP camps in Germany to the borders of Holland, Belgium and France.116 The Brichah selected 5,000 Jewish DPs and sent them on the road. The Mossad met the transports at the borders and directed them to Marseilles.117 The Mossad kept about 600 refugees for future transports and 200 children were placed in French homes and orphanages; the remaining 4,200 boarded the ship.118 The transfer of thousands of Jews from Germany to France was a major logistical and organizational effort and was an indication of the effectiveness of both the Brichah and Mossad in Europe.

Itzhak Ahranovitch, captain of the Exodus

116 Bauer, Flight, p.317
117 Bauer, Flight, p.317
118 P.318

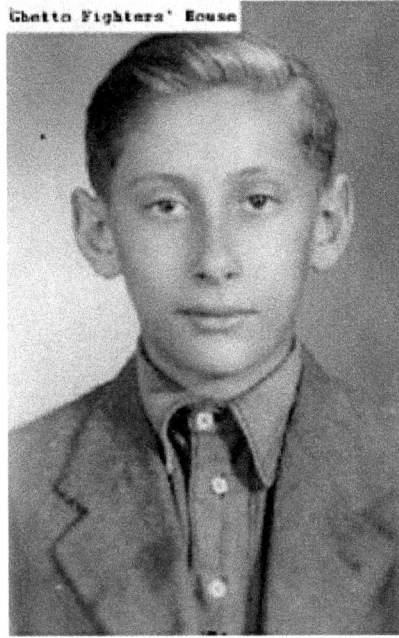

Shlomo Koren, passenger on the Exodus, at the Zabrze orphanage
(Lochamei Hagetaot, the Ghetto Fighters' Museum)

Included in the transport were hundreds of children from Jewish orphanages. Many of the children had been hidden by non-Jewish families and churches. Their own families had either been murdered by the Nazis or miraculously escaped and disappeared. The children had been redeemed or rescued through an intensive effort by Captain Yeshayahu Drucker, Rabbi Aaron Becker and Rabbi Yitzhak Herzog.

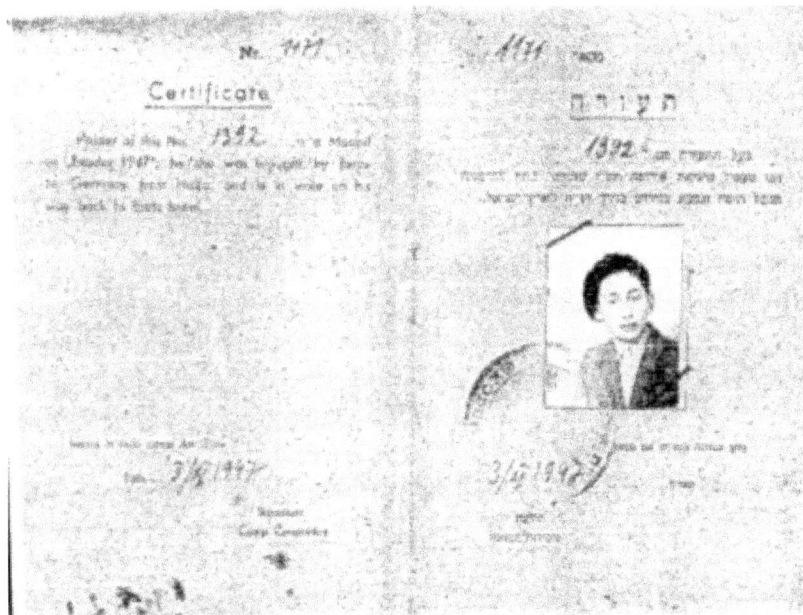

Numbered certificate issued to the passengers of the famous Exodus

*David Danieli, formerly Daniel Danielski, at the Zabrze
children's home in 1946. Danieli was a passenger on the Exodus.*

The *Exodus* sailed from the port of Sete, near Marseilles, on July 11, 1947, without permission. Ernest Bevin, the British foreign secretary, was in France at the time and begged French Foreign Minister Georges Bidault to stop the ship. Bidault consented and the order was issued to stop the departure of the ship. But someone leaked the information to the Mossad, which ordered the ship to leave the port immediately. The *Exodus* left the port without a French pilot.[119] As soon as it left the territorial waters of France, British destroyers followed it. On July 18, near the coast of Palestine but outside territorial waters, heavy machine gun fire was directed at the ship and two destroyers rammed the Exodus from both sides. The first landing party boarded the ship and was bombarded with tins of preserves and potatoes by the passengers, with no effect. The British marines and sailors, armed with side-arms and clubs, attacked the passengers and crew. They reached the bridge and viciously clubbed the *Exodus* captain, Second Officer William Bernstein,

---

119 Bauer, p.318

202

who died almost instantly as did two Jewish Shoah survivors. The ship was towed to Haifa, where the immigrants were forcefully taken off.

The Exodus is towed into the port of Haifa

Haifa's waterfront was like a battlefield with soldiers and policemen everywhere blocking access to the port area. The illegal refugees refused to move and were dragged on board the prison ships. Ambulances rushed seriously wounded refugees to the hospital. The Jewish population of Haifa was tense and nervous, hostility toward Britain was at a high point. Observers of the United Nations Commission of Inquiry witnessed the scenes, which influenced them to support the end of the mandate in Palestine.[120] On July 18, 1947, mourning signs appeared all over the city calling on the Jewish population to participate in the funeral procession of the young American Jewish naval officer. He was buried on July 18, 1947, in the Martyr section of the Haifa Jewish cemetery. The fact that he was an American created a great deal of negative coverage for Britain in the American press.

---

120 Bauer, Flight, p.185

William (Bill) Bernstein aboard the Exodus prior to its departure for Europe

William Bernstein was born January 27, 1923, in Passaic, New Jersey. At the age of 13 his family moved to San Francisco. He graduated from Galileo High School in San Francisco and attended Ohio State University. Although entitled to a deferment from military service as a pre-medical student, he volunteered for the U.S. Merchant Marines in World War II. He graduated from the Kings Point Merchant Marine Academy in 1944 as a second lieutenant. After the war, he received an appointment to the U.S. Naval Academy at Annapolis, but volunteered for Aliyah Bet and served as a second officer on the Exodus.

The Exodus Jewish survivors being directed to the prison ships
watched by lines of British soldiers. (Yad Vashem Archives)

People expected that the prison ships would sail to Cyprus where the refugees would be disembarked. But the British government decided to teach a lesson to the survivors of Hitler and send them back to the port of embarkation in France. British international standing had hit bottom. Bevin tried to involve France in his disastrous strategies regarding the Jewish refugees. On August 2, 1947, the three British prison ships entered the port of Port-de-Bouc and docked. The refugees refused to leave the ships. The British government urged France to forcefully remove the refugees from the ships, but the French refused to co-operate. They were willing to accept refugees who wanted to leave the ship but would not use force. The refugees were well organized and declared a hunger strike that gained attention from the entire free press, especially in France. The French government stood by their decision to help those who wanted to leave the ships and not interfere with the others.

Bevin did not know what do to. Meanwhile the refugees continued to get worldwide attention, especially in the United States. The ships remained in port for four weeks and on August 22, 1947, Bevin sent the refugees to the British zone in Germany. The decision rallied the entire free world against Britain. The idea of sending concentration camp survivors back to Germany was the height of cruelty and made no sense. The ships arrived at Hamburg and new clashes erupted between the Jews and the British soldiers. All passengers were finally forced into camps near the city of Lubeck, Germany. The Brichah would later transfer most of them into the American occupation zone in Germany. Many would join other illegal ships heading to Palestine. Bevin had won a very hollow victory.

Britain was convinced that the *Exodus* operation would stop further illegal ships from coming to Palestine or at least substantially reduce their numbers. The head of the Mossad in Paris, Avigur, read the map differently. He saw the British act in haste and in panic with the *Exodus* operation and decided to increase the number of illegal ships to Palestine.

On July 28, 1947, the Halalei Gesher Haziv, carrying 685 Eastern European Jews, was intercepted by HMS *Rowena*. Also, the *Shivat Zion*, carrying 411 North African Jews, was intercepted without resistance by the minesweeper HMS *Providence*. On September 27, 1947, the Af Al Pi Chen (434 passengers), was intercepted by HMS *Talybont* and taken after violent resistance. One person was killed and 10 were injured. All Jewish refugees were transported to Cyprus. Bevin did not want a repetition of the Exodus. At this point the passengers of the Exodus were still at sea. The Mossad response was clear and loud: "Illegal ships would continue to sail to Palestine."

The Mossad was, however, concerned with the possibility that the British would return passengers of big ships to their country of embarkation. So Avigur decided to play safe and bring refugees from Romania where there was a large reservoir of potential passengers due to the poor conditions in the country. Orders were issued to Shaike Dan to activate the Romanian Brichah office.

Shaike Dan

Isaiah Sheyke Dan Trachtenberg, better known as Shaike Dan, was born November 15, 1919, in Moldavie, Romania. He went to Palestine as a pioneer and joined a kibbutz. During World War II, Shaike Dan volunteered to parachute behind enemy lines in Romania on behalf of British Intelligence. This jump would begin a remarkable career of rescuing Jews aided by the many friends he made during the war, who became key figures in the security services of Eastern Europe. His jump had two objectives: to locate the prison camp where 1,400 allied air force crewmen, downed when bombing the Ploesti oil fields in Romania, were being held, and find ways to get them out of Romania so that they could go back into action. The second objective was to try to rescue Jews from Eastern Europe and get them to Palestine. There were 32 volunteer parachutists from Palestine. Some of them parachuted into Yugoslavia, linked up with partisan forces, and stole across frontiers with the help of local smugglers. Many of these volunteers were caught and some of them never returned.

Dan received orders to start negotiating for the release of Jews from Romania and the use of the port of Constantsa for their embarkation. Meanwhile two American ships received orders to prepare for crossing the Atlantic.

Refugee children being marched from Paducah (in background) to another ship at dock in Haifa

The Paducah renamed Geula or Redemption

The USS *Paducah* was launched on October 11, 1904 and commissioned 11 months later. It was named for the former mayor of Paducah, Kentucky, David A. Yeiser. The *Paducah* served as an escort for allied convoys in the Mediterranean during World War I and also saw action in World War II. It was decommissioned in 1945. A year later, Maria Angelo of Miami, Florida, purchased the ship and transferred it to the Mossad. The Mossad hired Merchant Marine Captain Rudolph Patzert to bring the *Paducah* from Miami to New York and then across the Atlantic. The crew was comprised of young Jewish volunteers. The final destination was the port of Bayonne, in southwest France, where the *Paducah* was transformed over several weeks into a crude but effective passenger liner. The ship was ordered to head to Varna, a Bulgarian port on the Black Sea. As mentioned previously, the Soviet fleet controlled the port of Constantsa and refused to share it with other groups, especially foreigners. The Soviets suggested that Romania use the ports in Bulgaria.

All through the Mediterranean, British destroyers cruised behind the *Paducah*. The *Paducah* arrived in Varna and soon after, on a moonless night, slipped away to Burgas, 50 miles down the coast. The Romanian Brichah sent 1,388 Jewish refugees to Burgas to board the *Paducah*. The British protested in Sofia against the presence of the illegal ship in Bulgaria but the Brichah had very good connections and the ship left, headed to the Dardanelles and the Mediterranean Sea with a British warship following. Five miles from the shores of Palestine, a British destroyer rammed the ship, now named *Geula*. Soldiers jumped from a specially built platform and boarded the ship. The Haganah sent orders from shore that there was to be no resistance. It would have been futile, resulting in unnecessary bloodshed. The engine room crew quickly disabled the engines. With the *Geula* immobile, the British towed the ship to a dock along the Haifa shoreline near a large prison ship. The passengers were marched down the gangplank and directed to the ship where they were transported to internment camps on the island of Cyprus.

The Northbound or Jewish State

The American Mossad ship Medinat Hayehudin or Jewish State

The *Northbound* was built in 1927 and saw naval action in World War II. The ship was purchased by the Mossad and also sent to Bayonne, France, for repairs. But the two Mossad ships, the *Geula* and the *Medinat Hayehudim*, were attracting too much attention. The *Geula* left port but the second ship was detained before it could sail. British agents informed the French police that the ship was owned by the same company that owned the *Exodus* that had caused extensive damage when it left the French harbor. The French insisted on payment for the damages. The Mossad appealed to the former French Prime Minister Leon Blum, who was Jewish, for help.

Léon Blum

André Léon Blum was born April 9, 1872 in Paris, France to a prosperous, assimilated Jewish family. Blum attended the École Normale Supérieure and The University of Paris and became both a lawyer and literary critic. He was a French politician, identified with the moderate left, He was heavily influenced by the Dreyfus affair of the late 19th century and became an important French Socialist leader rejecting the class conflict model of Marxist socialism, instead defining socialism as the highest use of the power of the state, under the guidance of well-educated experts like himself, "to define, protect, and guarantee the condition of the working class."[2] As Prime Minister in a "Popular Front" government of the left 1936-37, he provided a series of major economic reforms. Blum declared neutrality in the Spanish Civil War (1936–39) to avoid the civil conflict spilling over into France itself. Once out of office in 1938, he denounced the appeasement of Germany. When Germany defeated France in 1940, he became a staunch opponent of Vichy France. Blum made no effort to leave the country, despite the extreme danger he faced as a Jew and a socialist leader. Blum was arrested and sent to a French detention camp named Fort du Portalet in the Pyrenees.

Tried by Vichy on trumped-up charges, he was imprisoned in the Buchenwald and Dachau concentration camps. After the war he resumed a transitional leadership role in French politics, helping to bring about the French Fourth Republic, until his death in 1950.

Leon Blum used his connections and the ship was released and sailed for Burgas followed by British warships.[121] The ship docked in Burgas where the Romanian Brichah brought 2,700 Jewish refuges by train to the port. All the passengers had received permission from the Communist Party to leave Romania. They boarded the ship, which sailed to the Mediterranean Sea where British warships escorted it to the shores of Palestine. Once in Palestine, the British stormed the ship and sent all the passengers were sent to Cyprus as was the crew.

The fact that the passengers of both the *Geula* and the *Jewish State* were sent to Cyprus indicated to Avigur in Paris that the British were retreating from their announced position that all refugees would be sent back to the ports of embarkation. He decided to push for bigger ships with larger passenger capacity in order to flood Palestine and Cyprus with Jewish refugees. There were unlimited numbers of refugees awaiting their turn to sail to Palestine. In response the American Mossad purchased two huge ships in the spring of 1947, with an additional ship

---

121 Jews, p.139

purchased later in the year. The man who approved the purchase was Paul Schulman, the naval adviser of the American Mossad.

Leon Blum memorial in kibbutz Kfar Blum, Israel

Paul N. Schulman

Paul N. Schulman loved the sea and ships. He graduated from the U.S. Naval Academy and saw action in the Pacific during World War II. He resigned from the U.S. Navy in 1947 and joined the American Mossad under Schind's leadership and served as the naval expert assisting in purchasing and refurbishing vessels. Then, in May 1948, David Ben-Gurion asked Schulman to come to Israel to assist in the organization and establishment of the Israeli Navy. Schulman was appointed Commander of Israel's Navy in October 1948 and served in that capacity until March 1949, when he was appointed Naval and Maritime Advisor to the Prime Minister.

The *Pan Crescent* or *Atzma'ut* and the *Pan York* or *Komeimiut* were the two largest ships in the history of illegal immigration to Palestine. The ships had a capacity of about 15,000. While the ships were being prepared for their journeys to Europe, the British found out about the ships and applied pressure on the U.S. State Department to stop them from sailing. The efforts failed and the ships left for Europe. The *Pan Crescent* went to Venice, Italy, and the *Pan York* sailed to Marseilles. Both ships needed extensive repairs to accommodate large numbers of passengers. The British damaged *the Pan Crescent* by placing a charge along the side of the ship. The mayor of Venice spoke to Ada Sereni, Haganah leader in Italy, and assured her that the ship would be protected, repaired and permitted to sail on condition that the Haganah did not take revenge on British warships.

Ada Ascarelli Sereni was born in Rome on June 20, 1905, into one of Italy's wealthiest and most respected Jewish families (the Ascarelli's were descended from Spanish exiles). Ada's father, a lover of history with an extensive library, owned a herd of sheep in Sardinia and produced cheese that was exported to the United States. While still at school Ada fell in love with a fellow pupil, Enzo Sereni, a Zionist and socialist, like herself a member of the Italian Jewish aristocracy. After the birth of their daughter Hannah on July 4, 1926, the couple emigrated to Palestine, where they married on February 19, 1927.

Ada and Enzo spent their first year in Palestine in Rehovot, founding Kibbutz Givat Brenner in 1928 with a small group of Russian-born pioneers. Ada later worked as director of the Rimon juice and preserves factory. Enzo began to engage in communal service within the Labor movement. During World War II, he was among the initiators of a plan to parachute Jewish agents into Europe. He himself parachuted into the German lines on May 15, 1944, as a British army officer. Captured by the Germans, he was killed in Dachau on November 18, 1944. Ada approached Shaul Avigur to help find Enzo, and was invited to return to Italy under the guise of organizing social clubs for the soldiers of the Jewish Brigade. Her real assignment was to assist Yehuda Arazi in organizing illegal immigration to Palestine and to search for Enzo. Arriving in Munich, Ada visited the Dachau concentration camp and discovered proof of her husband's death. Her private mission was over.

Sereni returned to Italy, beginning a period of intensive activity dedicated to the clandestine immigration of Holocaust survivors to Palestine, in direct opposition to British policy. Her task was to purchase ships, fill them with Jews and organize all aspects of the voyage. At first serving as second-in-command to Yehuda Arazi, she replaced him as commander of the operation in 1947. Her fluency in Italian and familiarity with the country enabled her to establish excellent contacts. The fact that she was an Italian war widow opened many doors. She saw to it that the *Pan Crescent* sailed to Constantsa despite British protests. She continued in this position until May 14, 1948, when the state of Israel was established.

The Pan Crescent or Atzmaut

The Pan York or Kibbutz Galuyot

The British were desperate in their efforts to stop the ships and protested to the Romanian and US governments. British Foreign Secretary Bevin launched a worldwide campaign contending that the ships would carry hordes of Communists who would disrupt the entire Middle East and deprive the free world of oil supplies. The so-called Communist invasion, he argued, had to be stopped. The State Department and the Pentagon were ardently anti-communist. They had always supported British policies in Palestine and were now able to express their views in public. The American government began to pressure the Jewish Agency to cancel the operation. The vote to partition Palestine was coming up at the United Nations General Assembly. But Avigur insisted that the operation continue. Thousands of refugees were on the way, contracts were signed, ships were standing by and nobody knew when the Romanians or the Soviets would change their minds and stop the entire operation. Finally, the United Nations voted for the partition of Palestine. Avigur was notified to proceed.

Shaike Dan received the green light and began intensive final negotiations with the Romanian government, particularly with the Romanian Foreign Minister Hannah Rabinsohn Pauker.

Rabinsohn was born December 13, 1893, in Codăeşti, Vaslui County in Moldavia, into a poor, religious Orthodox Jewish family. Her father was a ritual slaughterer and a functionary in the synagogue, her mother a small-time food seller. They had four surviving children; an additional two died in infancy. As a young woman, she became a teacher in a Jewish elementary school in Bucharest. While her younger brother was a Zionist and remained religious, she opted for socialism, joining the Social Democratic Party of Romania in 1915 and later the Communist party. She and her husband Marcel Pauker became leading figures in the Romanian Communist Party.

She was the unofficial leader of the Romanian Communist Party right after World War II. She returned to Romania in 1944 when the Red Army entered the country, becoming a member of the post-war government, which came to be dominated by the communists. In November 1947, the non-communist Foreign Minister, Gheorghe Tătărescu, was ousted and replaced by Pauker, making her the first woman in the modern world to hold such a post.

Ana Pauker

The Soviets were determined to blacken the image of Britain and gave the Romanians permission to sell Jews to the Mossad, knowing that they would go to Palestine or Cyprus and further embarrass Britain. Negotiations went on and money was exchanged. Finally, lists of Jews who would be leaving Romania were established. Romania would provide trains that would take the refugees to Burgas where the boarding would take place, since the Soviet Navy would not give permission to use the port of Constantsa. The ships left Burgas on December 26, 1947, and headed to Palestine with British war ships following closely. Meanwhile, the Jewish Agency and the British Navy conducted negotiations regarding the landing of refugees. Finally, the Mossad agreed that the ships would head to Cyprus if British soldiers did not board the ships. On January 1, 1948, the ships and their British escorts arrived at the port of Famagusta in Cyprus. The unloading of the refugees took several days. Mossad-Brichah ships continued to arrive in Palestine and were intercepted by the British and sent to Cyprus. The Jewish population on the island grew and reached about 50,000. The last ship to arrive was the *Calimat* or *Mala*, which brought the remnants of the *Exodus* passengers from Europe to Israel. The ship docked in Haifa, Israel, on July 18, 1948.

The vital role played by the American ships and American sailors is little known[122]. They carried almost 32,000 Jewish survivors from Europe to the shores of Palestine in comparison to the total number of 72,000 Jewish survivors who reached the shores of Palestine between 1945 and 1948[123]. The American Mossad ships carried almost half of the total number of illegal passengers. The numbers are quite large, considering the short period of time that American Mossad existed and all the difficulties it faced. The American Mossad indeed answered the call of the Jewish people and like other American organizations such as the JDC extended all the help it could to the defeat of the blockade and the creation of the State of Israel.

---

122 Hochstein pp.30-310
123 Ibid., p.171

Chapter XV
Cyprus

Map of the Island of Cyprus

The island of Cyprus was placed under British administration in 1878 and annexed in 1914. The island's location in the Eastern Mediterranean Sea south of Turkey and northwest of Israel as militarily very important for the British colonial empire, particularly the proximity of the island to the Suez Canal, the main route to India. During WWII, Cyprus was an important naval base and an important supply center for the Allied forces.

As mentioned previously, the numbers of illegal ships grew with the strong partnership between American Jews, the Mossad and the Brichah[124]. The British refused to open more internment camps in Palestine and decided to send all future illegal refugees to Cyprus.

On August 13, 1946, the first transport of Jewish refugees arrived at Famagusta, Cyprus and were tra military escort to camp number 55[125]. The entire operation was kept secret and the press was not allowed to

---

record the event. A total of 12 camps would operate between August 1946 and January 1949 holding approximately 53, 510 Jewish Shoah survivors. The camps were located mainly near two sites about 50 kilometers apart, at Caraoles north of Famagusta and Dhekelia outside of Larnaca.

Conditions in the camps were very harsh, with poor sanitation, over-crowding, lack of privacy and a shortage of clean water. The prisoners were mostly young, 80% between 13 and 35, and included over 6,000 orphan children. About 2,000 children were born in the camps. The births took place in the Jewish wing of the British Military Hospital in Nicosia. Some 400 Jews died in the camps and were buried in Margao cemetery.

UNRRA or United did not operate in Cyprus nor did the International Red Cross and Jewish social welfare agencies were not permitted to operate in the camps. The Jewish Agency of Palestine had taken the position that the refugees were Jews coming to their homeland, no one had the right to deport them; and refused to have any official contact with the mandatory administration in Palestine or the Cyprus military authorities on the issue. Now, the Palestinian mandatory authorities were paying for the maintenance of the refugee camps, not Jewish organizations.

The Jewish Agency and the JDC knew they had to do something to alleviate the situation. The groups formed a committee of two people: Dr. Reuven Katznelson, a well-known physician in Mandatory Palestine, and Charles Passman, head of the JDC office in Jerusalem.[126] Both men were influential but not viewed as political. As mentioned earlier, Passman was an American citizen and a troubleshooter for the JDC. The two-man delegation flew to Cyprus but the British authorities on the island refused to acknowledge them. Dr. Katznelson returned home but Charles Passman stayed on and investigated the camps. He then informed the British authorities that he intended to hold an international press conference to expose the terrible conditions in the internment camps where Shoah survivors were forced to live, and would be raising the fact that an American humanitarian agency, the JDC, wanted to help but was not permitted by the British since the refugees were kept behind barbed wire for the sole crime that they had tried to reach Palestine.[127] Britain, already suffering from bad press in the United States, did not

---

126 Bogner, Deportation, p. 63
127 Bogner, Deportation, p. 80

relish the thought of more negative publicity and decided to meet with Passman. He was even permitted to visit the camps where he witnessed terrible and inhumane conditions. He established a list of priorities that was sent to the JDC in Paris and to the Jewish Agency in Jerusalem.

An internment camp in Cyprus (Yad Vashem Archives)

The Paris office of the JDC granted an emergency financial allocation to Passman to open and staff an office in Cyprus. Passman was also authorized to bring the necessary staff, including doctors, nurses and teachers, to organize various medical and social facilities in the camps. Most of the staff were brought from Palestine. So the Jewish Agency, the Mossad, the Haganah, and the political Zionist parties were all able to send their representatives to Cyprus. Contacts were also established with Brichah and Mossad leaders who were on the island mixed in with the refugees. Passman found it difficult to cope with his offices in Jerusalem and Cyprus and urged the JDC to appoint a director specifically for Cyprus to handle the growing needs of the refugees. The JDC appointed Morris Laub as director of Cyprus operations.

Morris Laub assumed his post on December 10, 1946.[128] He brought his family to Famagusta and began to effectively provide all the necessary assistance that the Jewish camp population needed. Laub was born in Przemysl, Galicia, Poland and educated in the United States. He was a conscientious Jew, familiar with Jewish literature and history, and spoke fluent Hebrew, Yiddish, the language of most of the internees, as well as English.

He spent much of his time dealing with the British authorities on the island who were not inclined to be cooperative. The smallest concession required many hours of discussions with military officials who went by the book and were suspicious of his But he managed to establish medical and educational facilities and organized sports activities. He also received permission to have the ORT train youngsters in manual skills they would later use in civilian life in Palestine. He rarely dealt directly with the Jewish population or its leaders.

Laub was familiar with Palestine and the workings of the Jewish Agency but he lacked the intimacy that was needed to handle the multitude of problems among the camp population. The British permitted the Jews internal autonomy. Most of the population belonged to Zionist parties that formed the camp administrative councils. The Brichah and Mossad had agents in the camps as did the Haganah and the Irgun, which organized semi-military formations in the camps. To all of them, Laub was an outsider, an American Jew who helped them, but they questioned whether he could be trusted with smuggling or tunnel-digging operations. The answer was always doubtful and Laub knew it. He therefore began to look for an assistant who was very familiar with the Palestinian situation but also spoke English fluently.

Laub flew to Jerusalem where he was introduced to **Yehoshua Leibner**. The two "Galitzianers" (both originally came from Galicia, Poland) hit it off. Leibner was born on July 1, 1910, in Krakow, Poland, and died on July 29, 1956 in Israel. In 1921 he immigrated with his family to the United States where he attended secondary school. By 1928 he was a prominent activist of the Zionist pioneering youth movement and joined an American Jewish training farm that prepared youngsters to move to Palestine. He married Pearl (later Pnina) Horowitz and they moved to Palestine where they established kibbutz Ein Hashofet, which belonged to the Hashomer Ha-Tzair movement. The kibbutz sent him on many missions to the US where he organized Jewish youth. He also

---

128 Bogner, Deportation, p. 53.

represented the Jewish Agency on several missions abroad. Leibner was familiar with the lweaders of the Haganah and its elite force the Palmach. He was also familiar with the American Jewish scene since he had spent a great deal of time there representing the kibbutz movement. during his stay in the US met and became friendly with Louis D. Brandeis, the U.S. Supreme Court justice and Zionist.

Yehoshua Leibner (photo from the Ghetto Fighters Archives}

Laub was impressed with what he saw and submitted Leibner's name to the JDC headquaters in Paris. The latter confirmed his appointment.

The British military authorities that accepted him. The Jewish Agency was pleased with the appointment as were the British authorities.The kibbutz Ein Ha-Shofet granted him and his family a leave of absence and they left for Cyprus on April 12, 1946. They arrived at Famagusta and Leibner started to coordinate the various Zionist existing parties and associations. The fact that he represented the Jewish Agency in Palestine carried a great deal of weight and greatly helped him in his tasks. Unlike Laub who spent most of his time with the British authorities on the island, Leibner spent most of his time with the Jewish refugees. He also supervised the Palestinian Jewish staff at the camps and transmitted the latest requests from Palestine. In effect he was responsible for creating an Israeli atmosphere in the camps with an emphasis on studying the Hebrew language and culture.

Tent Camp for Cyprus Jewish Shoah Refugees

A number of escape attempts took place while the camps were active. The most significant was in August 1948, when an estimated 100 inmates escaped a detention camp through a secret tunnel that had been dug over a period of six months. The British believed that the escapees were aided by Palestinians who were rescuing needed technical or military men. Hochstein and Greenfield in their book *The Jews' Secret Fleet* also mention the event. One man managed to escape while being transported from court to prison. In January 1949, as the British began deporting the final batch of inmates from Cyprus to Israel, an unspecified number of Jews who had escaped the camps earlier and remained at large on Cyprus turned themselves in so they could be sent to Israel.

Each month, the British granted a limited number of certificates to enter Palestine, and Leibner coordinated the list of people who were selected to leave the island. The demand for such certificates frequently resulted in heated debates and discussions among the various political parties. The camps frequently received or dispatched emissaries to and from Palestine who needed official assistance. Laub was not involved in these activities and did not want to involve himself since he dealt with the British and had to fight hard to obtain benefits for the refugees. The running of the camps themselves was greatly influenced by Leibner, who dealt with many individual problems. Leibner's door was always open, according to Laub.[129]

The JDC tended to the many needs of the Jewish detainees in the camps while the Jewish Agency provided the spiritual sustenance and hope that they would reach the shores of Palestine. Leibner assured them daily they would reach their homeland. Indeed, many reached Palestine legally and illegally. He urged the remainder of the detainees to learn trades and Hebrew so that they would become productive citizens of the land of Israel. Most of the young detainees enlisted in the Haganah formations in the camps, ready to join the battle for independence. British hostility to the detainees continued to the last possible moment.

From November 1946 to May 1948, Cyprus detainees were allowed into Palestine at a rate of 750 per month. During 1947-48, special quotas were given to pregnant women, nursing mothers and the elderly. Released Cyprus detainees amounted to 67% of all immigrants to Palestine during that period. Following Israeli independence, the British began deporting detainees to Israel at a rate of 1,500 per month. The *Pan Crescent* and the *Pan York* were used to transport the detainees to Palestine.[130] They amounted to 40% of all immigration to Israel during the war months of May-September 1948. The British kept about 11,000 detainees, mainly men of military age, imprisoned throughout most of the war. On January 24, 1949, the British began sending these detainees to Israel, with the last of them departing for Israel on February 11, 1949.

Even when Britain handed over the Palestine mandate to the United Nations, it kept the Jewish refugees in the camps on Cyprus. When the State of Israel was proclaimed on May 14, 1948, many of the Jewish refugees in Cyprus, especially young men, were still behind barbed wire. Britain used every device to keep the Jews in the Cyprus camps. . On February 11, 1949, Morris Laub and Yehoshua Leibner were the last JDC officials to leave Cyprus when all the camps were closed JDC operations ceased.

---

129 Laub, Morris. A Barrier to Freedom, Judah Magnes Museum, 2911 Russel Street Berkeley , California., USA. p 35
Hochstein. Jews' p.149130

The Leibner family returned to the kibbutz. Yehoshua resumed tending to his sheep. He soon passed away. His family donated to Yad Vashem in Jerusalem all the artifacts (shown in photo) that he received in Cyprus from the Jewish refugees.

Chapter XVI
Epilogue

The largest organized covert mass migration in the twentieth century brought a quarter of a million Jews from Eastern and Central Europe to the DP camps in Germany, Austria and Italy. The movement started slowly in several places, hardly noticeable at first. It became "Brichah", an organized underground effort that took Shoah survivors from all over Eastern Europe on difficult journeys with the goal of settling in Palestine. Jewish Polish resistance members and Warsaw ghetto fighters led the way, knowing that Jews were not safe anywhere in Europe. They were challenged by the fact that Jews could not legally move from country to country and that the British were greatly restricting Jewish immigration to the Mandate of Palestine. Moving large numbers of people across borders, through difficult terrain, caring for and feeding them, and attending to their education and religious needs was an enormous task.

The Jewish world responded and organizations such as the American Jewish Joint Distribution Committee, the Mossad, the Haganah, the Jewish Agency for Palestine, Jewish military personnel from the US and England, all played major roles in the massive effort. The United Nations Relief and Rehabilitation Agency also had major responsibility for the refugees.

To most Jews in the DP camps it was clear that they must organize and fight for their survival. Illegal ships crammed with refugees and forced into Cyprus camps attracted world attention and raised the idea of a Jewish state in Palestine in the eyes of the world. The number of Jewish survivors in the camps of Germany, Austria and Italy kept growing and no one wanted them except for Palestine. The British were determined to keep them out. Every illegal ship made headlines. Britain refused to listen, eventually losing all of Palestine when the Jewish State of Israel was created. Most of the DP camps disappeared very rapidly since most of the residents went to Palestine. The Brichah and the Mossad organizations were dismantled with the closing of the camps. Most of the Brichah members and the Mossad agents that dealt with transporting Jews across Europe retired and returned to their homes to resume their normal lives.

Incomplete list of Jewish DP camps in Austria

After the liberation of Vienna in April 1945, there were 17,000 Jews in the city, most of whom were Hungarian Jews or other refugees. Between 1945 and 1952, their numbers were augmented by other Jewish displaced persons, whose needs were met by the displaced persons (DP) camps administered by the U.S. Army, the Central Committee of Liberated Jews, the UNRRA, and later the International Refugee Organization (IRO).

Austria and Vienna were divided into American, British, French, and Russian zones. Jewish refugees gravitated towards the U.S. Zone, regarding it as a more desirable haven than the territories of the other occupation forces. A transient population, the Jewish DPs looked towards the American Army for services and protection, rather than towards the Austrian government. The DP camps were also maintained by the UNRRA organization in 1946-1947 and then by the IRO organization in 1948. The US military also provided massive amounts of aid to the refugees.

The Austrian DP camps were also administered by the Central Committee of Liberated Jews that was affiliated with the World Jewish Congress, the Central Committee had its headquarters in Salzburg, and by 1948, represented approximately 25,000 Jewish DPs concentrated in the following camps.

- Ebelsberg camp
- Ebensee camp
- Enns camp
- Gratz camp
- Hanlein camp
- Insbruck camp
- Judenburg camp
- Linz camp
- Saafelden camp
- Salzburg camps;
- Salzburg; DP Hosp. (U.S. zone) - In the town of Salzburg were a number of Jewish DP camps:
- Riedenburg (Machne Yehuda) on the "Neutorstrasse, Ecke Moosstrasse."
- Franz-Josefs-Kaserne or Camp Herzl between

- Schrannengasse and Paris-London-Strasse.
- Mülln Camp 6 DP in Müllner Hauptstrasse 38.
- Maxglan or Beth Beit Bialik cmp in Salzburg.
-

Beth Bialik 1946; source: Yad Vashem

Beth Bialik; kitchen staff; source: Yad Vashem

- Gnigl or Beth Trumpeldor in the part of Salzburg
- Parsch or New Palestine in the Wiesbauerstrasse 9 in Salzburg-Parsch (is also the part of Salzburg)
- Wallnerkaserne or Givat Ha-Avoda camp 1946 in the small village called "Saalfelden" am Steinernen Meer

Vienna camps

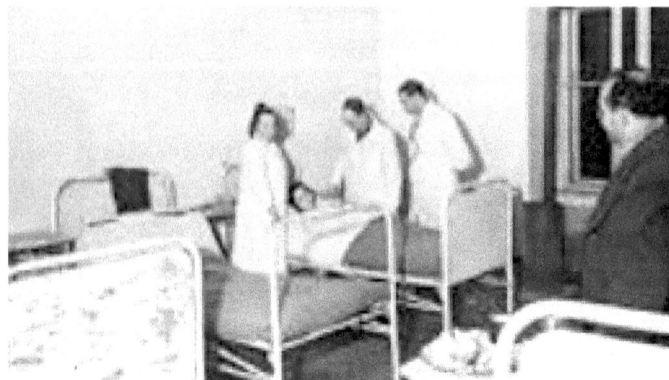

The Rothschild Hospital in Vienna provided medical care to the many Jewish refugees who transited Austria. The hospital had several sub camps.

- Rothschild Hospital, Severingasse, Stadteil Alsergrund, UNRRA camp 350, Durchgangslager, Wien IX
- Rupertsusplätz, Dombach, Stadheil Hemals, former school, Wien XVII
- Arzbergengasse No. 2 Stadteil Hemals, subcamp of Rothschild Hospital, former school Wien XVII
- Alserbachstrasse Stadteil Alsergrun transit camp Wien IX.
- Wegscheid camp
- Wels camp

Incomplete list of Jewish DP camps in Germany.

The displaced persons camps and centers in Germany came into existence in 1945 as a result of the liberation of masses of inmates from the Nazi concentration camps and forced labor units. The term "Displaced Person" (and its acronym "DP") was used by the United Nations Relief and Rehabilitation Administration (UNRRA) and by the Allied military commands to describe the persecutees driven by the Nazis from their native countries into Germany and Austria. Of the nearly 6,000,000 DPs who at the end of the war were found in Central Europe, there were only about 50,000 Jewish survivors. But while most of the DPs were being repatriated at a rapid pace, the Jewish survivors from Eastern Europe did not want to return to their countries of origin and demanded that they be allowed to emigrate to Palestine. A report to President Truman by his special envoy Earl G. Harrison submitted on August 1, 1945 supported the assertion that the Jewish DPs were non-repatriable, that they should be considered as Jews rather than nationals of their native countries and that 100,000 immigration certificates to Palestine should be provided for them through the Jewish Agency. These recommendations were accepted by the military government in the American zone where there was the highest concentration of Jewish DPs and as a result, separate camps and centers were set up by UNRRA for the Jews (although the first Jewish DP camp, in Feldafing, was organized prior to the Harrison report).

At the same time the Jewish DP population began to grow quickly as a result of the flight of Jewish survivors from Poland which continued through 1946 and became especially intensive after the pogrom in Kielce, Poland (July 4, 1946). Also, in the spring of 1947 some 20,000 Rumanian Jews took refuge in Austria and Germany. This infiltration of refugees from Eastern Europe brought the total number of Jewish DPs to 184,000 in February of 1947.

The American authorities recognized the need to receive the refugees and establish for them a "temporary haven" in the American zone. This policy was in force until April 12, 1947 when any further infiltration by the refugees into the American zone was barred by the military. The British zone was closed off to the refugees much earlier, on December 5, 1945. \

The establishment of the State of Israel in May 1948, aided by the introduction in the U.S. of the Displaced Persons Act of 1948 brought about the solution to the DP problem. By 1951 a great majority of Jewish DPs had emigrated to Israel and to the U.S. The last of the DP camps was closed in 1953.

The Jewish DP group in the French zone was the smallest of all zones comprising in 1947 some 1800 persons.

Camps

- Airing camp
- Amberg, community
- Ansbach camp
- Aschaffenburg camp
- Augsburg, community
- Bamberg camp
- Babenhausen camp
- Bad Aibling camp
- Bad Hersfeld camp
- Bad Mergentheim camp
- Bad Reichenhall, camp
- Bad Salzshirf camp
- Bensheim camp
- Berchtesgaden, rest home
- Bergen Belsen camp
- Berlin-Düppel camp
- Biberach camp
- Cham camp
- Deggendorf, camp
- Dornstadt camp
- Eggenfelden, camp
- Eichstätt (Formally known as either Eichstädt or Aichstädt) camp
- Ellwangen camp
- Erlangen camp
- Eschwege, camp
- Esslingen am Neckar camp
- Feldafing, Camp

Brichah - Hebrew for Escape or Flight

- Foehrenwald, Camp
- Frankfurt, community and camp
- Fulda, community
- Frankfurt-Zeilsheim camp
- Funk Kaserne (UNRRA's Emigration and Repatriation Center in Munich)
- Gabersee camp
- Gauting, hospital
- Giebelstadt, camp
- Gersfeld, community
- Hasenecke, camp
- Heidelberg, community
- Heidenheim, camp
- Hofgeismar, camp
- Jagelkaserne near Kassel camp
- Krailing-Planegg, community
- Lampertheim, camp
- Landau, community
- Landsberg, camp
- Lubeck camp
- Leipheim camp
- Munich, region
- Neu-Freiman, camp
- Neu-Ulm, camp
- Plattling, community
- Pocking Waldstadt, camp
- Poppendorf, camp
- Regensburg, region
- Rochelle, camp
- Salzsuflen camp
- Schaustein camp
- Schwabach, community
- Schwabach, region
- Schwaebisch Hall, camp
- Straubing, community
- Stuttgart, region, 1946-1950
- Tirschenreuth, camp
- Vilseck, camp
- Wetzlar, camp
- Windsheim, camp
- Zeilsheim, camp
- Ziegenhain, camp

Incomplete list of Jewish DP camps in Italy

By 1947, the Jewish DPs in Germany, Austria and Italy numbered 250,000. Between 1945 and 1950, around 40,000 Jewish Displaced Persons passed through the Italian peninsula. The precise number is difficult to estimate due to continuous new arrivals and departures, as Italy developed into a major assembly center for refugee emigration (both legal and clandestine) to Palestine.

The majority of refugees entered Italy from the North-East border through the mountain passes (mainly the Brenner pass), where they arrived with the help of the Brichah that connected Eastern Europe to the DP camps in Germany and Italy. The illegal departures for Palestine were then organized by the Italian section of Mossad organization. Between 1945 and May 1948, 34 illegal ships sailed from Italian shores to Palestine.

The main refugee resettlement center was located in Via Unione in Milan. This center was created with the support of Raffaele Cantoni, president of the Union of Italian Jewish Communities, and it functioned from 1945 to 1947. From Via Unione, refugees were redirected to the various DP camps in Italy

Bari Transit camp in Italy

- Senigallia,
- Bagnoli, camp
- Bari, camp
- Barletta, camp
- Bologna, camp
- Casere, camp
- Chiari, camp
- Cinecitta', camp
- Cremona, camp
- Genova, camp
- Grugliasco, camp
- Fermo, camp
- Jesi,
- Merano, camp
- Milano, camp
- Modena, camp
- Palese, camp
- Pontebba, camp
- Reggio Emilia, camp
- Rivoli, camp
- Santa Cesarea, camp
- Santa Maria al Bagno, camp
- Santa Maria di Leuca, camp
- Tricase, camp
- Trani camp

The DP camps were both be "mixed camps", where Jewish DPs cohabited with refugees from various nationalities, and separate Jewish camps. Many refugees also lived in "kibbutzim" or communal groups and training farms for potential farmers in Palestine of which there were more than 60 in Italy. Approximately 5,000 refugees were labeled as "out of camps DPs" and lived in private homes in the main cities. In addition, a few children's homes were created for orphans, the most well-known being Selvino.

Map listing some of the major Jewish D.P. camps in Europe.

All these Jewish D.P. camps were united in their fight to open the gates of Palestine where most of them wanted or hoped to settle. This huge Jewish population will play a decisive role in breaking the British naval blockade and opening the gates to Palestine.

Chapter XVII
Appendix I

An Incomplete list of the members of the Brichah organization 1945-1948. Some members never gave their real names while others gave code names. Excuse misspellings of names and places.

Last Name	First Name	Code name	G
ABRAHAM	Hersh		M
AMSTERDAM	Shimon		M
ANSHEL	Shnulick		M
ANTECOL	Moshe		M
APFEL	Zacharia		
APPELBOIM	Moshe		M
APPELBOIM	Haim		M
APPELHOLTZ	Menucha		M
APPELHOLTZ	Haim		
APPFEL	Zacharia		M
ARGOV	David		M
ARGOV	Levi		M
ARGOV	Levy		M
ARIK		Brigade	M
ARMON	Aryeh		M
ARNER	Yaacov		M
ARNER	Rachel		F
ARNON	Aryeh		M
ARTZI-HERTZIG	Itzhak		M
ARYEH		Undersh	
ASHMAN	Frida		F
ASHMAN	Chaim		M
ASHMAN	Frida		F
ASSA	Lea		F
ASSA	Aaron		M
ASSA-SHINDLER	Leah		G
AST	Zaharia		M
AST	Awraham		M
AUERBACH	Moshe	Agami	M
AUERBACH	Moshe	Agami	M
AVEL	Zacharia		M
AVIROV	Itahak	Pasha	M
AWIROW	Itzhak	Pasha	M
AXELROD	Batia		F
AZAPHRAN	Siomka		M
AZARIAH	Zvi		M
BACHNAT	Michael		M
BACKLATCHUK	Beno		M
BAGROL	A		M
BAHAT	Michael		M

BAKIN	Shimon		M
BAKIN	Shmuel		M
BAKIN	Bebka		F
BAKIN	Esther		M
BALTAN	Chaim		M
BALTZAN	Chaim		M
BAR GRA	Yaacov		M
BAR ISHAY	Nina		F
BAR YEHUDA	Michal		M
BARAK		Esh	
BARASH	Itzhak		M
BARASH	Bobby		M
BARDA	Awraham		M
BAREL	David		M
BAR-GRA		Canada	
BAR-GRA	Yaacov		M
BARITOR	Shimon		M
BARNEA	yechezkel		M
BARSHATZ	Itzhak		M
BARUCH	Shoshana		F
BAR-YEHUDA	Michael		M
BARZEL	Amnon		M
BARZILI	Mickey		M
BARZILI	Moshe		M
BASH	Lina		F
BASH	Zeev		M
BASHAN	Eli		M
BASHAN	Joshek		M
BASSMAN	Rivkah		F
BASSOK	Haim		M
BAT ISRAEL	Yafa		F
BAUER	Arieh		M
BEATUS	Felix		M
BECK	Zeev		M
BECK	Gad		M
BECKER		Religious	
BEILIN	David		M
BEILIN	Ada		F
BEIN	Salek		M
BEIN	Risheck		M
BEITMAN	Guta		F
BEITMAN	Nachman		M
BELLES	Romek		M
BELZITZER	Shimon		M
BEN ARI	Mordechai		M
BEN DAVID	Moshe		M
BEN DROR	Yossef		M
BEN DROR			
BEN EPHRAIM	Itzhak	Meno	M

BEN GERSHON	Haim		M
BEN HAIM	Mulia		M
BEN HAIM	Max		M
BEN HAIM	Ephraim		M
BEN HALOM	Rafi	Fridel	M
BEN MOSHE	Yehuda		M
BEN NATHAN	Erika		F
BEN NATHAN	Asher	Arthur	M
BEN NUN	Hanah		F
BEN SHALOM	Rafi		M
BEN SIMCHA			
BEN TZUR	Pinhas		M
BEN TZUR	Yeshayahu		M
BEN URI	Chaim		M
BEN YAACOV	Bolek		M
BEN YOSSEF		Inding	
BEN ZVI	Isar	Shimon	M
BEN ZVI	Isser		M
BENTZLOWITZ	Pinhas		M
BENYAMINI	Sarah		F
BENYAMINI		Agudah	
BEN-ZVI	Iaaer	Shimon	M
BERNSTEIN	Pesia		F
BERNTZWEIG	David		M
BETZALELI		Minkow	
BIATOS	Felix		M
BIDERMAN	Ossi		M
BIELSKI		Hatzair	M
BIGUN	Yehoshua		M
BILU	Haftel		M
BINDY	Yehoshua		M
BIRAN	Pinchas		M
BIRENTZWEIG	David		M
BIRGER	Zeev		M
BIRNBAUM	Shaul		M
BIRNBAUM	Yasha		M
BITESH			
BLACHASH	Kalman		M
BLAS	Romek		M
BLATMAN	lLiuba		F
BLAUSCHIELD	Gamliel		M
BLECKENFIELD	Eli		M
BLEICHER	Sarah		F
BLUMENFELD	R		M
BLUMENFELD	Shlomo		M
BLUMENKRANTZ	Nahum		M
BLUMFELD	Shmuel		M
BLUMOWICZ			M
BOBROV	Zvi		M

BODENYEV	Joseph	M
BORENSTEIN	Aryeh	M
BOUKIN	Michael	M
BOUKIN	Reuven	M
BOXER	Zvi	M
BOYM	Leibl	M
BOYM	Carola	F
BOYM	Leibl	M
BRAND	Zvi	M
BRANDES	Yehosua	M
BRANDT	Shlomo Jozek	M
BRANDWEIN	Tzila	F
BRAT	Hanke	F
BRAT	Zvi	M
BRAUN	Simcha	M
BRAUN	Yossef	M
BRAUNER	Shlomo	M
BREITBERG	Moshe	M
BREITBERG	Hanah	M
BREITNER	SHIMON	M
BRETMAN		
BROCHINSKI	Miriam	F
BRONCA	Gratz	
BRONEK	Stettin	
BRONSTEIN	Samek	M
BRONSTEIN	Munia	M
BRONSTEIN	Paula	F
BROOK	Sabina	F
BROOK	Shoshana	M
BROYER	Eliezer	M
BRUCKNER	Alter	M
BRUK	Shoshana	
BUCHBINDER	Yaacov	M
BUDENYAV	Yossef	M
BUKIN	Reuven	M
BUKIN	Michael	M
BURSHTEIN	Mordechai	M
CARMELI	Ptachya	fF
CARMI	Itzhak	M
CHAIM	Abraham	M
CHAIM	Salfelden	
CHAOS	Poli	F
CHAOS	Ika	F
CHERMATZ	Julek	M
CHMIELNIK	Chaim	M
CJERES	Boris	M
COHEN	Simcha	M
COHEN	Zvi	M
COHEN	Frida	M

COHEN	Miriam		M
COHEN	Michael		M
COHEN	Yochanan		M
COHEN	Chanah		M
COHEN	David		M
COHEN	Eliyahu		M
COHEN	Isser		M
COHEN	Yochanan	Gideon	M
COMIN	Baruch		M
COMIN	Ariela		F
CROLIN	Eliyahu		M
CZARNY	Eliyahu		M
DAGAN	Abram		M
DAN	Yehuda		M
DAN	Chaim		M
DAN	Yossef	Freilichman	M
DANTZIGER	Reuven		M
DANY		Graz	
DAVID		Bratislava	
DAVID		Vienna	
DAVID		klatzko	
DAVID		Stettin	
DAVID	Dov		M
DAVIS	Moshe		M
DAWIDMAN	Itzhak		M
DAWIDOWICZ	M		M
DAYAN	Arik		M
DAYAN	Zorik		M
DEAN	Polack		M
DEGANI	David		M
DEKEL	Ephraim		M
DEMBITZ	Eliezer		M
DERECH	Milo		M
DEUTCH	Otto		M
DIAMANT	Tamara		F
DIAMANT	Sarah		F
DIM	POOLadak		
DINOR	Dov		M
DOLEK		Stettin	
DOLEK			
DOR	Ben Zion		M
DORA		Stettin	
DORA	Yehudit		F
DOVELAH		Kattowice	
DRESSLER	Aryeh		M
DREZNIN	David		M
DUBINSKI	Dwora		F
DUBINSKI	Simcha		M
DUVDEVANI	Yechiel		M

DWORKIN	Yerachmiel		M
DWORKIN	Mophet-Yocha		
DZINEK	Elsh		
ECKSTEIN	Haya		F
ECKSTEIN	Haim		M
EHERENPREISS	Joseph		M
EHRENHAFT	Sarah		F
EHRENPRACHT	Joseph		M
EHRENPREISS	I		M
EHRNBLATT	Sarah		F
EINHORN-STRASBERG	Dina	Dina	
EINHORN-STRASBERG	Rina		F
ELDAR	Arieh		M
ELIASH		killed in action	M
ENGLANDER	Juzek		
ENGLANDER		Jozek	M
EPHRAIM	Abraham		M
EPHRAIM	Adam		M
EPHRAT	Gershon		M
EREZ	Yochanan		M
ERIK		Brigade	
ERNA	Yaacov		M
ERTRACHT	Yossef		M
ESHOL	Aryeh		M
FALIK	David		M
FARBER	Fishel		M
FARGERICHT	Abraham		M
FARKASH	Laci		M
FEFFERMAN			
FEIGENBAUM	M		
FEIN	Esther		F
FEINBOK	Israel		M
FEINGOLD	Max		M
FEINMAN	Gideon		M
FEISHTER	W		M
FEIVEL	Rafi		M
FELDMAN	Raphael		M
FELDMAN	Mulyah		F
FELDMAN	Raphael		M
FELLER	Neta		F
FERBER	Rivkah		F
FERBER	Fishel		M
FERBER	Israel		M
FEURSTEIN	Dov		M
FILDOS	Rivkah		F
FINDLING	Mark		M
FINMAN	Gideon		M
FLAM	Haim S		M

FLAVOS	Shmuel	M
FLEISHMAN	Yaacov	M
FLINKER-KLEINBERG	Regina	F
FOGEL	Mordechai	M
FORGRET	Awraham	M
FRANK	Ernest -E[hrai	M
FRANK	Ephraim	M
FRANKEL	Zacharia	M
FRANKEL	Zalman	M
FRANKFURTER	Yehoshua	M
FREDDY		
FREIDER	Emanuel	M
FREILICHMAN	Yossef	M
FREIMAN		
FREITEL	David	M
FRIDA	Emanuel	M
FRIDMAN	Yaacov Janek	M
FRIDMAN	Nati	M
FRIDMAN	Fredo	M
FRIED	Uri	M
FRIEDEL	Leib	M
FRIEDMAN	Shlomo	M
FRIEDMAN	Franczik	M
FRIEDMAN	Nati	M
FRIEDMAN	Noah	M
FRIEDMAN	Mordechai	M
FRIEDMAN	Leibl	M
FRIEDMAN	Israel	M
FRIEDMAN	Itzhak	M
FRIEDMAN	Yossef	M
FRIEDMAN	Tadek	M
FRIEDMAN	Herbert	M
FRIEDMAN	Dova	F
FRUTER	Dov	M
FUCHS	Miriam	M
FUCHS	Misha	M
FUCHS	Benyamin	M
FUCHS	Miriam	F
FUGGER	Gita	F
GAFNI	Elchanan	M
GARDASH	Budapest	
GARFINKEL	Boris	M
GARFINKEL	Yossef	M
GARFUNKEL	Sulka	F
GEFEN	Tamar	F
GEFEN	Shlomo	M
GEFEN	Abba	M
GEISSER	Menashe	

GEITER	Menashe	M
GEITHEIM	Yossef	M
GELBER-YACOBI	Bruria	F
GELBLUM	Irena	F
GELIBTER	Bronek	M
GELLER	Martin	M
GELLER	Milek	M
GELLER	Liuba	F
GELLER	Itzhak	M
GELLER	Zeev	M
GENOSSAR	Menashe	M
GERSHON	Nahum	M
GERSHONOVITZ	Menachem	M
GERSON	Alter	M
GERTEL	Chaim	M
GEWISSER	Menashe	M
GIBMAN	Moshe	M
GIDEON		
GILADI	Baruch	M
GINGER	Menashe	M
GINGER	Gute	M
GINTER	Moshe	M
GINZBURG	Zvi	M
GINZBURG	Pini	M
GITELMAN	Shimon	M
GITELMAN	Shimshon	M
GLAKSBERG	Sarah	F
GLASS	Michael	M
GLASS	Shraga	M
GLASSER	Israel	M
GLASSER	Yossef	M
GLIBTER	Bronek	
GLICKER	Henia	F
GLIGSBER	Sarah	F
GLIGSBERG	Sarah	F
GLOBMAN	Rene	F
GLUZMAN	Yossef	M
GOBERG	Itzhak	M
GOBIONDESKI	Israel	M
GOLAN	Yaacov	M
GOLAN	Yehosua	M
GOLAN	Esther	F
GOLDBART	Yossef	M
GOLDBERG	Zvi	M
GOLDBERG	Haim	M
GOLDBERG	Duba	F
GOLDBERG	Ilka	F
GOLDBLUM	Itzhak	M
GOLDBLUM	Irena	M

GOLDFARB	Poppy		M
GOLDFINGER	Itzhak		M
GOLDMAN	Shlomo		M
GOLDMAN	Yossef		M
GOLDMAN	David		M
GOLDMAN	Nahum		M
GOLDSHER	Jomek		M
GOLDSHER	Ruth		M
GOLDSTEIN	Shlomo		M
GOLDSTEIN	Yossef		M
GOLDSTEIN	David		M
GOLDSTEIN	Baruch		M
GOLDSTEIN	Reisel		F
GOLDSTRUM	Zeev		M
GOLMAN	Raphael		M
GOLMAN	Yashke		M
GONINDESKI	Israel		M
GORA	Abraham		M
GORDON	Shlomo		M
GORDON	Zeev		M
GOREN	Don		M
GOREN-GRINSHPAN	Ron		
GOREV	Hasia		F
GORMAN	Levi		M
GOTESMAN	Awraham		M
GOTTLIB	Simcha		M
GOVSMAN	Moshe		M
GRANICH	Elchanan		M
GRANIT	Aryeh		M
GRATZ	Julia		F
GRAYEK	Stephan		M
GRAYEK	Shulem	Stefan	M
GREEN	Moshe		M
GRINBERG	Pasco		M
GRINBERG-BAR-GRA	Kanda		M
GRINBLAT	Yossef		M
GRINFELD	Shmil		M
GRINGOTT	Lazar		M
GRINGROSS	Shenia		M
GRINSTEIN	David		M
GRINSTEIN	Yaacov		M
GRINSTEIN	Zvi		M
GRISHA		Stettin	M
GROSS	Sarah		F
GROSS	Nehemia		M
GROSS	Moshe		M
GROSSMAN	Santo		M
GROSSMAN	Shoshana		F

244

GRUBBER	Moshe	M
GRUNWALD		
GUREWITZ	Gershon	M
GUTKIND	Aryeh	M
GUTMAN	Mordechai	M
GUTMAN	Ezra	M
GUTMAN	Moshe	M
HABER	Michael	M
HACOHEN	Tuvia	M
HACOHEN	Rachel	M
HADDAS	David	M
HAIFETZ	Yaacov	M
HAIMOWICZ	Isachar	M
HAITZES	Bruria	F
HALB	Walbrzych	
HALBERTAL	Awaham	M
HALBERTAL	Chaim	M
HALEVI	Yehuda	M
HALEVI	Sami	M
HALPERIN	Yossef	M
HALPERIN	Rachel	F
HALPERIN	Yossef Zvi	M
HALPERT	Eliezer	M
HAMEIRI	Shmuel	M
HAMEL	Itzhak	M
HAMMEL	Lina	F
HAN	Parsi	M
HARAMATY	Zvi	M
HARARY	Dov	M
HARARY	Gita	F
HARARY	Tzemach	M
HAREL	David	M
HAREL	Tziporah	F
HAREUVANI	Yehuda	M
HARRY	Yehudit	M
HARRY	Tziporah	F
HARZAHAV	Zvi	M
HASSENWALD	Yaacov	M
HAUCHBAUM	Shlomo	M
HAZAN	Mendel	M
HECHT	Awraham	M
HEFTEL	Dov	M
HELLER	Adash	M
HELLER	Sarah	F
HELLER	Bumek	M
HELLER	Awraham	M
HELPHANT	Zeev	M
HEMEL	Lena	F
HENDLER	Oskar	M

HEPHTER	Shmulik		M
HERBST	Mimish		M
HERBST	Itzhak	Mimush	M
HERMAN	Gavriel		M
HERMETZ	Yulek		M
HERSH	Aaron		M
HERSHKOWIC	Israel		
HERSHKOWITZ	Israel		M
HERTZBERG	Shlomo		M
HERTZENBERG	Gica		F
HERTZIG	Shimon		M
HILFESTEIN	Yossef		M
HILZERNET	Bobby		M
HIRSH	Aaron		M
HIRSHBERG	Zeev		M
HIRSHBERG	Heniek		M
HIRSHPRUNG	Abraham		M
HIRT	Silvia		F
HIRT	David		M
HOFFMAN	Itzhak		M
HOLIK		Eish	
HONIG	Sarah		F
HONIG	Yossef		M
HONIG	Zilka		F
HONNENBERG	Polia		F
HOOTER	Michael		M
HOROWITZ	Zvi		M
HOROWITZ	Yossef		M
Inhaber	Janek		M
ISRAEL		Stettin	
ISRAEL		klatzko	
ITZHAK		Eish	
ITZHAK		Esh	
ITZHAKI	Michael		M
ITZHAKI	Dworah		F
ITZHAKI		Halavan	
JABLONKA	Gedalia		M
JACOBI	Gdalia		M
JACOBI	Bruria		M
JAFFA	Aryeh		M
JAFFA	Mulka		M
JAFFA		Krakow	
JAKUBOWICZ	Elisheva		F
JAKUBOWICZ	Moshe		M
JANOWSKI	Uri		M
JANOWSKI	Jerachmiel		M
JANOWSKY			
JASHPAN	Abraham		M
JECHEDOWICZ	Galia		F

JECHEDOWICZ	Henia		M
JEDINOWITZ	Ephraim		M
JOEL	Yona		M
JOHANES	Dov		M
JOSEPH		klatzko	
JOSKE		Gedenwald	
JOSKOVIC			M
JUCHT	Meir		M
JUCHT	Tzipora		F
JUCHT	Meir		M
JUDOWICZ	Aryeh		M
JUNGERMAN	Pinchas		M
JUSSEK	Hana		F
KADMON	A		
KAGANOVITCH	Moshe		M
KAGANOWICZ	Sima		F
KAGANOWICZ	Moshe		M
KAHANA	Meir	Rabbi	M
KAHN	David		M
KAK	Betzalel		M
KALMAN		Stettin	
KAMINSKY	Dov		M
KAMINSKY	Uriel		M
KAMINSKY	Baruch		M
KANGON	Bruria		F
KAPLAN	Motel		M
KAPLOWITZ	Yehuda		M
KAPUT	Silvia		F
KARAKOWSKA	Miriam		F
KARMIL	Moshe		M
KARMIL	Akiva		M
KARMIL	Itzhak		M
KARMIL	Israel		M
KARP	Eduard		M
KARPENS	Gershon		M
KASHIV	Itzhak		M
KASPI	Avraham		M
KASPIT	Itzhak		M
KASPIT	Awraham		M
KASTENBAUM	Hesiek		M
KATCHUBA	Shulamit		F
KATCHUBA	Hillel		M
KATZ	Gershon		M
KATZ	Eisik		M
KAUFMAN	Itzhak		M
KAUFMAN	Mara		F
KAUFMAN	Deika		F
KERNBERG-KORN			M
KERSH	Elka		F

KESHET	Israel	M
KESSEL	Mussiah	F
KIEVSKY	Antek	M
KIHN	Shlomo	M
KIMCHI	Max	M
KLARMAN	Nahum	M
KLARMAN	Yossef	M
KLAVIR	Yehuda	M
KLEIDMAN	LIONKA	M
KLEIMAN	Julek	M
KLEIN	Zvi	M
KLESS	Valcon Geniah	F
KLESS	Shlomo	M
KLE-VULKAN	Genia	F
KLORMAN	Lionke	M
KOCHBA	Eliezer	M
KOLMAN	Israel	M
KOPELBERG	Pinhas	M
KOPITER	Moshe	M
KOPLOWITZ	Yehuda	M
KORCZAK	Ruzhka	M
KORISKI	Leibl	M
KORN	Frida	F
KORNBLIT	Pinhas	M
KORNBLUM	Anna	F
KORNITZKY	Yossef	M
KOSSOVER	Sonia	F
KOTZER	Zvi	M
KOVNER	Vitka-Kempner	F
KOVNER	Abba	M
KOWALSKI	Itzhak	M
KOWALSKI	Yaacov	M
KOZLOWSKY	Israel	M
KOZUCH	Benyamin	M
KRAUSS	Poli	F
KRAUSS	Erica	F
KRAWCZIK	Ruth	F
KRAWTCHIK	Misha	M
KREIZER	Itzhak	M
KREMER	Milo	M
KREPINKES	Rivkah	F
KRETCHMER	Naphtali	M
KRIKON	Moshe	M
KRIKON	Zv	M
KROCHMAL	Ruth	M
KROCHMAL	Maxx	M
KROLICKI	Shoshana	F
KROLICKI	Yoel	M
KROLITZKI	Shoshana	M

KROLITZKI	Chaim		M
KROLL	Arieh		M
KROLOWSKI	Israel		M
KUBA		Nachod	
KUPPERBERG	Tziporah		M
KUPPERBERG	Itzhak		M
KUPPERMAN	Pinhas		M
KUPPERSTEIN	Meir		M
KURTZ	Moshe		M
LAHAV	Tzivia - Bri		F
LAMPERT	Tzila		F
LAMPERT	Aryeh		M
LAMPERT	Linka		F
LANDAU	Fruma		F
LANDAU	Israel		M
LANDAU	Bobo Zeev		M
LANDAU	Ze'ev	Buba	M
LANDSBERG	Aaron		M
LANGER	Yaacov		M
LANIR	David		M
LAOR	Dan		M
LASHOWITZ	Katriel		M
LASKER	Peretz		M
LAUFFER	Moshe		M
LAVIE	Yossef		M
LAZAR	Haim		M
LAZAR	Zeev		M
LAZAR	Chaim		M
LECHOWITZKY	Hedwa		F
LECK	Dora		F
LEDERMAN			
LEIBOWICZ	Shlomo		M
LEIBSON	Sarah		F
LEIZER	Zeev		M
LEIZERIN	Yossef		M
LEIZERIN	Dora		F
LEMBERG	Baszek		M
LEO		Driver	
LEONEK			
LEV	Fima		F
LEV	Shragai		M
LEV	Fima		M
LEV	Gershon		M
LEVANA	Zahava		F
LEVI	Yehuda	Pitzi	M
LEVINE	Rachel		F
LEVINE	Mishke		M
LEVINE	Yehuda		M
LEVINE	Baruch		M

LEVINE	Benek		M
LEVINGER	Zvi		M
LEVINGER	Zalman		M
LEVIPENSE	Moshe		M
LEVITAN	Reuven		M
LEVY	Sami		M
LEVY	Moshe		M
LEVY	Itzhak		M
LEVY	Yehuda		M
LEWANOWSKI	Pesia		F
LEWKOWICZ	Joana		F
LEWKOWICZ	Bronislaw		M
LEWTOWSKY	Zvi		M
LEZNIK	Aryeh		M
LIBERMAN	Yaacov		M
LIBERMAN	Sarah		F
LICHTENSTEIN	Fanny		F
LICHTENSTEIN	Dani		M
LICHTIG	Aryeh		M
LICHTMAN	Awraham		M
LIDKOWSKY	Eliezer		M
LIDKOWSKY	Awraham		M
LIPSHITZ	Raphael		M
LIPSHITZ	Yehudit		M
LIPSHITZ	Zalman		M
LIPSHITZ	A.A		M
LITVAK	Zvi		M
LITVAK	Yossef		M
LITVAK	Leika		F
LITVAK	Itzhak	Katowice	M
LIVNI	Awraham		M
LONGIN	Itzhak		M
LOTEM	Epraim		M
LUBETKIN	Tzivia		F
LULU		Marano	
LUPOVIC	Chico		M
LURIA	Ephraim		M
LURIA	Betzalel		M
LURIA	Kalman		M
LUST	Ephraim		M
LUSTGARTENMEIR	Shimek		M
LUSTIG	Yochanan		M
LUTENBERG	Zvi		M
LWOW	Pinhas		M
LWOW	Michael		M
LWOW	Lola		F
MAGEN	Pertzig		M
MAGGID	Haim		M
MAIMON	Yehusa	Poldi	M

MAIMUN	Poldak Wasserman	M
MALACHI	Hanina	M
MALI	Pinhas	M
MALKOWITZ	Shlomo	M
MALOCK	Yehiel	M
MALTZ	Mitek	M
MAN	Sarah	M
MAN	Shlomo	M
MAN	Gershon	M
MANCOTAH	Yehuda	M
MANKOTA	Yehusa	M
MANN	Shlomo	M
MANOR	Nahum	M
MARGALIT	Yaacov	M
MARK	Moshe	M
MARK	Shoshana	F
MARKUS	Yossef	M
MARKUS	Isac	M
MARKUS	Awraham	M
MARKUS	Yossef	M
MARPHUGO	Haim	M
MARTIN	L	M
MAX	Haim	M
MAZYAH	Haya	F
MECHTIGER	Hela	F
MEIR	Zelig	M
MEIR	ZVI	m
MEIRFELD	Chaim	M
MEIRI	Shmuel	M
MEIRI	Moshe	Ben	M
MEIRI	Haim	M
MEIRKE		Zaalpeden
MELETZ	Mitek	M
MELLER	Yossef	M
MELLER	David	M
MELNIK	Zvi	M
MELNIK	Itzhak	M
MELTZER	Shimon	M
MELVILLE	Max	M
MENACHEM	Sharon	M
MENDEL		Krosno	M
MENDELSON	Nahum	M
MEZRITCHER	Abrasha	M
MICHAEL		San Martin
MICHAELI	Shlomo	M
MICHAELI	Renee	F
MICHAELI	Beby	M
MICHANOWSKY	Lionek	M
MIKLOSH		Dr.

MILBERG	Itzhak		M
MILGROM	Shmuel		M
MILLER	Yossi		M
MILLER	Yoel		M
MINDEL	Libka		F
MIREMOWICZ	Rachel		F
MIRIAM		Eckron	
MIRON	Yaacov		M
MITTELMAN	Asher		M
MITTELMAN	Max	Mietek	M
MOKSAY	Michael		M
MONDZIEK		Liber	
MONIEK		ZSaltzburg	
MOOR	Yaacov		M
MORAWCZIK			
MOSHE		Klacko	
MOSHE		Stettin	M
MOSHKOWICZ	Yerachmiel		M
MOTEK		Bratislava	
MOTEL		Curly	M
MOTILOFF	Yossef		M
MOTULA	Yaacov		M
MOZOWITZKI	Yashka		M
MUNKATCH	Mordechai		M
NACHOWITZ	Raphael		M
NACHOWITZ	Israel		M
NADEL	Rachel		M
NADEL	Martin		M
NADEL	Moshe		M
NAHUM		Krakow	
NARKISS	Zvi		M
NATHAN		Zbonshin	
NATHAN		Budapest	
NAVON	Aryeh		M
NECHEMA		Zagreb	
NEIMAN	Mordechai		M
NESHER	Aryeh		M
NETZER	Moshe		M
NETZER	Zvi	Alexander	M
NEUFELD	Akiva	Noy	M
NEUMAN	Ruth		F
NEUMARK	Mitek		M
NEUMARK	Israel		M
NEUMARK	Hela		F
NEUSTADT	Paula		F
NEVO	Yehudit		M
NIR	Akiva		M
NISHMAT	Sarah		F
NISHRY	Dov		M

NISSAN	Mordechai		M
NISSENBAUM	Yossef		M
NISSENBLAT	Hanan		F
NISSENBLAT	Hanah		M
NISSENLEWICZ	Zeldah		F
NUDELMAN	Yaacov		M
NUSSBAUM	Genia		F
NUSSBAUM	Asher		M
NUSSENBLAT	Hannah	Hanka	F
NUSSINOWITZ	Haim		M
NUTY		Vienna	
OFFER	Yoav		M
OFFER			M
OFFER	Aaron		M
OFFRI	Aaron		M
OICHENWALD	Janek		M
OLIBICKY	Zvi	Henik	
OLIWITZKI	Zvi	Heniek	M
ORLINSKI	Riszek		M
OSTROWER	Zishe		M
OZICHOWSKI	Nahum		M
OZICHOWSKY	Nachum		
PALGI	Yoel		M
PASTER	Lipa		M
PATRAN			
PEARL	Ben Tzion		M
PEARLS	Yaacov		M
PEER	Shlomo		M
PEER	Esther		F
PELED	Haim S		M
PELED	Aryeh		M
PELED	Chaim		M
Perilis	Yaacov		M
Perla		Budapest	
PERLMUTER	Shlomo		M
Perlmutter	Yehoshua		M
PETER	Sarah		F
PHIL	Shoshana		F
PHIL	Moshe		M
PHIL	Jozek		M
PHILO	Awraham		M
PICHOWITZ	Tziporah		F
PICHOWITZ	Jurek		M
PICK	TadIK		M
PINCHO	Shalom		M
PINES	Zvika		M
PINSKER	Shlomo		M
PIPI		Stettin	
PODHORTZER	Shlomo		M

POLACZEK	Shlomo		M
POLDA	Awraham		M
POLDAK		Esh	
POLDI		Marano	
POMERANTZ	Shmuel		M
POMERANTZ	David		M
PORT	Meir		M
POSLANETZ	Yossef		M
POSLANTZ	Yossef		M
POTYK	Shmuel		M
POZNER	Hanah		F
PRAT	Yehoshua		M
PRESSMAN	Sarah		F
PRINTZIG	Victor		M
PRISANT	Zvika		M
PROSSER	Dov		M
PRUSMAN	Sarah		F
PULMAN	Hawkah		F
RABEL	Amos		M
RABER	Yehudit		M
RABINOWICZ	Shlomo		M
RABINOWICZ	Reuven		M
RABINOWICZ	Zelig		M
RABINOWICZ	Velvele		M
RABINOWICZ	Awraham		M
RABINOWICZ	Yaacov		M
RABINOWICZ	Shimon	hanita	M
RABINOWICZ	Zeev		M
RABINOWICZ	Shimon	hanita	M
RABINOWITZ	Reuven		M
RABINOWITZ	Zelig		M
RACHEL		Bratislava	
RACKOVER	Shulem		M
RADIAH		Budapest	
RAFEK	Slavko		M
RAJCHMAN	Alexander	Shani	M
RAKOWER	Shalom		M
RAM	Itzhak		M
RAND	Zvi		M
RAPAPORT	Munia		M
RAPAPPORT	Monia		M
RAPHAEL	Gideon		M
RAPHSON	Rivkah		F
RAPHSON	Michael		M
RASHISH	Pinhas		M
RATER	Aryeh		M
RATZKO		Lawyer	
RAZI		Bratislava	
REICH	Herman-Gav		M

REICHMAN	Siano Alexander	F
REICHMAN	Avrahan	M
REICHMAN	Guta	F
REITZES	Bruria	F
REIZER	Silvia	F
REIZER	David	M
REIZER	Ephraim	M
RESNIK	Nissan	M
RESNIK	Aryeh	M
REUVENI	Yehuda	M
REVES	Peretz	M
RIDDELNIK	Israel	M
Riklis	Awraham	M
RIM	Poldek	M
RISHEK	Capitan	
RITTER	Reuven	M
RITTER	Zeev	M
ROCHMAN	Zvi	M
ROGALIN	Itzhak	M
ROGOWSKI	Abrashke	M
ROITER	Moniek	M
ROKEACH	Israel	M
RONAL	Ephraim	M
ROSA	Stettin	
ROSEBERG	Linka	F
ROSEBERG	Lulu	M
ROSEBERG	Yossef	M
ROSEBERG	Wladislaw	M
ROSEBERG	Dov	M
ROSEN	Yonah	M
ROSENBAUM	Moshe	M
ROSENBAUM	Ephraim	M
ROSENBERG	Raphael ReJo	M
ROSENBERG	Yaakov	M
ROSENBERGER	Samy	M
ROSENBERGER	Cesia	M
ROSENBERGER	Razi	M
ROSENBERGER	Silvia	M
ROSENBLAT	Gad	M
ROSENFELD	Rasha	M
ROSENFELD	Yaacov	M
ROSENFELD	Yonah	M
ROSENFELD	David	M
ROSENMAN	Dov	M
ROSENTHAL	Haim	M
ROSMAN	Mordechai	M
ROSMAN	Abraham	M
ROSNER	Driver	
ROTARO	Zeev	M

ROTEM	Kazik		M
ROTENBERG	Nachman		M
ROTGOLD	Gershon		M
ROTH	Moshe		M
ROTMAN	Motek		M
ROUEN		Zagreb	
ROZA			M
ROZENTZWEIG	Rosa		F
ROZENTZWEIG	Rivkah		F
ROZENTZWEIG	Moshe		M
ROZMAN	Mordechai		M
RUBIN	Yaacov		M
RUBIN	Beinish		M
RUBINOWICZ	David		M
RUBINSTEIN	Eliexer		M
RUBINSTEIN	Eli-gadol		M
RUBINSTEIN	Eliezer		M
RUCHMAN	Pasha		M
RUDELNIK	Israel		M
RUTGARTEN			
RUZICKI	Shimon		M
Sabo	Israel		M
SADEH	Eliezer		M
SADEH	Abraham		M
SADEH	Uyochanan		M
SADEH	Avraham		M
SADELIS	Gavick		M
SALEK		Bratislava	
SANDIUK	Eliezer		M
SANEK		Partisan	
SAPHIR	Meir		M
SAPIRSTEIN	Leibel		M
SAPIRSTEIN	Awrahm		M
SARA		Stettin	
Sarah	Tamara		
SARID	Aryeh L		M
SASSON	S		
SCHECHTER	Pinhas		M
SCHECHTER	Yossef		M
SCHECHTER	David		M
SCHECHTER	Bracha		F
SCHIFF	David	Dudek	M
SCHNEIDER	Munio		M
SCHOCHAT	Nahum		M
SCHOCHAT	Ziana		F
SCHOCHET	Nach	Jingi	M
SCHOCHET	Zalman		M
SCHUMACHER	Yafa		F
SCHUMACHER	Meir		M

SCHUSTER	Yaacov	M
SCHWARTZ	Fruma	F
SCHWARTZ	Yaacov	M
SHWARTZ	Sanek Ba	M
SCHWARTZ	Yaacov	M
SCHWEITZER	Uri	M
SCOTT	Kopel	M
SEGAL	Pessah	M
SELA	Miriam	F
SELA	Itzhak	M
SELA	Michael	M
SELA	Benyamin	M
SHACK	Zeev	M
SHADELMAN	Sashka	M
Shalat	Mark	M
SHALOM	Stettin	
SHAMIR	Mlalka	F
SHAMIR	Nahum	M
SHANIYA	Miriam	F
SHANY	Hillel	M
SHAPIRA	Tzila	F
SHAPIRA	Yechiel	M
SHAPIRO	Cila	F
SHARFSTEIN	Haim	M
Sharon	Aryeh	M
SHARON	Vienna	
SHARON	Menachem	M
SHATZ	Mendel	M
SHAUL	Krakow	
SHAVIT	Pnina	F
SHAVIT	Yair	M
SHAVIT	Eliezer	M
SHEFER	Shmuel	M
SHEFER	Leah	F
SHEFER	Grisha	M
SHEIKE	Insbruck	
SHEINWALD	Israel	
SHELET	Mark	M
SHENBAUM	Pesia	M
SHENBERG	Zalman	M
SHENBERG	Shenia	F
SHENBERG	Shlomo	M
SHENFELD	Yoochevet	F
SHENKMAN	Kuba	M
SHENOON	Avinoam	M
SHERMAN	Hanina	M
SHERMAN	Haim	M
SHEVACH	Zeev	M

257

SHEVACH	Avigdor		M
SHEVAH	Ze'ev		M
SHIBA	Hanah		F
SHIFF-RABINOWITZ	Sarah		F
SHILO	Zeev		M
SHILO	Ephraim		M
SHIMEK		Zalpeden	
SHIMONOW	S		
SHIMONOW		Krakow	
SHIMSHON		Insbruck	
SHKLAR	Haim		M
SHLEIN	Amos		M
SHLEIN	Mlkah		F
SHLEIN	Micha		F
SHLEZINGER			
SHLOMO		Klacko	
SHLOMO		Walbrzych	
SHLOMO		Belgrade	
SHLOMOWITZ	Rivkah		F
SHLOMOWITZ	Lesiek		M
SHLOMOWITZ	David		M
SHLOMOWITZ	Gita		F
SHLOMOWITZ			
SHLOSBERG	Haim		M
SHMETER	Yaacov		M
SHMULEVITCH	Tushia		F
SHMULEWITZ	Menahem		M
SHNAPPS	Pinhas		M
SHNER	Sarah		F
SHNIRSKA	Mira		F
SHNITZER	Moshe		M
SHOR	Yecutiel		M
SHOR-AMI	Shmuel		M
SHORI	Eliyahu		M
SHPERN	Siomka		F
SHRAGA		Accordeon	
SHRAGA	Esther		F
SHREIBER	Itzhak		M
SHTALMAN	Moshe		M
SHTEINMAN	Jozek		M
SHTEINMAN	Moshe		M
SHTERNFELD	M		M
SHTILER	Arieh		M
SHULAMIT		Greece	M
SHULAN	David		M
SHWEISGOLD	Shlomo		M
SHWORDT	Leibush		M
SIGAL	EDUARD		M

SKALINA			M
SKICINSKI	David		M
SKONES	Max		M
SKOP	Kapel		M
SKUTZANDEK	David		M
SLAVKO	Radek		M
SLOVO	Aryeh		M
SMALI	Mlkah		F
SONIA		Rzeszow	
SOPHI		Gratz	
STANCIGER	Aryeh		M
STASHEK	STIEF		M
STASZEWSKI	Shlomo		M
STAV	Staszek		M
STEIN	Eliezer		M
STEINBUCH	David		M
STEINFELD	Zeev		M
STEINMAN	Moshe		M
STEINMAN	Hanoch		M
STEINMAN	Baruch		M
STEINMERZ	Moshe		M
STERN	Sarah		F
STETIN	Borah		M
STETIN	Yanek		M
STETIN	Joseph B		M
STILTZER	Aryeh		M
STOKLISKY	Itzhak		M
STRACHMAN	Zeev		M
STRASSBERG	Dinah		M
STRELSKI	Haim		M
STURM	Yossef		M
SURKISS	Mordechai		M
SUSSMAN	Lina		F
SWEDSKA	Mira		F
TABASHNIK	David		M
TALMI	Matityahu		M
TALMI	Yehuda		M
TALMI	Hawa		M
TANETZAV	Zvi		M
TANNENBAUM	Ruth		F
TANNENBAUM	Sasha		M
TARMON	Asher		M
TARNOPOLSKI	Hawa		F
TARNOPOLSKI	Meir		M
TAUB	Benjamin		M
TAUMAN	Nehame		F
TAUMAN	Btzalel		M
TCHATCHKES	Fishel		M
TCHITINSKY	Klaman	Katzetnik	M

TEABY		Merano	
TEICHNER	Feleck		M
TEITELBAUM	David		M
TELOR	Eliyahu		M
TENEH	David		M
TESTLER	Ephraim		M
TIBI		Marano	
TISHLER	Aryeh		M
TOR	Sonia		F
TOR	Awrahan		M
TOUNIN	Asariah		M
TREICHOLTZ	Bronislaw		M
TREIMAN	Pinek		M
TREIMAN	Fink		M
TREPOWICZ	Shimeck		M
TREPPER	Rivkah		M
TRICHTER	Peretz		M
TRICHTER	Poldi		M
TURKEL	Matityahu		M
TZARFATI	Yaacov		M
TZATISNKY	Kalman		M
TZATZKES	Fishel		M
TZEITAG	Pibieh		M
TZIMAND	David		M
TZIPRIS			
TZUCKERMAN	Naomi		F
TZUK	Yehoshua		M
TZUNDEK	Shimon		M
TZUR	Amram		M
TZWIBEL	Yaacov		M
TZWINGEL	Yehoshua		M
VAGEN	Itzhak		M
VAN		Aso	
VARDI	Yaacov		M
VARDI	Ruth		F
VARDI	Shmuel		M
VARDY	Nathan		M
VARPHOGY	rri		M
VERED	Abraham	Vertzoizer	M
VERED	Hanoch		M
VERED-WERTZEISER	Awraham		M
VERED-WERTZEIZER		Awraham	M
VERMAN	Munio		M
VERMAN	Nathan		M
VERSES	Abraham		M
WALDMAN	Arieh		M
WALDMAN	A		M
WALLACH	Nhum		M

WALLDMAN	Awraham	M
WANCHOTZKI	Genia	G
WANG	David	M
WANG	Dorka	F
WANGLISHEWSKY	Uri	M
WARSZAWCIK	Hasia	F
WASSSERSTRUM	Asher	M
WEINBERG	Itzxhak	M
WEINER	Shaike	M
WEINGARTEN	Awraham	M
WEINMAN	Shlomo	M
WEINSHELBAUM	David	M
WEINSTEIN	Yossef	M
WEINSTEIN	David	M
WEINSTEIN	Aeyeh	M
WEINSTOCK	Aryeh	M
WEINSTOCK	Avital	F
WEISAND	Moshe	M
WEISAND	Chaim	M
WEISMAN	Shragai	M
WEISS	Shalom	M
WEISS	Kalman	M
WEISS	Moshe	M
WEISS	Yossef	M
WEISS	Awraham	M
WEISS	Hella	F
WEISSHANDEL	Moshe	M
WEISSKOPF	Moshe	M
WEISSMAN	Nachman	M
WEITZMAN	Zelig	M
WEITZMAN	Awraham	M
WEIZER	David	M
WEIZLER	Chaim	M
WEOSZEBCIK	Hasia	F
WERBER	Itzhak	M
WERMAN	Munia	M
WERNIK	Itzhak	M
WERNIK	Netka	F
WERTZHEIGER	Abrasha	M
WIDRA	Reuven	M
WIDRA	Max	M
WIDRA	Awraham	M
WIENER	Budapest	
WIENER	Baruch	M
WIERNIK	Nechema	F
Wiessman	Nachman	M
WIGOHAUS	Awraham	M
WILCZINSKY	Israel	M
WINKLER-YATIR	Yael	F

WINTZBERG	Carola	F
WINTZBERG	Karol	
WINTZELBERG	Karol	M
WITZMAN	Zelig	M
WIZENBERG	Yossef	M
WLADARSKI	Hanan	M
WOLBERSTEIN	Moshe	M
WOLFSON	Yossef	M
WOLKOWICZ	Shlomo	M
WROBEL	Pessah	M
WROCLAWSKY	Gershon	M
WURTZEL	Chaim	M
YAFAH	Krakow	
YAFAH	Mulkah	M
YAFAH	Aryeh	M
YANAI	Jacob	M
YASKY	Haim	M
YEHOSHUA		
YEHOSHUA		M
YOSSI	Zaltzburg	M
ZAGBAUM	Mashe	F
ZAGMIROWSKI	Tanchum	M
ZAGRZE	Moshe	M
ZAHAR-ZLOTO	Zvi	
ZALEWSKI		
ZALMANOWICZ	Dov	M
ZAMOROWSKY	Tanhum	
ZANBERG	Motek	M
ZANDBAR	Dov	M
ZANDBAR	Gertha	F
ZEEV	Marano	
ZEIDEL	Hillel	M
ZEIDEN	Eliyahu	M
ZEIDLER	Shragai	M
ZEIDMAN	Aaron	M
ZEIDMAN	Bolek	M
ZEIRA	Meir	M
ZELIG	Bratislava	
ZELIKOWICZ	Zigmund	M
ZELINSKI		
ZELTZER	Eliexer	M
ZEPKA	Mendel	M
ZIEGLER	Moshe	M
ZIGBAND	Rachel	F
ZIGELBERG	Yossef	M
ZIGNUND	Wilach	
ZILBER	Israel	M
ZILBER	Moshe	M
ZILBERBERG	Yosef	M

ZILBERBERG	Zerach		M
ZILBERFARB	Shalom		M
ZILBERFARB	Zeev		M
ZILBERMAN	Salek		M
ZILBERSTEIN	Shoshana		F
ZILBERSTEIN	Mark		M
ZIMAN	Rosa		F
ZIMRY	S		
ZINGER	Sonia		M
ZINGER	Moshe		M
ZINGER			M
ZISKIND	Ida		F
ZISKIND	Ira		M
ZISKIND	Shlomo		M
ZLOTER	Aryeh		M
ZLOTER	Zvi		M
ZOHAR-ZLOTO	Zvi		M
ZONNENSHEIN	Kalnan		M
ZOSIEN			
ZUCKERMAN	Antek		M
ZVI		Krakow	
ZVULON		Cordova	
ZYSZEK		Driver	

Chapter XVIII
Appendix II

Names of American and Canadian volunteers that served aboard the Mossad ships that sailed from American ports and transported Jewish Shoah survivors from Europe to Palestine.

Last name	First name	Name of ship
ABADIE	Eddie	JEWISH STATE
ABELLS	R.(Hess)	JEWISH STATE
ABRAMS	Sydney	GEULA
ABRAMSON	Lester	ARLOSOROFF
ARANOFF	Murray	EXODUS
ASH	William	WEDGWOOD
ASSANOWICZ	Ajzik	WEDGWOOD
BACANER	Marvin	WEDGWOOD
BAIRD	Pierre	GEULA
BALL	Louis	GEULA
BARKAN	Mordechai	WEDGWOOD
BARNEA	Yisrael	HAGANAH
BAUM	David	HAGANAH
BAUM	Mordechai	HAGANAH
BAUM	Ralph	HAGANAH
BEERI	Shmuel	EXODUS
BELKIN	Gidon	CALAMIT
BELMAN	Shimshon	WEDGWOOD
BEN-YISRAEL	Yakov	HATIKVAH
BERG	Bertram	JEWISH STATE
BERGMAN	Elihu	BEN HECHT
BERKOVITS	Jeno	BEN HECHT
BERNSTAIN	Jack	BEN HECHT
BERNSTEIN	Arthur	ARLOSOROFF
BERNSTEIN	Jack	ARLOSOROFF
BERNSTEIN	William	EXODUS
BINDER	Louis	BEN HECHT
BLAKE	David	GEULA
BLOCKMAN	Mordechai	WEDGWOOD
BRAISLEY	Lou	JEWISH STATE
BRAVERMAN	Hy	HATIKVAH
BREEN	Shabtai	LANEGEV
BRETTSCHNEIDER	Louis	GEULA
BROWNSTEIN	Albert	GEULA
BUIZA	Miguel	GEULA

BUXENBAUM	Philip	GEULA
CALIC	Yitzhak	CALAMIT
CHRISTIE	Paul	GEULA
COHEN	Eli	WEDGWOOD
CUSHENBERRY	Walter	BEN HECHT
DREYFUS	Jochahnan	CALAMIT
EDMONDON	Howard	JEWISH STATE
EISEN	David	HAEMEK
ENDIN	Dave	JEWISH STATE
ETROS	Duke	ARLOSOROFF
EUGEN	Alexander	ARLOSOROFF
FENDEL	David	HAGANAH
FLEIGLER	Heine Fra	WEDGWOOD
FORMAN	Ben	EXODUS
FRANK	Yakov	HAGANAH
FREUNDLICH	Eli	BEN HECHT
GALIL	Irving	MALA
GALILI	Hal	HATIKVAH
GARVA	Richard	GEULA
GEORGE	Apply Sh	HAGANAH
GIBRALTAR	Jared	JEWISH STATE
GILBERT	Peter	GEULA
GILDEN	Joe	HATIKVAH
GOLDMAN	George	GEULA
GOLDSTEIN	David	MALA
GOLDSTEIN	Myron	EXODUS
GOOEN	Marlin	GEULA
GORDON	Sam H	HATIKVAH
GOTLIB	David	WEDGWOOD
GOTTLIEB	William	WEDGWOOD
GRAUL	John	EXODUS
GREAVES	Walter	BEN HECHT
GREENFIELD	Murray S	HATIKVAH
GREER	David	GEULA
GUTMAN	DavidLeo	BEN HECHT
HALEVI	Awraham	HAGANAH
HEGGIE	James	BEN HECHT
HERSHKOFF	Albert	BEN HECHT
HERSHKOWITZ	Harry	BEN HECHT
HILB	Gad	ARLOSOROFF
JACKS	Stanley	JEWISH STATE
KAHAN	Laz	JEWISH STATE
KALLNER	Moshe	GEULA
KALM	Eli	EXODUS
KAPLAN	David	BEN HECHT
KAPLANSKY	Eddy	JEWISH STATE
KASHNER	Arye	HAGANAH

KATZ	Moshe	WEDGWOOD
KATZ	Harold	HATIKVAH
KATZ	Moshe	WEDGWOOD
KAUFMAN	Paul	WEDGWOOD
KAYE	Paul	HATIKVAH
KAZICKI	Benjamin	BEN HECHT
KELLENER	David	GEULA
KEONIGSBERG	Louis	JEWISH STATE
KIRSTEN	Uri	WEDGWOOD
KITE	Arnold	GEULA
KRAMER	Joseph	aARLOSOROFF
KOCHAVI	David	EXODUS
KOGAN	Bernard	WEDGWOOD
KOHLBERG	Lawrence	GEULA
KOLOMENTZEV	Arye	EXODUS
KULBERSH	Benny	GEULA
KURT	Baruch	EXODUS
KUSNITSKY	Siegfried	JEWISH STATE
LABACZEWSKI	Augustine L	HATIKVAH
LAVINE	Frank	EXODUS
LEBOW	Aaron	JEWISH STATE
LEIDNER	Harold	EXODUS
LERNER	Sol Alvin	WEDGWOOD
LESTER	Aaron	EXODUS
LEVINE	Phil	CALAMIT
LEVINE	Aaron	ATZMAUT
LEVITAN	Hyman	BEN HECHT
LEVY	Bernie	HATIKVAH
LEWIS	Josh	HATIKVAH
LEWIS	Morris	JEWISH STATE
LIBERSON	Joe	CALAMIT
LICHTMAN	Jacob	WEDGWOOD
LIEBERMAN	Marvin	BEN HECHT
LILIBY	Haakom	BEN HECHT
LINSKY	Baruch	ARLOSOROFF
LIPSCHUTZ	David	GEULA
LITWIN	Wallace	BEN HECHT
Livingston	David	ARLOSOROFF
LIVNI	Avi	ATZMAOUT
LOMBARD	Daniel	GEULA
LOWENTHAL	David	ATZMAOUT
LUCE	Norman	BEN HECHT
LUTZ	Abbot	EXODUS
MALKIN	Aryie	WEDGWOOD
MALOWSKY	Danny	EXODUS
MALTESE	Dani	CALAMIT
MANDEL	Henry	BEN HECHT

MARGOLIS	Reuven	EXODUS
MARKOWITZ	Louis	BEN HECHT
MARKS	Bernie	EXODUS
MCDONALD	Hugh	HATIKVAH
MELTZER	Irving	JEWISH STATE
MENDELSON	Mendy	WEDGWOOD
MILLER	Hans	HAGANAH
MILLER	Milton	WEDGWOOD
MILLMAN	Dave	EXODUS
MILLMAN	William	EXODUS
MILLS	Dov	EXODUS
MITTELMAN	PHILIP	WEDGWOOD
MONASH	Zvi	HAGANAH
MYERS	Chaim	TEL HAI
NACHLIELI	Yaakov	YUCATAN
NADLER	Nat	EXODUS
NAFTAL	Al	EXODUS
NEMOFF	Alexander	HATIKVAH
NEWMAN	Benny	CALAMIT
NICOLAI	Ben Robe	CALAMIT
NIEDER	Bailey	GEULA
PEKOFSKY	M	ARLOSOROFF
PERETZ	Adrian	HAGANAH
PERLSTEIN	Menachem	HATIKVAH
PHILIPS	Yaakov	HATIKVAH
PLEET	Haim	WEDGWOOD
POMARANTZ	Alexander	WEDGWOOD
PRAGER	Isidore	CALAMIT
RABINOWITZ	Charles	JEWISH STATE
RAMATI	Hillel	LATRUN
RATNER	Zev	WEDGWOOD
RAUFF	Zvi	WEDGWOOD
RAV		ARLOSOROFF
REICH	Philip	WEDGWOOD
REUBEN	Arnie	HATIKVAH
RIFKIN	Shephard	BEN HECHT
RITZER	Stanley	EXODUS
ROFE	Roger	EXODUS
ROMERO	Marvin	GEULA
ROSENBERG	John	WEDGWOOD
ROSENFELD	Buddy	GEULA
ROSTOKER	Leonard	ORLOSOROFF
ROTTER	Gerald	GEULA
RUBIN	Paul	CATRIEL JAFE
RUBIN	Hyman	HATIKVAH
RUBINSTEIN	P.	HATIKVAH
SANDIN	John	GEULA

SCHELAZNICKI	Manfred	JEWISH STATE
SCHIFF	Reuben	GEULA
SCHILER	Shmuel	EXODUS
SCHINDLER	Ralph	GEULA
SCHLIEFSTEIN	Leonard	HATIKVAH
SCHULMAN	Sam	ATZNAUT
SCHWARTZ	Shulim	WEDGWOOD
SCHWARTZ	Harry N	BEN HECHT
SEGAL	Zeev	EXODUS
SELA	Yehuda	HAGANAH
SELIGMAN	Dov	WEDGWOOD
SELOVE	Lou	EXODUS
SHACHORI	David	GEULA
SHANKMAN	Israel	JEWISH STATE
SHAPIRO	Aaron	HAGANAH
SHEFFI	Abe	HAGANAH
SHMERLING	Doc	ARLOSOROFF
SHUSHMAN	Benjamin	HAGANAH
SHWARTZ	Max	HAGANAH
SIEGEL	Abe	EXODUS
SILVER	Martin	MALA
SILVERSTEIN	Larry	ARLOSOROFF
SKLAR	Lennie	EXODUS
SOLOWICZ	Sholon	GEULA
SORENSEN	Erling	BEN HECHT
STANCZAL	Frank	EXODUS
STARER	Reuben	ARLOSOROFF
STYRAK	Edward	BEN HECHT
SUSSGAL	Ben Ami	GEULA
SYGAL	Awraham	EXODUS
TALLER	Archie	CALAMATI
TILOLLOW	Willie	ARLOSOROFF
TSUK	E. (Phil)	ARLOSOROFF
WARDI	Teddy	EXODUS
WEIHAUS	Sid	ATZNAUT
WEINGARTEN	Irving	BEN HECHT
WEINGRAD	Al	WEDGWOOD
WEINSTEIN	Manny	HATIKVAH
WEINSTEIN	Cy	EXODUS
WEINTRAUB	Sonny	HATIKVAH
WEISAFT	Harry	EXODUS
WEISS	Charles	HATIKVAH
WEISS	Marvin	HATIKVAH
WEISS	Mike	Unknown
WIESMAN	Samuel	HAGANAH
WINKLER	Jack	HATIKVAH
WINKLER	Jack	BEN HECHT

WITTENHOFF	Jehuda	WEDGWOOD
WURM	David	
YELLIN	Saul	HATIKVAH
YELLIN	Sid	BEN HECHT
YERIEL	Jack	JEWISH STATE

Chapter XIX
Bibliography

Albrich, Thomas and Ronald Zweig, Editors, *Escape through Austria.* London: Frank Cass, 2002.

Arens, Moshe, *Flags over the Warsaw Ghetto.* Gefen Publishing Company, 2011.

Avriel, Ehud, *Open the Gates*. New York: Atheneum, 1975.

Bauer, Yehuda, *Flight and Rescue*: Brichah. New York: Random House, 1970.

Bauer, Yehuda, *The Brichah-She' erit Hapletah 1944-1948. Jerusalem*: 1990

Bauer, Yehuda, *Out of the Ashes*. Oxford: Penguin, 1989.

Berman, Gizel, *My Three Lives*. Niche Press, 1999.

Bogner, Nahum, *Isle of Deportation* 1946-1948, Am Oved, Hebrew.

Cichopek-Gajraj, Anna, *Beyond Violence*. Cambridge University Press: 2014.

Cohen, Yochanan, *Brichah-Poland Report. Jerusalem*: Yad Vashem.

Dekel, Efraim, Bri'ha: *Flight to the Homeland*, New York: Herzl Press, 1972.

Hochstein, Joseph M. and Murray S. Greenfeld*, The Jews' Secret Fleet.* Jerusalem: Gefen Publishing House Ltd.

Israel Defense Ministry, *The Brichah Movement from Europe to Israel.* Israeli Defense Ministry 1998.

Jacobson letter to JDC office in New York of August 26, 1946.

Kahane, David Rabbi*, After the Deluge.* Jerusalem: 1981, Hebrew.

Kahane, David, Rabbi, *Lwow Ghetto Diary*. Jerusalem, 1978.

Kovner, Abba, *On The Narrow Bridge*. Tel Aviv: 1981, Hebrew

Kochavi, Arieh J., *Post Holocaust Politics; the British, the USA and the Refugees* 1945-1948. UNC Press, 2014.

Laub, Morris, *Last Barrier to Freedom: Internment of Jewish Holocaust Survivors on Cyprus, 1946 to 1949*. Berkeley, Ca: Judah L. Magnes Museum, 1985.

Leibner, William, interview with Mordechai Lustig.

Leibner, William, *Mass Exit Transport of Jewish Children from Poland.* Jerusalem: Yad Vashem, 2010.

Leibner, William, *Zabrze-Hindenburg-Zabrze Yizkor Book*. Jerusalem: Yad Vashem.

Leibner, William, interview with Anna Neufeld.

Leibner, William, interviewed Shlomo Korn.

Leibner, William, interview David Danieli.

Lustig, Mordechai, *The Red Feathers*. Israel.

New York Post front page dated October 2 1945.

Rosner, Leo, *The Holocaust Remembered – A Child Survivor's Account of Imprisonment and Redemption, 1939 to 1945*, 2003.

San Francisco Jewish Community Publications Inc. JWeekly.com 2 *"Deaths of 260 in 1940 ship explosion commemorated"*. 14 December

Smok, Martin - movie entitled *"Bricha"*.

Warhaftig Zorach, *The Uprooted Jewish Refugees and Displaced Persons after Liberation: From War to Peace, Vol. 5. New York*: Institute of Jewish Affairs of the American Jewish Congress and World Jewish Congress, 1946.

YIVO materials pertaining to the Jewish D.P. camps in Germany, Austria and Italy

Index

A

Abadie, 264
Abells, 264
Abraham, 18, 29, 236
Abramovitz, 127
Abrams, 264
Abramson, 264
Aftergut, 86
Agami, 19, 20
Ahranovitch, 199, 200
Akselrod, 166
Alexander, 6, 45, 92
Alexander, 111
Alfi, 111
Alon, 111, 146
Alon-Haft, 146
Amarant, 13, 17, 28
Amsterdam, 76, 236
Angelo, 209
Anielewicz, 41
Anshel, 236
Antecol, 236
Antonescu, 11, 24, 25, 27
Apfel, 236
Appelboim, 236
Appelholtz, 236
Appfel, 51, 236
Appfelholtz, 51
Aranoff, 264
Arazi, 170, 171, 172, 174, 175, 176, 215
Argov, 66
Argov, 76, 236
Arik, 236
Arlosoroff, 179, 193, 194, 195
Armon, 236
Arner, 236
Arnon, 236
Artzi-Hertzig, 29, 236
Aryeh, 236
Ascarelli, 215
Ash, 199
Ash, 264
Ashkenazi, 166
Ashman, 29, 236
Assa, 76, 236
Assanowicz, 264
Ast, 18, 236
Auerbach, 19, 27, 28, 43, 49, 194
Auerbach, 29, 236
Augoshewitz, 146
Augushewitz, 146
Avel, 236
Avigur, 20, 169, 170, 189, 206, 212, 215, 217

Avirov, 236
Avriel, 144, 145, 270
Awirow, 51, 236
Axelrod, 236
Ayalon, 111
Azaphran, 236
Azariah, 236

B

Babetlerder, 117
Bacaner, 264
Bachnat, 236
Backlatchuk, 236
Bagrol, 236
Baharav, 198
Bahat, 236
Baird, 264
Bakin, 237
Ball, 264
Baltan, 76, 237
Baltzan, 237
Bar Gra, 237
Bar Ishay, 237
Bar Yehuda, 237
Barak, 237
Barash, 237
Barda, 237
Barel, 237
Bar-Gra, 237
Baritor, 237
Barkan, 264
Barnea, 237, 264
Barshatz, 237
Bar-Shatz, 181
Baruch, 237
Bar-Yehuda, 237
Barzel, 237
Barzilai, 181
Bash, 237
Bashan, 146, 237
Bassman, 237
Bassok, 237
Bat Israel, 237
Bauer, 51, 237
Baum, 264
Beatus, 237
Beck, 237
Becker, 39, 201
Becker, 237
Beeri, 264
Beilin, 146, 237
Bein, 72
Bein, 146, 237
Beitman, 237
Belkin, 264

S

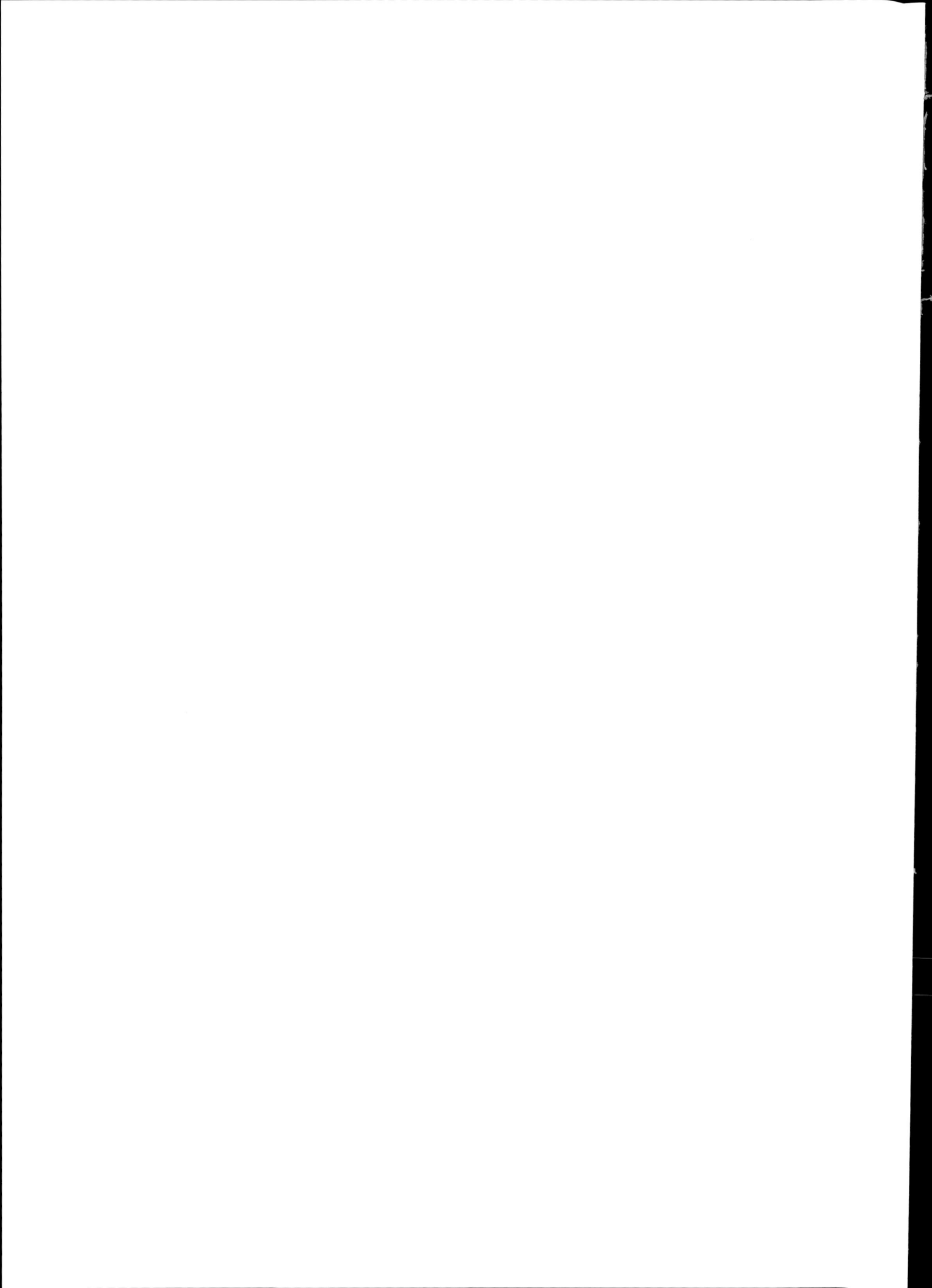